"*Bodega Bakes* is filled with fanciful, creative recipes and photos that are a treat for all the senses. Visually dazzling and with taste combinations that honor Paola's Dominican heritage as well as the humble corner store of New Yorkers, this is a beautiful book to enjoy and inspire."
  —**JACQUES PÉPIN**, chef, culinary instructor, and television personality

"This book is filled with recipes that I can't wait to make over and over again! It's a love story of family and community, blending flavors from childhood memories with classic techniques in an approachable and creative way. Paola's signature style of baking shines bright on every page and opens up our hearts and minds to be more accepting of cultures that may not be our own. She is a true original—baking a difference every day!"
  —**CHERYL DAY**, author of *Cheryl Day's Treasury of Southern Baking*

"*Bodega Bakes* is like baking in the kitchen with Paola, live and in Technicolor. It screams 'Git in there, trust yourself, and have FUN!' It's a total vibe."
  —**CARLA HALL**, author of *Carla Hall's Soul Food*

"Growing up in Queens, New York, corner stores (aka bodegas) were a neighborhood's oasis. They were filled with the necessities that we needed because *our* neighborhoods didn't have access to a variety of amenities like other communities. From socks and batteries to pickled pig's feet in jars and cold cut sandwiches, my bodega helped to inform my spending power and shape my palate. This love letter to the Bronx, in all its Latina flair, is the cookbook my inner-city child has been waiting for. Thank you, Paola."
  —**MASHAMA BAILEY**, coauthor of *Black, White, and The Grey*

"It's been a true delight following Paola's journey to the creation of this wildly beautiful cookbook. Her brilliant, deeply personal desserts defy tradition and bring so much joy to those among us lucky to have had the chance to taste them. Now everyone can serve themselves an extra-big slice. *Bodega Bakes* overflows with imagination, purpose, and indulgence, and I can't get enough!"
  —**GAIL SIMMONS**, author of *Bringing It Home*

Bodega
Bakes

Bodega Bakes

Recipes for Sweets and Treats Inspired by My Corner Store

Paola Velez

with Emily Timberlake

UNION
SQUARE
& CO.

NEW YORK

I dedicate this book to my mother, Lala; my husband, Hector; my wonderful in-laws, Rebecca and Hector Sr.; and to Titi Liz, Tío Luis, Tía Chichi, Tía Masina, and all my friends and family for cheering me on throughout this whole journey. I also dedicate this book to my grandparents, Mama Paulina, Abuelo Frank, and Doña Ofelia, who are no longer here with us—I know that you're watching over me and guiding my steps as I navigate life. Thank you for loving me and making me who I am today. *(Dedico este libro a mi abuelos, Mamá Paulina, Abuelo Frank y Doña Ofelia. A pesar que ustedes ya no estén aquí fisicamente, sé que sus espíritud y sus enseñanzas continúan conmigo siempre, guiándome y protegiéndome. Con Diosito primero, y el apoyo de mi familia, todo es posible.)*

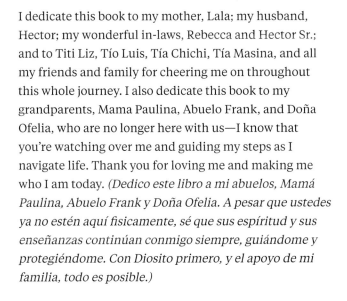

Contents

Doña Dona, Baked & Fried Delights   166

The Flan Familia   214

Ponlo en el Freezer! (Put It in the Freezer!)   244

Basics   277

Acknowledgments   283

Index   285

Foreword

Show up and mean it. This is what Paola reminds me every time I see her curls, her curiosity, her flavor, her HER.

Dessert has a powerfully deep and long-standing connection in our lives. It is sacred, timeless, indulgent. It's a special occasion. It's the thing we use to show up for others, for ourselves. It's the thing we turn to when we need help saying "congrats!" or "that stinks" and everything in between. Yet baking for a living can be a little—or a lot—challenging. A near impossible task, surviving and thriving as a baker can be tricky. It's a passionate pursuit, perhaps even an optimistic one, where details are never-ending and margins are razor-thin. But you'll never hear that from the people who do it, because we're focused on the bigger prize. To do it well, to do it masterfully, it boils down to one's ability to show up, time and time again, bull's-eye on the why, center of the heart, right to the taste buds, as Paola Velez does.

My first introduction to the powerhouse that is Paola was within the walls of Milk Bar. We had just opened our bakery in Washington, DC, and Paola was a member of our new team: no easy task. Day after day, Paola showed up not just ready to do the work, but to do it with a brightness, curiosity, and sense of wonder. She was there to learn through doing, to form human connections, ensuring that the collection of talent yielded a *team*. She baked, she asked questions, she challenged the status quo, and she never stopped smiling. I knew she was destined for greatness.

To dine in a restaurant that Paola has her whisk in is to have a front seat to what makes Paola so singular. Bold flavors, playful combinations, skillful executions that could come from no one else. Paola has a tremendous ability to show up as

herself, to express herself through dessert, and to bring a point of view that is hers and hers alone to the table. In a world of trends and copycats and influencers, it's easy to get lost, but Paola always shines brightly as her strong and hilarious, wise and playful self, and she channels that into her dessert, continuously raising the bar on creativity.

But what really makes Paola the one-in-a-million person she is comes from her ability—or, perhaps better said, need—to show up for others. When restaurants were shuttered in the early days of the COVID-19 pandemic, Paola sprang into action, putting her skills to work to raise money for the hospitality community—and she did so in her typical no muss, no fuss way. Her compulsion to run toward the problem is beyond admirable, and her generosity runs bone-deep. When the Black Lives Matter movement stirred a need in our country to bring change, she rallied our culinary community again, inspiring the entirety of us, giving our skills a voice and purpose during a time of need by forming Bakers Against Racism. Baking is an inherently altruistic act: You bake something to give it away. And so Paola tapped into professionals and home bakers alike, people who share that generosity of spirit, and gave them something to funnel their energy into: their baked goods. Millions of dollars later, the world BAR touched is certainly better, the true power of Paola, of bakers, of dessert resounds.

To know Paola Velez is to see the world in Technicolor. Paola walks a tightrope of exacting pastry technique meets Americana flair meets Afro-Dominican flavor—and she does so with astounding heart and oh-so-much style. Who else on this planet could dream up PB&J Pots de Crème with guava jelly? (I'll take two.) She so naturally

does what all great artists set out to do—create something that is uniquely an expression of true self—and the results are irresistible. This book will breathe energy into your life, teach you to view the ingredients around you in new and inspiring ways, and inspire you to wake up, show up, and make the world a better place. I know it has for me.

—*Christina Tosi, chef/founder, Milk Bar*

Introduction

Before we start making magic together, allow me to introduce myself: My name is Paola, and I'm a Bronx-born Afro-Latina pastry chef and community organizer who did not plan on becoming either.

I was born at Montefiore Hospital on East 210th Street and went to PS/MS 95 on Hillman Avenue. I loved going to school, and I loved growing up in the Bronx, which has the highest percentage of Hispanic and Latino residents of any county in the entire American Northeast. But for me, the Bronx is even more special than that powerful fact. Growing up, it felt like everyone in the neighborhood knew and cared for each other. I had friends from all backgrounds—Nigerian friends, Dominican friends, Puerto Rican friends, Catholic, Jewish, and everything-in-between friends.

I was a total nerd. The first time I felt truly seen was when Steve Urkel, the lovably dorky neighbor on *Family Matters*, appeared on my television screen. I was big on chess club, math club, and slam poetry. Our house was always littered with science projects and Play-Doh.

As lovely as it sounds (and as lovely as so much of it was), this is the part where I tell you that my early years weren't a total breeze. Like many first-generation Americans, I had the hardest time figuring out who I really was, how exactly I fit in. It seemed weird to me that I could love mofongo and anime at the same time. I hardly spoke any Spanish. And to be perfectly honest, like many first-generation Americans, I still have a hard time with it. (I like to say that both English and Spanish are my second languages.)

My mom, Lala, had me only two years after immigrating to the States. In the Dominican Republic, she had trained to become a biochemist. Here, in her adopted home country, she worked for our family's local restaurant chain, Mary-Ann's, doing everything from hostessing to accounting. There were nine Mary-Ann's locations in and around Manhattan. Most days after school, I would ride the subway to one of the outposts, take a seat in a booth, and watch Mom do her job while I did my homework. My cousins once told me that I was almost born in a Mary-Ann's because even through her pregnancy, my mom didn't feel right taking time off. She had a work ethic like few people I've ever met, and an incredible skill for running a business. She sacrificed everything for me.

There were no American traditions for her to pass on to me, but she still tried her darndest to help me assimilate. While she watched Telemundo and Univision, she made sure her daughter's eyes were glued to PBS, *The Fresh Prince*, and *Martin* (Mart-iiiiiiiiiiiin!). She and my stepdad, a Nuyorican, would take me on adventures to the Met and the Natural History museum. The three of us would visit Queens, Manhattan, and other parts of the Bronx, and eat at restaurants featuring cuisines from all around the world. This introduced me to different cultures in an authentic way. Chinatown was one of my favorite neighborhoods to explore with my family. Not just to feast on Peking duck on Canal Street, but also to indulge in the amazing bakeries. I still think about the walnut bars I used to buy—they seemed to me like a pecan pie condensed into a perfect three-inch rectangle. That was the first time I realized that "sweet" baked goods didn't have to be overly sugary or cloying.

As much as I loved exploring every corner of New York City, my favorite place was always the bodega around the corner. Just hearing that word strikes a chord. *Bodega*. People in Paris might call it a tabac. Folks in Tokyo visit konbinis. For me, my family, and my friends, our local corner store and unofficial community anchor was the bodega: a densely inhabited mini market where Jarritos, Cap'n Crunch, shampoo, gossip, and chopped cheeses peacefully coexist—along with Joselito from the neighborhood holding court and shouting about the news. I never had to worry about being short a

dollar—the bodega owner would always smile and say, "I got you, you can pay me back next time." He knew that my mom and I didn't always have the means to make ends meet, and the nicest part was, he never collected on those IOUs.

Up until my teens, my world mostly consisted of school, the neighborhood park, the local slice shop, C-Town supermarket, and the bodega—which gave me a window into places beyond the one I knew and became a source of great culinary inspiration.

My happy-place bodega will forever be the one across the street from my old middle school in Van Cortlandt Village. Sadly, it's gone now, but I can still map every inch of those 400 square feet in my mind. Two things I loved about it were its open floor plan and super mellow and kind cat. (This is important. If the bodega cat doesn't like you, to be honest, you should just find a new bodega, because it's hella awkward.) People were always mingling and telling stories. The bodega provided a daily dose of adventure that fed my appetite for discovery.

I'll start with the candy selection. In my youth, my bodega had so many options: traditional American classics like M&M's, Latin American brands that no one else carried, and, most important, Warheads that only cost a nickel. For some reason, Dominicans have a thing for cough drops, which we refer to as "Menta Halls" and eat like candy. Those were in ample supply, too. Whenever I craved something savory, the answer was always Muenster on a toasted roll with a bottle of malta, a nonalcoholic soda made from hops and barley. This bold, dark brown refreshment is an acquired taste, even for folks in the Caribbean for whom it is a birthright.

I remember it all so fondly, but in retrospect, the bodega was so special to me because they sold Dominican and Puerto Rican pastries and desserts. I didn't grow up eating johnnycakes; I picked up yaniqueques (Dominican fried dough). People went to Zabar's for rice pudding; we hit the bodega for majarete (corn pudding). The flan there was outstanding. On hot days, it was easy to narrow down the options: I'd just make a beeline to the freezers to snatch an esquimalito, a colorful ice pop that came in a plastic tube.

As naturally connected as I felt to these foods, I couldn't figure out if I fully belonged to the islands that produced them or to the place where I was born. My mom was pushing me toward America—which I understood, because it was for the sake of my own survival. It also didn't help that I was an anxious kid. Very anxious. Depressed, in fact. And if you know something about Hispanic families, you know we don't love to talk about mental health struggles. We also generally have a hard time accepting that younger generations who were born and raised in the States—and who didn't go through the struggle of emigrating—often want to pursue more creative paths.

My mom wanted me to become an engineer, not to get paid seven dollars an hour and face rejection from almost every kitchen job I applied to. My mom didn't want me to have to choose between feeding myself and paying rent, which ended up happening fairly regularly for several years. It didn't matter to the restaurant industry that I finished culinary school in nine months when it was supposed to take two years. Or that during my externship at Mary-Ann's, I wound up running all nine locations almost immediately, managing folks who'd been around long enough to remember when I was little. I even found time to lighten up Mary-Ann's flan recipes.

Lala was supportive, but also worried about me. She knew what the culinary industry was like. But I couldn't help myself. I needed to give it a try.

So what happened? How did I end up a pastry chef?

Culinary school was all about mastering savory techniques: French cuisine and the mother sauces. I learned how to be a prep cook and a line cook, but I didn't start baking in earnest until I met Hector,

my now-husband. As much as I love baking and pastry—it's what I'm known for, and why you're reading this book—the truth is, I got into this because I wanted a morning schedule so I could go on dates with Hector in the evening.

I taught myself how to bake mostly on my own, at home. I like to say I trained at YouTube University. At the beginning, I got the classics under my belt; I could give you a mean chocolate chip cookie and an absolutely jaw-dropping apple pie. But little by little, I started to play, drawing inspiration from all my lived experiences.

I learned how to trust my instincts. Instead of making a straightforward snickerdoodle, I infused the dough with the flavors of sorrel, the delightful Jamaican drink that's beloved well beyond Jamaica. Instead of making a classic chocolate chip cookie, I baked a version with a gooey tres leches core, a subtle nod to molten lava cakes. Classic pinwheel cookies turned into delightful moringa-soursop swirls.

(By the way, if you're wondering if Lala approves of my career path, this is what she has to say whenever I hand her a new batch of bakes: "Jyes, I like it!" Which in Lala means "I'm very proud of you.")

Not every combination was a hit; not every reference point fit. But eventually I realized that I wasn't robotically following someone else's instructions anymore. I was coming to understand who I was, and that I didn't want to tell anyone else's story but my own. A story where plátanos maduros, sticky buns, and Cosmic Brownies all play leading roles.

He's going to be embarrassed to read this, but I have to acknowledge that Hector has been a major influence guiding me toward this moment. Hector, the man who checked with my mom before asking me out. The guy who works crazy hours and would still go pick me up from work late every night (technically morning), even though our schedules couldn't have been more different. The incredibly

Miss Daisy Lebron, owner of my favorite childhood bakery,
Bizcocho de Colores (see page 131).

positive force who—at a point when I was ready to call it quits, having encountered far too many people in the industry who did not make me feel welcome—said go for it when I said I wanted to give professional cooking one last shot, as a pastry chef.

This book would not be possible without the love and support of Hector and people like him, and mentors like Jacques Torres and Christina Tosi, who showed me how wide, wonderful, and *kind* the world of pastry can be.

I'm not going to lie. There was a time, not very long ago, when the idea of writing a cookbook was the furthest possible thing from my mind. I almost threw in the towel a second time. It was 2020. I had spent three months on the phone every single day, trying to do something for my staff members who had lost their jobs due to the COVID-19 pandemic. By the end of those three months, it finally sank in for me: I was out of a job, too. I couldn't even get unemployment benefits, as the system was completely overwhelmed by applicants.

Over the years, I had skipped out on so many birthday parties and family gatherings. Worked my butt off, day after day, night after night, sometimes for no pay at all. And then the pandemic ripped it all away. I was in a bad place. I didn't touch flour or sugar for the longest time. It got dark. I had just earned a James Beard Award nomination, but I was convinced my career was over.

I don't know what happened, but one day, something flipped. Despite everything that was going on, I realized how lucky I still was and decided to refocus my frustration—to try to help those more unfortunate than I was, in particular the undocumented workforce. They were hurting the same hurt, but to a far greater degree.

I looked for local organizations with missions that aligned with the causes near and dear to me. There were many worthy, wonderful organizations, and speaking to each one gave me hope. In the end, I was very taken by the people and practices of Ayuda, a nonprofit in DC that has spent more than fifty years caring for low-income immigrants as they make their lives in America.

That is the cause I endeavored to support with my first pandemic pop-up, Doña Dona. I made four types of doughnuts and made them available for preorder, with the idea that folks would come pick them up at a local restaurant. It helped me organize, keep costs under control, and maximize the amount I could donate to Ayuda. I hired a talented Dominican artist named Agustina to create an amazing graphic that cast me as a muñeca sin rostro, one of those famous Dominican dolls without faces. This was in May 2020, and I didn't know if there would be much interest. When I launched the weekend pop-up, it sold out . . . five weeks in a row.

That fifth and final Saturday would have been a small moment of celebration. Instead, May 25, 2020, was a national tragedy—the day George Floyd was murdered. I can tell you exactly what I was thinking in the aftermath: *It could happen to Hector*. In the dizzying, sad, scary, and heavy days that followed, I fielded lots of calls from people who sounded like they wanted me to help them help others so they could feel better. I decided I was going to do something else.

I called up my friends and fellow chefs Rob Rubba and Willa Pelini. I created a new social media account, which I called Bakers Against Racism, and Rob designed a graphic. All three of us shared the account on our own accounts, along with a call to action. We asked our fellow bakers to join our activation. We had no idea if anyone *would* join us, but our goal was to get eighty chefs and bakers to raise $1,200 each in a sort of decentralized bake sale. I had identified organizations across the country fighting for social justice and equality that I knew would benefit from our support and shared my lists with all the participating chefs and bakers. I encouraged them to use my lists as a starting point, but to do their own research to learn about the unique issues and organizations in their local communities.

Drawing on my many years managing food costs and teams, as well as the experience I'd just had with the Doña Dona series, I also developed and shared detailed guides about how to make a successful pop-up (that are still available on the Bakers Against Racism website today, if you're interested!). I knew folks would find them useful, especially those who'd been forced to pivot after the pandemic shut their businesses down.

We had no expectations, only a need to do something, anything. Even so, there's a small part of your brain that can try to trick you into thinking, *It's a bake sale, dude, how much do you really think this can do?*

Hector and I answered nine hundred emails on the first official day. Turns out, there were more than two thousand people across the world interested in participating, way beyond what seemed at the time like a "lofty" goal of

eighty in our vicinity. By June, we'd collectively raised $1.9 million for social justice causes. We, not me. Bakers Against Racism continues to grow bigger and bigger with each activation. Its success depends on the power of the collective. I feel so lucky to be part of something that has grown beyond the trio that started it into a global phenomenon, with participants on four continents, that now belongs to everyone. There's a reason we chose the tagline "Baking the *world* a better place."

I'm grateful for these experiences, and grateful to have the chance to tell you a whole lot more over the next few hundred pages.

So, what can you expect from this book?

It's not in my nature to talk a big game, but I can tell you that *Bodega Bakes* is a collection of recipes that you can't find elsewhere: a mix of my classical training and love of Americana filtered through the Bronx and the islands of the Caribbean. It's filled with novel, accessible, irresistible flavor combinations. Because, as Ina would say, I like to turn the volume up. I'm talking about tropical opera cakes, guava and lemon bars, and dulce de leche babkas. A tamarind-and-pecan pie. My version of a sticky bun, featuring ripe plantains—which Guy Fieri says is the best sticky bun he's ever tried.

If you're wondering about the level of difficulty, this should all be a breeze. I mean that. I'm very serious when I say that I will make sure that anyone who tries to cook from this book will be successful. Over the course of my career, I've always been willing to hire anyone no matter their skill level, as long as they have a good attitude. I know that with a little time and care, I can bring them up to the same level as somebody who has been doing the job for ten years. This book is no different. I'm here to

hold your hand. My one-bowl cakes, for example, prove that you don't need to be a three-Michelin-star chef to prepare a mind-blowing dessert.

But this book isn't just about baking and eating, bursts of vivid color, and heart-warming stories about my abuela. When you google "Dominican pastry chef" these days, you'll only see one face. I hope that this work—these flavors and traditions, which may not be familiar to some of you reading this, as well as the way I use them to explore questions of family, diaspora, community, love, sacrifice, and change—marks a big step toward making sure that many more faces show up on that image search, and soon. Because more points of view mean more delicious recipes you haven't already seen everywhere else.

Take my famous Thick'em (page 33), which combines all the good parts of a crispy cookie and the gooey parts of a softly baked cookie to create a big, beautiful delight. It's a treat with crunchy edges and a molten center, and the most requested recipe in my repertoire—one which I've held off on sharing until now. I've been waiting for the right moment. (You can't blame me. I first started dreaming this up all the way back in summer camp, where they served something called "The Big Cookie." They made it in a cast-iron pan and topped it with ice cream. The edges were perfection. But the rest of the affair was trash, tbh. So I decided to fix the issue.)

Most people who try a Thick'em insist that there is a secret or trick that makes this chocolate chip cookie stand out. They beg me to tell them. The truth, which I can now reveal, is that I stick to pantry staples: vanilla, dark and milk chocolates, salt.

You know, stuff you can pick up at the bodega.

Paola's Pantry

No matter where you come from, something tells me you'll encounter ingredients you've never tried before while baking from this book. Nothing could make me happier.

One thing I should call out right from the top is that not all my inspirations come from the bodega, even though I wouldn't blame you for expecting as much, given the book's title. Some of my fondest memories are of my abuela's home in the Dominican countryside, where my family raised chickens for their eggs and grew all sorts of fruits, vegetables, cacao, and even coffee beans. Every morning I'd put on my long-sleeve shirt and little booties to avoid getting stung by bees (I'm allergic) as I grabbed fresh fruits and avocados from the fields. The only foods we had to venture elsewhere to get were pork from my cousin's pork stand, roasted chicken from my other cousin's chicken stand, and ice cream from Helados Bon.

I hope some of the magic of these memories comes through for you in the pages and recipes in this book, because they're just so special to me.

DULCE DE LECHE

Dulce de leche has always been essential to my baking—and my life. By now, it's a staple well beyond South America and the Caribbean. I'm not gonna lie, dulce de leche is the sweetest of the sweet. But that doesn't stop me from eating it by the spoonful. Look for dulce de leche in the baking aisle of your supermarket, or make it following the recipe on page 281.

BROWNED BUTTER

I like to use browned butter to provide depth of flavor—especially for my Thick'ems (see pages 33–39). But in addition to that, browning butter reduces the butter's liquid content and provides a more stabilized fat for your dessert. I like to brown a few cups of butter at a time and keep it stored airtight in the refrigerator—see page 277 for my technique. Of course you should use it in your baked goods—cakes and cookies—but just imagine a browned butter cacio e pepe. (You're welcome!)

BLACK PEPPER

One of my signature moves is to incorporate black pepper into sweets that would otherwise be too cloying. This comes in very handy when you're the type of person who loves caramel and sweetened condensed milk and wishes they could consume more of it without experiencing palate fatigue.

VANILLA BEAN PASTE, PURE VANILLA EXTRACT, AND DOMINICAN IMITATION VANILLA EXTRACT

Thick vanilla bean paste gives you the concentrated flavor of vanilla without having to spend on a pod. I love using it because of that lovely flavor, but also for aesthetic reasons—sometimes you just want to see those beautiful vanilla freckles, and this is how you get there. Well-stocked supermarkets should sell vanilla bean paste, but if you can't find it there, look online. Pure vanilla extract is made by steeping whole vanilla beans in a mixture of alcohol and water. Feel free to use it, if that's your preference, but I'm not about to frown upon imitation vanilla—especially not Dominican imitation vanilla, which is a little sweeter and more fragrant and helps make our desserts distinct. It can be found at well-stocked international markets, but your best bet is probably buying it online. If you can't find a Dominican brand of imitation vanilla, look for Mexican brands, which I support as well!

IMITATION LEMON EXTRACT

If you don't have fresh lemons or regular lemon extract, go right ahead and use an imitation lemon extract, such as McCormick brand. Look for it in the baking aisle of most grocery stores.

ROSE WATER

Rose water appears in just one recipe in this book—Rose Water & Coconut Macaroons (page 67)—but I want to shine a light on this ingredient, which Hispanic cultures appreciate for the quiet, floral quality it lends to baked goods, balancing out acidity and bringing focus to sweet elements. It's also a lovely example of the Middle Eastern influence in Dominican cuisine.

MALTA

Rich, hoppy, and intense, malta is a nonalcoholic soda made from hops and barley. It's also an acquired taste, one that a lot of folks never come around to acquiring. I love drinking the stuff, and the unique depth it brings to my Chocolate Malta Cake (page 164).

MARIA COOKIES

The best damn biscuity cookies, these subtly sweet treats have been a part of my life since as far back as I can remember. They're a constant presence in Latin households, enjoyed alone and in abundance; to accompany coffee or tea, and, in my case, to dazzle as part of two of my favorite cakes (pages 139 and 153). Maria cookies are available in the international aisle of many supermarkets, and in markets specializing in Latin American ingredients.

LADYFINGERS

As you'll learn when you read about my Black & White Cookie Charlotte (page 223), I grew up very close to the Stella d'Oro factory in the Bronx. Ladyfingers trigger something warm and nostalgic for me, and I can put down an entire box of them in one sitting.

BAKER'S ANGEL FLAKE COCONUT FLAKES

Very finely ground coconut makes all the difference when you want the bits to disperse evenly in a mixture or batter, keeping the texture as smooth and elegant as possible. You can find Baker's Angel Flake coconut in the baking aisle of most grocery stores. If you can't find them, use regular unsweetened coconut flakes and pulse them in a food processor with a bit of powdered sugar to help break them up.

BLACK (NOIR) COCOA POWDER

In recipes like my Triple Chocolate Noir Thick'ems (page 34), I call for noir cocoa powder, so you can access peak chocolaty richness. To me, its rich chocolate flavor and color are reminiscent of Oreos. Try adding a pinch to a braise or a stew, and watch the flavor become more complex. A beautiful ingredient. You might have to buy this online or at a specialty chocolate shop. If you don't have noir cocoa powder, you can most certainly use a Dutch-process cocoa powder, such as Hershey's.

COFFEE LEAVES

I grew up drinking coffee-leaf tea because we grew coffee plants in our backyard in the Dominican Republic. So of course I like to utilize the whole plant. You'll see coffee leaves featured in the Té de Hoja de Café Madeleines (page 47). The best place to find these is the internet. If you can't find them there, check out an Ethiopian market. So much amazing coffee is cultivated in Ethiopia, and Ethiopian cooking uses coffee leaves in delicious ways.

NASTURTIUM LEAVES

A lot of restaurants these days will garnish with nasturtium leaves to give dishes a natural feel. I blend them and add them to desserts like the Nasturtium Coconut Cream Pie (page 108) so you get not only a green burst of color but also peppery notes that help balance out the richness in the dessert. If you can't find any (or don't grow them on your balcony like I do), use peppercress or arugula (which won't have quite the same peppery zing) instead.

HIBISCUS

Hibiscus, or sorrel, as it's known in Jamaica and other parts of the Caribbean (it's called jamaica in Mexico and other Spanish-speaking countries) tastes as good as it looks and imparts a lot of flavor, brightness, and vitamin C. I roll my Sorrel Snickerdoodles (page 58) into a sugar mixed with hibiscus powder, use the ground leaves to bring sweet-sour notes to donut icing (see page 203), and celebrate the flowers' bright and brilliant red hue as a garnish for Hibiscus-Pineapple Sorbet (page 265). Look for dried edible hibiscus flowers in the tea aisle of your supermarket, or at international markets. You can make hibiscus powder by pulsing the dried flowers in your blender or in a clean coffee grinder.

GUAVA PASTE

If it's not part of your rotation already, you are about to become very well acquainted with guava paste, which is a birthright for most people of Caribbean descent. We keep it in the pantry at all times to enjoy with sliced cheese and crackers, and we love what happens when it's paired with cream cheese in a turnover (see page 110). It's essential in my Beginner's Guide to Dominican Cake (page 131) and Passion Fruit & Guava Mascarpone Tart (page 117). Unopened guava paste can be stored in a cool, dark place like your pantry cabinet, but once opened, you should move it to the fridge. Look for it at international markets, especially those specializing in Latin American ingredients.

WARMING SPICES

This is a big one for me: I wholeheartedly embrace the liberal use of warming spices in Dominican desserts—I'm talking about cinnamon, ginger, allspice, and cloves, which provide a magnificently cozy effect in my Majarete (page 232), Bulla Snickerdoodles (page 52), and Tres Leches Thick'ems (page 38).

MORINGA

A fruit packed with antioxidants and other nutrients, moringa in powdered form looks similar to matcha—and makes the Moringa-Soursop Swirl Cookies on page 62 such a joy to behold (and consume). Look for culinary moringa powder online.

SOURSOP

This is a tropical fruit that we used to grow in my backyard in DR, whose flavor will remind you of strawberries and citrus. The pureed variety is showcased in both the Peach, Cinnamon & Soursop Cobbler (page 114) and the Moringa-Soursop Swirl Cookies (page 62). Buy frozen soursop puree in Latin markets or international markets specializing in subtropic cuisines.

PLANTAINS

When you get to chapter five, you're in plantain city. Plantains are an essential ingredient in my sticky buns (see pages 169–180) and many other recipes throughout the book. You can find fresh plantains pretty much anywhere in the country . . . but for baking, I actually prefer to work with frozen plantains. If you do use fresh plantains, you're going to have to let them get suuuper ripe, almost blackened, and that takes time. Worse, it might attract fruit flies. Nobody wants that. Look for frozen plantains, which will already be peeled and chopped into pieces, alongside the other frozen fruit at the supermarket. I don't even defrost the plantain pieces when I use them in my sticky buns—I just let them thaw in the saucepan and add a couple of minutes to the cooking time.

PUFF PASTRY

If you'll be using store-bought puff pastry, a high-quality brand like Dufour is preferred, but any puff pastry will work in a pinch. Or you can make your own following the recipe on page 277, which is the BEST option.

SANDING SUGAR

Sanding sugar is a little coarser than granulated sugar, so when you bake it, it doesn't dissolve into the pastry. Think of it as a finishing sugar.

SUPERFINE SUGAR

Superfine sugar (known as caster sugar in the UK) is finer than granulated sugar, but not as fine as powdered sugar. If you don't have it and don't want to buy it, you can sub granulated sugar, which shouldn't affect the recipe too much.

GELATIN

I typically make pastries with gelatin leaves or sheets, but they're a bit harder to source than unflavored gelatin powder. So for the recipes in this book, I call for gelatin powder from packets; each packet typically contains ¼ ounce (7 g) of gelatin, or roughly 2½ teaspoons. Use any brand—Knox is one widely available example.

Scrape & Pack What Ya Momma Gave Ya

and Other Notes About These Recipes

Notes About Ingredients

All **eggs** are large eggs unless otherwise specified. All **salt** is kosher unless otherwise specified. You can use any kosher salt you like, but if your favorite is Morton's, you should halve the amount called for in these recipes. I do all my baking with Diamond Crystal kosher salt, which is less dense and therefore seems less salty than Morton's. All **lime juice** and **lemon juice** is fresh.

Notes About Equipment

BAKING SHEET SIZES

All baking sheets are 9 by 13-inch rimmed baking sheets, except when I call for a rimmed eighth sheet pan, which is roughly 6 by 9 inches, or a half sheet pan, which is 13 by 18 inches.

LINING BAKING SHEETS AND GREASING BAKING PANS

I line baking sheets with parchment paper to make cleanup easier. I line 9 by 13-inch baking pans and the pans I use to form frozen desserts (like you'll find on pages 247–274) with enough overhanging parchment to make lifting bars/semifrios/etc. out of the pan easier. Snip the corners so the parchment perfectly lines the walls of the baking pan, then trim away any excess.

Sometimes I will tell you to line a baking pan with parchment *and* grease it. I do this when something is super sticky and I want you to play

it safe. You can definitely use cooking sprays—I sometimes call for a spray-style cooking oil—or you can butter or oil the pan the old-fashioned way, if that feels right.

STAND MIXER

Ideally, if a recipe calls for a stand mixer fitted with the paddle attachment, that's what you should use. But you certainly don't have to miss out on the fun if you don't have one. You can use a hand mixer instead, especially for softer cookie doughs, cake batter, meringues, and icings. If you're making something with a very firm dough, such as brioche or my Thick'ems, you'll have better luck using your hands than a hand mixer. (Sometimes the batter is just so thick and abundant, those poor lil electric beaters can't handle it. It's sad to see them struggling.)

As long as your butter is super soft, it shouldn't take much longer to cream butter with a hand mixer than with a stand mixer. If your butter is cold, it might need a bit more time—a hand mixer is simply less powerful than a stand mixer.

And if you want to do it all by hand, I'm here to tell you that you can. My mom doesn't have a mixer at home, so sometimes even I do it manually. Here's what I do: I get the butter really soft, and then I put on a glove (sometimes, if I'm feeling very unhinged, I'll do it *without* a glove). I mash the butter and sugar together with my gloved hand, using my body heat to really warm it up further and help it incorporate with the sugar. It won't look creamed at this point. Then I get a firm rubber spatula (not one with a flippy-floppy tip) and use that to really press the butter into the sides of the bowl. I stir vigorously like that for 10 to 15 minutes and eventually the color changes, becoming paler, and there it is—creamed butter and sugar. I'm not gonna lie to you: It's an awful process, so difficult, 0 out of 10 stars. I am not meant for it. But if you are, God bless you.

COOKIE-SCOOP SIZES

You'll notice a range of cookie-scoop sizes in this book. Don't sweat it if you need to eyeball the measurement with a spoon, tablespoon, or even a cup measure, then portion the dough to the correct size and roll it into a ball with your hands.

PIPING BAGS

For ease and control, I highly recommend using piping bags. They are the best, and once you buy one or two, you'll never look back. Personally, I would avoid using a zip-top bag, particularly for firm frosting, because they're messy and harder to control. You don't want your plastic bag bursting on you—that would be sad. In a pinch, you can use parchment paper to make a cornet instead, a technique we learn in culinary school. I'm not going to lie, it can be pretty difficult at first—but with practice, you can learn anything! I suggest going to YouTube (you know how much I love YouTube University) and searching for "pastry cornet tutorials." Soon you'll be like me, making cornets lightning-quick and with any shape of triangle. (Making good parchment paper cornets might actually be my superpower.) You can use your cornet for royal icing, chocolate work, or any other delicate touches, like writing "Happy Birthday," or "I Quit" on your resignation cake.

THERMOMETERS

A deep-fry or candy thermometer is the best way to ensure your cooking oil is at the perfect temperature to fry the donas on pages 181–194. And a standard instant-read thermometer is great for checking if doughy pastries like sticky buns are fully cooked.

Notes About My Cup Measurement

To state the very obvious, I want you to make these recipes effortlessly—and correctly—so I made something for you: The chart opposite shows what 1 cup of all-purpose flour means for me compared to what 1 cup of all-purpose flour means for some of my baking heroes. It may also help explain why certain recipes you've made in the past haven't worked out, even though you've followed the measurements with the greatest care.

For my 1 cup, you have to pack with firmness and consistency, and use a butter knife, offset spatula, or anything with a straight edge to make sure the flour and the edge of the measuring cup are completely level. The surface should look like pristine, very flat sand. **Each of my cups of flour weighs 140 g.**

Do I encourage you to buy a kitchen scale? I'm a professional chef and baker, so you know the answer is yes, because it lowers the margin for error. But I'm also the person who likes to say things like "Pastry is often referred to as a science, but I see it more as a séance"—which means I am equally fond of keeping things loose and leaning on intuition. This is why I've included volume measures in my recipes for those of you who are not yet willing to join the kitchen scale club.

Notes About Techniques & Storage

BEATING EGG WHITES

Grease is the enemy, at least when you're beating egg whites, and laziness in this matter will be the end of you. So listen closely: Keep the bowl very, very clean before dropping your egg whites in and

1 US IMPERIAL CUP IN GRAMS

. . . ACCORDING TO ME & SOME OF MY BAKING HEROES

AP FLOUR

122 GRAMS — **The Petite Martha**
LIGHTLY SPOONING & FAIRY-TALE LEVELING

The Darling Dorie — **136 GRAMS**
CUTE & CONFIDENT PACKING & EVEN LEVELING

140 GRAMS — **The Paola**
SCRAPE & PACK WITH WHAT YA MOMMA GAVE YA

The Ina Garten — **150 GRAMS**
INA MEASURES WITH HER HEART AND SOUL—IN INA WE TRUST

whipping them. If you feel like your bowl is a little greasy, add a bit of vinegar or lemon juice and wipe with a paper towel. Same goes for your stand mixer's whisk attachment or your hand mixer's beaters.

There are two types of meringue: Egg whites without sugar are used as a stabilizer. When you whip them to soft peaks, which takes about 5 minutes, they will be fluffy and soft, and very airy, like a sponge. Egg whites with sugar are different—they'll become glossier and more compact or dense as you whip. When you stop whipping and pull up your whisk attachment or beaters, the egg whites will billow down, creating a layered-on-itself shape that looks like soft-serve ice cream. Medium peaks take about 7 minutes and will be stiffer than what's described above. Firm peaks take about 10 minutes, and when you lift up the whisk, the peak should stand straight up—not collapse on itself like with soft peaks.

When I use a stand mixer to whip egg whites, I generally start on low speed and gradually increase the speed every minute or two until I get to high. This reduces the risk of mess. No stand mixer? Use a hand mixer (but again, make sure your beaters and bowl are degreased!) or, if you're brave, a whisk and some old-fashioned elbow grease.

TEMPERING EGGS

Tempering eggs is the process of gradually adding heat to raw eggs so they don't scramble when added to a hot mixture. (If you just plopped eggs into a pot of hot liquid, the eggs would curdle and you'd get a lumpy texture and eggy taste.) To temper eggs, place the eggs in a heatproof bowl and whisk them lightly. Get a ladleful of hot liquid and, while whisking the eggs continuously, slowly stream in the hot liquid and whisk until well combined. You should have a nice liquidy consistency with no gloopy eggs. Now you can safely pour that tempered egg mixture into the pan with the rest of the hot liquid without worrying that the egg will scramble.

Tropical Bark, page 78

MELTING AND TEMPERING CHOCOLATE

When it comes to melting chocolate, the microwave is your friend. Place the chocolate in a microwave-safe bowl and microwave on high in 15-second bursts, stirring after every interval. Don't overdo it, though—the residual heat will help melt the rest of the chocolate at the end.

Tempering is a process in which you slowly heat chocolate to a specific temperature and then cool it back down, allowing the chocolate molecules to crystallize evenly. Why should you care whether your chocolate molecules crystallize evenly? Well, I'm not here to tell you what you should care about in your life. You can make most of the recipes in this book without tempering. But we professional pastry chefs rely on tempering to provide structure (that appealing snap when you break the chocolate) and to make the chocolate aesthetically pleasing (a shiny, even color). If you don't temper your chocolate, you might see white streaks throughout—this is where the cocoa butter solids have separated from the cacao.

BLOOMING GELATIN

When you're working with powdered gelatin, you need to bloom before using it. Sounds fancy, but "blooming" just means hydrating and softening it in a liquid. To do this, put your cold liquid in a small bowl and sprinkle the gelatin over the surface; stir to incorporate, then let it stand for 5 minutes. You'll know the gelatin is bloomed when the mixture is thicker and almost jellylike. Keep in mind that the granules won't dissolve completely at this point—you need heat to do that, which is why I heat the gelatin later, either on the stovetop or by folding in something like warm pastry cream. I always try to bloom gelatin in liquid that's already being used in the recipe—in other words, I don't add more moisture.

SCORING BARS AND CAKES

When it comes to scoring bars and cakes, I like to use a warm knife to make cutting easier. I warm my knives under hot running water, or, if I need to keep the knife warm over time, in a large container of hot water; I keep a kitchen towel handy to wipe off any excess water before cutting.

SIFTING FLOUR

You don't have to do it! So don't worry about it.

DON'T WANT TO BAKE IT ALL?

Some of these recipes—the cookies in chapter one, for example—have pretty big yields. You might not have enough baking sheets (or hungry people in your life) to bake them all at once. The good news is, almost all of my cookie doughs freeze beautifully for up to 1 year.

For larger cookies like my Thick'ems, I recommend wrapping each cookie dough ball individually in plastic wrap to avoid freezer burn, then storing the wrapped dough balls in an airtight container.

Smaller cookies, like my lemon cookies, don't necessarily need to be individually wrapped. I like to store them in small or medium zip-top bags: Arrange them in the bag in a 4- or 5-inch square, with the edges just touching, so they freeze in a little block and you can just snap off however many cookies you want to bake at a time. You'll thank me when you have a freezer full of cookies ready to be baked at a moment's notice.

Galletas para Todos

(Cookies
for All)

OG Chocolate Chip Thick'ems

I used to sell these to raise funds for disadvantaged young women in Brooklyn, so they could buy feminine products. Back then, I was barely scraping by, but I had been taught that that was no excuse. Maybe I wasn't making the big bucks, but I had time, and time is a currency.

Line one large or two small baking sheets with parchment paper.

In the bowl of a stand mixer fitted with the paddle attachment, beat the browned butter, brown sugar, and granulated sugar on medium-low speed until aerated and paler in color, 4 to 5 minutes. With the mixer on medium-low speed, add the eggs one at a time, mixing until evenly incorporated and scraping down the sides and bottom of the bowl after each addition. Add the vanilla and mix to incorporate.

In a large bowl, whisk together the flour, salt, and baking soda to combine. Add the dry ingredients to the mixer bowl with the wet ingredients and pulse the mixer on and off, almost like you're trying to jump-start a car, so the flour gets gradually incorporated without flying all over your kitchen. When the dry ingredients are mostly combined, turn off the mixer and add the dark and milk chocolates and the butterscotch chips. Mix on medium-low speed until all the flour is incorporated and the chocolate and butterscotch are evenly distributed.

Using a 6-ounce cookie scoop or ¾-cup measuring cup, scoop balls of dough onto the prepared baking sheets, leaving about 2 inches between the cookies and at least 1 inch between the cookies and the edges of the pan. Use your fingers to lightly flatten the tops—this will help the cookies spread as they bake instead of staying domed. Cover with plastic wrap and refrigerate overnight. (If you don't want to bake them all at once, freeze some of the dough as directed on page 29.)

The next day, preheat the oven to 350°F.

Bake the cookies for 15 to 18 minutes, until crispy and golden brown on the outside but still gooey on the inside. Remove from the oven and let rest on the baking sheet for 4 to 5 minutes. These are best served warm, but no one has ever turned their nose up at one that was room temp, either.

MAKES 8 THIIIIIICCKKK COOKIES

- 1 cup (225 g) Browned Butter (page 277), at room temperature
- 1 cup plus 2 tablespoons lightly packed (235 g) light brown sugar
- ¾ cup (150 g) granulated sugar
- 2 large eggs
- 2¼ teaspoons vanilla bean paste or vanilla extract
- 3¼ cups (450 g) all-purpose flour
- 1 teaspoon kosher salt
- ½ teaspoon baking soda
- 6 ounces (170 g) dark chocolate, chopped, or 1 cup (170 g) semisweet chocolate chips
- 3 ounces (85 g) milk chocolate, chopped, or ½ cup (85 g) milk chocolate chips
- ¼ cup (40 g) butterscotch chips

Triple Chocolate Noir Thick'ems

MAKES 8 THIIIIIICCKKK COOKIES

1 cup (225 g) Browned Butter (page 277), at room temperature

1 cup plus 2 tablespoons lightly packed (235 g) light brown sugar

¾ cup (150 g) granulated sugar

2 large eggs

2¼ teaspoons vanilla bean paste or vanilla extract

3¼ cups (450 g) all-purpose flour

¼ cup (25 g) black (noir) cocoa powder

1 teaspoon kosher salt

½ teaspoon baking soda

6 ounces (170 g) dark chocolate (62% cacao), chopped, or 1 cup (170 g) semisweet chocolate chips

3 ounces (85 g) dark chocolate (70% cacao), chopped

3 ounces (85 g) milk chocolate, chopped, or ½ cup (85 g) milk chocolate chips

¼ cup (40 g) butterscotch chips

If a Brooklyn Blackout Cake is your kind of cake, then this is your kind of cookie. We've got dark chocolate, we've got milk chocolate, we've got noir cocoa powder, and then a little butterscotch, in the form of a warm cookie almost the size of a baby's head.

Line one large or two small baking sheets with parchment paper.

In the bowl of a stand mixer fitted with the paddle attachment, beat the browned butter, brown sugar, and granulated sugar on medium-low speed until aerated and paler in color, 4 to 5 minutes. With the mixer on medium-low speed, add the eggs one at a time, mixing until evenly incorporated and scraping down the sides and bottom of the bowl after each addition. Add the vanilla and mix to incorporate.

In a large bowl, whisk together the flour, cocoa powder, salt, and baking soda to combine. Add the dry ingredients to the mixer bowl with the wet ingredients and pulse the mixer on and off, almost like you're trying to jump-start a car, so the flour gets gradually incorporated without flying all over your kitchen. When the dry ingredients are mostly combined, turn off the mixer and add the dark and milk chocolates and the butterscotch chips. Mix on medium-low speed until all the flour is incorporated and the chocolate and butterscotch are evenly distributed.

Using a 6-ounce cookie scoop or ¾-cup measuring cup, scoop balls of dough onto the prepared baking sheets, leaving about 2 inches between the cookies and at least 1 inch between the cookies and the edges of the pan. Use your fingers to lightly flatten the tops—this will help the cookies spread as they bake instead of staying domed. Cover with plastic wrap and refrigerate overnight. (If you don't want to bake them all at once, freeze some of the dough as directed on page 29.)

The next day, preheat the oven to 350°F.

Bake the cookies for 15 to 18 minutes, until crispy and golden brown on the outside but still gooey on the inside. Remove from the oven and let rest on the baking sheet for 4 to 5 minutes, then serve warm.

Matcha
Thick'ems
(page 36)

Raspberry, White
Chocolate & Cranberry
Thick'ems (page 37)

Triple Chocolate
Noir Thick'ems
(opposite)

Matcha Thick'ems

MAKES 8 THIIIIIICCKKK
COOKIES

1 cup (225 g) Browned Butter
    (page 277), at room
    temperature
1 cup plus 2 tablespoons lightly
    packed (235 g) light brown sugar
¾ cup (150 g) granulated sugar
2 large eggs
2¼ teaspoons vanilla bean paste or
    vanilla extract
3¼ cups (450 g) all-purpose flour
3 tablespoons culinary matcha
    powder (use more if you love
    intense matcha flavor)
1 teaspoon kosher salt
½ teaspoon baking soda
9 ounces (1 cup/255 g) toasted white
    chocolate chips (see Note)
3 ounces (85 g) white chocolate
    (discs, fèves, or chopped from
    a bar)
2 tablespoons chopped
    butterscotch chips

NOTE: *You can buy toasted white
chocolate, like Valrhona Dulcey
blond chocolate fèves, or you can
buy plain white chocolate chips
(or bars, which you'd chop) and
toast them yourself: Spread the
chips or chopped chocolate over a
parchment-lined baking sheet and
bake at 200°F for 40 minutes, until
the color changes from white to tan
and the flavor intensifies and cara-
melizes. Remove from the oven and
let cool before using.*

I'm pretty sure you can add matcha to almost anything, and I'm not
just talking about beverages, cakes, or icings. The other day, I folded
some into empanada discs before frying them, and I definitely
didn't regret it. But I digress. These Matcha Thick'ems are a divine
union of the aforementioned green tea powder, beautiful browned
butter, and milky chocolate. I really like how the golden bits of this
cookie, which taste like the purest, toastiest hōjicha, balance out
the sweetness and keep you coming back for more bites.

Line one large or two small baking sheets with parchment paper.

In the bowl of a stand mixer fitted with the paddle attachment, beat
the browned butter, brown sugar, and granulated sugar on medium-
low speed until aerated and paler in color, 4 to 5 minutes. With the
mixer on medium-low speed, add the eggs one at a time, mixing until
evenly incorporated and scraping down the sides and bottom of the
bowl after each addition. Add the vanilla and mix to incorporate.

In a large bowl, whisk together the flour, matcha, salt, and baking
soda to combine. Add the dry ingredients to the mixer bowl with the
wet ingredients and pulse the mixer on and off, almost like you're trying to jump-start a car, so the flour gets gradually incorporated without flying all over your kitchen. When the dry ingredients are mostly
combined, turn off the mixer and add the toasted white chocolate,
chopped white chocolate, and butterscotch chips. Mix on medium-
low speed until all the flour is incorporated and the chocolate and
butterscotch are evenly distributed.

Using a 6-ounce cookie scoop or ¾-cup measuring cup, scoop balls
of dough onto the prepared baking sheets, leaving about 2 inches
between the cookies and at least 1 inch between the cookies and the
edges of the pan. Use your fingers to lightly flatten the tops—this will
help the cookies spread as they bake instead of staying domed. Cover
with plastic wrap and refrigerate overnight. (If you don't want to bake
them all at once, freeze some of the dough as directed on page 29.)

The next day, preheat the oven to 350°F.

Bake the cookies for 15 to 18 minutes, until crispy and golden brown
on the outside but still gooey on the inside. Remove from the oven
and let rest on the baking sheet for 4 to 5 minutes, then serve warm.

Raspberry, White Chocolate & Cranberry Thick'ems

I love baking these during the holidays, but I don't want that detail, or the cranberry sauces you associate with the colder months, to fool you—it's all brightness here. Think of this recipe as a warm hug with a side of sunshine.

Line one large or two small baking sheets with parchment paper.

In the bowl of a stand mixer fitted with the paddle attachment, beat the browned butter, brown sugar, and granulated sugar on medium-low speed until aerated and paler in color, 4 to 5 minutes. With the mixer on medium-low speed, add the eggs one at a time, mixing until evenly incorporated and scraping down the sides and bottom of the bowl after each addition. Add the vanilla and mix to incorporate.

In a large bowl, whisk together the flour, salt, and baking soda to combine. Add the dry ingredients to the mixer bowl with the wet ingredients and pulse the mixer on and off, almost like you're trying to jump-start a car, so the flour gets gradually incorporated without flying all over your kitchen. When the dry ingredients are mostly combined, turn off the mixer and add the raspberry chocolate chips, white chocolate chips, and dried cranberries. Mix on medium-low speed until all the flour is incorporated and the chocolate and butterscotch are evenly distributed.

Using a 6-ounce cookie scoop or ¾-cup measuring cup, scoop balls of dough onto the prepared baking sheets, leaving about 2 inches between the cookies and at least 1 inch between the cookies and the edges of the pan. Use your fingers to lightly flatten the tops—this will help the cookies spread as they bake instead of staying domed. Cover with plastic wrap and refrigerate overnight. (If you don't want to bake them all at once, freeze some of the dough as directed on page 29.)

The next day, preheat the oven to 350°F.

Bake the cookies for 14 to 16 minutes, until crispy and golden brown on the outside but still gooey on the inside. Remove from the oven and let rest on the baking sheet for 4 to 5 minutes, then serve warm.

MAKES 8 THIIIIIICCKKK COOKIES

1 cup (225 g) Browned Butter (page 277), at room temperature

1 cup plus 2 tablespoons lightly packed (235 g) light brown sugar

¾ cup (150 g) granulated sugar

2 large eggs

2¼ teaspoons vanilla bean paste or vanilla extract

3¼ cups (450 g) all-purpose flour

1 teaspoon kosher salt

½ teaspoon baking soda

12 ounces (340 g) raspberry chocolate chips, such as Valrhona Inspiration Framboise

12 ounces (340 g) white chocolate chips

¾ cup (105 g) chopped dried cranberries

Tres Leches Thick'ems

MAKES 8 FILLED COOKIES

FILLING

4 ounces (115 g) cream cheese, at
    room temperature
6 tablespoons (90 mL) sweetened
    condensed milk
1 large egg yolk

DOUGH

1 cup (225 g) Browned Butter
    (page 277), at room temperature
1 cup plus 2 tablespoons lightly
    packed (235 g) light brown sugar
¾ cup (150 g) granulated sugar
2 large eggs
2¼ teaspoons vanilla bean paste or
    vanilla extract
3¼ cups (450 g) all-purpose flour
¼ cup (30 g) malted milk powder
1 teaspoon kosher salt
½ teaspoon baking soda
12 ounces (340 g) milk chocolate
    chips

A lava cake in cookie form. It's not like I need to say more, but just in case, here's what's going on: The milk chocolate Thick'em is spiked with a little malt powder and then stuffed with a frozen puck of sweetened condensed milk and queso crema (cream cheese) that will melt as it bakes and ooze out when you take a bite. Sometimes I'll add a sprinkle of cinnamon at the end for the full tres leches feeling. (You know I love my warming spices.) Because of the time you need to make and cool the different components, this is a three-day bake. I don't say that to scare you off—trust me, they are totally worth the wait!

MAKE THE FILLING: At least one day before you plan to bake your cookies, line a plate with parchment paper. In a large bowl, whisk together the cream cheese, condensed milk, and egg yolk until combined. Scoop 1-tablespoon portions of the filling onto the plate, wrap in plastic wrap, and freeze for 24 hours.

THE NEXT DAY, MAKE THE DOUGH: Line one large or two small baking sheets with parchment paper.

In the bowl of a stand mixer fitted with the paddle attachment, beat the browned butter, brown sugar, and granulated sugar on medium-low speed until aerated and paler in color, 4 to 5 minutes. With the mixer on medium-low speed, add the eggs one at a time, mixing until evenly incorporated and scraping down the sides and bottom of the bowl after each addition. Add the vanilla and mix to incorporate.

In a large bowl, whisk together the flour, malted milk powder, salt, and baking soda to combine. Add the dry ingredients to the mixer bowl with the wet ingredients and pulse the mixer on and off, almost like you're trying to jump-start a car, so the flour gets gradually incorporated without flying all over your kitchen. When the dry ingredients are mostly combined, turn off the mixer and add the chocolate chips. Mix on medium-low speed until all the flour is incorporated and the chocolate is evenly distributed.

Using a 3-ounce cookie scoop or ⅓-cup measuring cup, scoop the dough into 16 balls and place them on a couple of large plates. Working with one at a time, grab a dough ball, then grab a portion of the frozen filling. Place the filling in the center of the dough ball, then grab a

second dough ball and sandwich the filling between the dough. Seal the edges tightly to enclose the filling so it won't leak when baking. Use your hands to lightly flatten the top and bottom of the cookie—it'll look more like a deflated ball than a hockey puck. Place the assembled cookie back on the plate and repeat with the remaining dough and filling. When all your cookies are shaped, wrap the plates in plastic wrap and freeze overnight.

The next day, preheat the oven to 350°F.

Bake the cookies for 17 to 20 minutes, until crispy and golden brown on the outside but still gooey on the inside. Remove from the oven and let rest on the baking sheet for 4 to 5 minutes, then serve warm.

Classic Snickerdoodles

MAKES 16 COOKIES

1 cup (2 sticks/225 g) unsalted
    butter, softened
2 cups (400 g) granulated sugar
¼ cup lightly packed (50 g) light
    brown sugar
2 large eggs
½ teaspoon coconut extract
2¾ cups (385 g) all-purpose flour
2 tablespoons plus 1 teaspoon
    ground cinnamon
2 teaspoons cream of tartar
1 teaspoon baking soda
½ teaspoon kosher salt

A classic snickerdoodle recipe to start, so you can appreciate what makes this legendary cookie so special: the tang and chew provided by the cream of tartar, and the comforts of cinnamon sugar. If there's a Paola touch to call out, it's the coconut extract, but this one's really about honoring tradition. We'll have time to get a little wacky in the two variations that follow (pages 27 and 30).

Preheat the oven to 400°F. Line two large baking sheets with parchment paper.

In the bowl of a stand mixer fitted with the paddle attachment (or using one of the alternate methods on page 25), beat the butter, 1½ cups (300 g) of the granulated sugar, and the brown sugar on high speed until light and pale, 8 to 10 minutes. Reduce the mixer speed to medium and add the eggs one at a time, mixing until combined and scraping down the sides and bottom of the bowl after each addition. Add the coconut extract and mix until combined.

In a medium bowl, whisk together the flour, 2 tablespoons of the cinnamon, the cream of tartar, baking soda, and salt to combine. Add the dry ingredients to the mixer bowl with the wet ingredients and pulse the mixer on and off, almost like you're trying to jump-start a car, so the flour gets gradually incorporated without flying all over your kitchen. When the dry ingredients are mostly combined, mix on low to incorporate them fully.

Using a 2-ounce cookie scoop (or a large spoon—your portions should be ¼ cup), scoop portions of the dough and put them on a plate.

In a small bowl, combine the remaining ½ cup (100 g) granulated sugar and remaining 1 teaspoon cinnamon.

Roll the cookies in the cinnamon-sugar to coat completely, then place them on the prepared baking sheets, leaving at least 2 inches between the cookies and 1 inch between the cookies and the edges of the pan. (If you don't want to bake them all at once, freeze some of the dough as directed on page 29.)

Bake for 9 to 10 minutes, until golden. Remove from the oven and let cool on the baking sheets for 3 minutes, then transfer to a wire rack to cool completely before serving.

Lala's Mantecaditos

No matter how often I bake these butter cookies for my mom—or how many I bring—they vanish almost immediately. Lala is getting faster and faster at demolishing my care packages. She cannot be contained. Lucky for me, I can keep up, since they're so easy to prepare. In between visits, I just make batches of the dough, pop them in the freezer, and wait for the inevitable phone call.

Of course, you may not have to keep up with someone as mantecadito-obsessed as Lala, but it's always nice to know there are butter cookies waiting to go into the oven at a moment's notice.

MAKE THE DOUGH: Preheat the oven to 350°F. Line two large baking sheets with parchment paper.

In the bowl of a stand mixer fitted with the paddle attachment (or using one of the alternate methods on page 25), combine the butter and powdered sugar. Pulse the mixer on and off a few times to start incorporating the sugar so it doesn't fly all over the place, then mix on medium speed for 3 to 5 minutes, until fluffy and pale.

In a medium bowl, lightly whisk together the flour, salt, and nutmeg. Add the dry ingredients to the mixer bowl with the butter mixture and pulse the mixer on and off, almost like you're trying to jump-start a car, so the flour gets gradually incorporated. When the flour is mostly combined, mix on medium-low for about 5 minutes, until the dough is sticky and a little glossy. Scrape down the sides of the bowl to catch any flour that didn't get mixed in.

Set a very large piece of parchment paper on the countertop, then use a spatula to transfer the dough to the parchment. Use your hands to form the dough into a rough log shape, then wrap the log in the parchment. Using a ruler, your bench scraper, or a butter knife, shape the dough (working through the parchment to avoid sticking) into a more symmetrical log that is 18 inches in length and 1½ to 2 inches in diameter. Refrigerate the dough for 10 to 20 minutes to get it firm enough to cut.

Unwrap the dough and slice it into 1-inch-thick rounds. This next step is optional, but I like to shape the rounds so they're more like little mounds with shallow divots than flat discs. To do this, I grab

continues ▶

MAKES 18 COOKIES

DOUGH
1 cup (2 sticks/225 g) unsalted butter, softened
1 cup (125 g) unsifted powdered sugar, plus more as needed
2¼ cups (315 g) all-purpose flour
¾ teaspoon fine sea salt or table salt
½ teaspoon ground nutmeg

ICING
¾ cup (95 g) powdered sugar
1 to 2 tablespoons fruit juice (see Note, page 43)
Pinch of citric acid
Pinch of kosher salt

the rounds in between my index finger and my thumb and gently squeeze so that the dough rises up a bit. Then I make a little dip in the middle with my thumb. It should look like a short mountain with a little crater in the middle.

Arrange the cookies on the prepared baking sheets, leaving at least ½ inch between the cookies and ½ inch between the cookies and the edges of the pan. (If you don't want to bake them all at once, freeze some of the dough as directed on page 29.)

Bake for 15 to 20 minutes, until slightly golden on the bottom. (If the bottom is very dark, the cookies are overbaked. Note that this cookie will remain pale on top.) Remove from the oven and transfer to a wire rack to cool completely.

MEANWHILE, MAKE THE ICING: Place the powdered sugar in a small bowl and create a well at the center. Add the fruit juice, citric acid, and salt to the well and whisk until all the ingredients are incorporated and the icing is fluid enough to slowly run off your whisk.

Transfer the icing to a piping bag fitted with a small round tip (alternatively, just use a fork or spoon to drizzle the icing). Freeform drizzle the icing over the mantecaditos in the pattern of your choice.

NOTE: *The fun thing about this icing is that you can use whatever fruit juice you have in your fridge—grape juice, orange juice, fruit punch, cranberry juice . . . If you have V8 Splash and want to make a V8 Splash cookie, I'm here to make that happen for you.*

The Lemon Cookies

MAKES 24 COOKIES

1 cup (2 sticks/225 g) unsalted
    butter, softened
1 cup lightly packed (200 g) light
    brown sugar
¾ cup (150 g) granulated sugar
1 large egg
¼ cup (25 g) lemon zest
1 teaspoon fresh lemon juice
1 teaspoon vanilla bean paste
Pinch of citric acid
2½ cups plus 2 tablespoons (370 g)
    all-purpose flour
1 teaspoon baking soda
½ teaspoon kosher salt
Maldon salt, for sprinkling

They call me the cookie lady. The kids in my family do, at least, because they've come to expect that I'll show up with a big batch of these soft and fluffy delicias every time there's a holiday gathering. I am always happy to oblige. Think of these as a cross between a sugar cookie and extra-sour lemonade.

Preheat the oven to 325°F. Line two large baking sheets with parchment paper.

In the bowl of a stand mixer fitted with the paddle attachment (or using one of the alternate methods on page 25), beat the butter on medium-low speed until fluffy and pale yellow in color, 3 to 4 minutes. Add the brown sugar and granulated sugar and mix on low until incorporated, light, and fluffy, about 3 minutes. Scrape down the sides and bottom of the bowl to make sure all the sugar and butter are combined and there are no visible clumps of either—do not skip this step.

With the mixer on low, add the egg, lemon zest, lemon juice, vanilla, and citric acid and mix until incorporated.

In a medium bowl, whisk together the flour, baking soda, and kosher salt. Add the dry ingredients to the mixer bowl with the butter mixture and pulse the mixer on and off, almost like you're trying to jump-start a car, so the flour gets gradually incorporated. When the flour is mostly combined, mix on low until the dry ingredients are well incorporated, 2 to 3 minutes.

Using a 1¼-ounce cookie scoop (or a spoon—your portions should be 2½ tablespoons), scoop the dough onto the prepared baking sheets, leaving at least 1½ to 2 inches between the cookies and ½ to 1 inch between the cookies and the edges of the pan. With damp fingers, press down the tops of the cookies and sprinkle with Maldon salt. (If you don't want to bake them all at once, freeze some of the dough as directed on page 29.)

Bake for 14 to 16 minutes, rotating the baking sheets halfway through, until lightly golden with a very fragrant lemon aroma. Remove from the oven and let cool on a wire rack before serving.

Té de Hoja de Café Madeleines

Coffee leaves don't taste like coffee. They are their own thing, with a beautiful flavor profile, and they're actually quite good for you. I know this because I used to get sick a lot growing up. During trips to DR, when my immune system would get wobbly, they'd serve me coffee-leaf tea every morning. The taste of it will always remind me of my grandmother. Meanwhile, I fondly remember Hector's grandmother eating madeleines for breakfast, so I decided to fuse those inspirations into a single, wonderful daytime treat.

In the bowl of a stand mixer fitted with the whisk attachment (or using one of the alternate methods on page 25), beat the eggs and granulated sugar on high speed until doubled in size and super fluffy, about 8 minutes. Add the vanilla and lemon zest and mix on low speed until incorporated. Increase the speed to medium-low, then add the browned butter and mix until the mixture is glossy, 2 to 3 minutes.

Add the flour, powdered sugar, ground coffee-leaf tea, baking powder, and salt and fold gently with a rubber spatula until the batter is smooth.

Transfer the mixture to a piping bag, tying the top closed with a rubber band (if you don't have a piping bag, just cover the bowl so it's airtight). Refrigerate for at least 8 hours or up to overnight.

Preheat the oven to 425°F. Grease the cavities of two madeleine pans with browned butter and dust lightly with flour, shaking any excess flour from the pan.

Cut off the tip of the piping bag and pipe the batter into the prepared madeleine pans, filling them about three-quarters of the way (make sure not to overfill the cavities, as the batter will spread). If you don't have a piping bag, use a spoon to fill the molds.

Place the pans in the oven, immediately reduce the oven temperature to 400°F, and bake for 8 to 10 minutes, until the madeleines are golden brown and a hump forms in the middle of each, and a cake tester inserted into the center comes out clean. Remove from the oven and transfer the madeleines to a wire rack to cool.

Enjoy with a freshly brewed cup of hoja de café, if you like.

MAKES 24 MADELEINES

3 large eggs

¾ cup (150 g) granulated sugar

1½ teaspoons vanilla extract

Zest of 1 lemon

½ cup plus 1 tablespoon (130 g) Browned Butter (page 277), at room temperature, plus more for greasing

1 cup (140 g) all-purpose flour, plus more for dusting

1 cup (125 g) unsifted powdered sugar

1½ tablespoons ground coffee-leaf tea, plus more for serving (see Note)

1 teaspoon baking powder

Pinch of fine sea salt or table salt

NOTE: *Look for ground coffee-leaf tea at markets specializing in Ethiopian or Dominican ingredients, or online.*

Black Pepper Espresso Dulce de Leche Shortbread Cookies

MAKES 18 FILLED COOKIES

SHORTBREAD

1 cup (2 sticks/225 g) unsalted
    butter, softened
½ cup (65 g) unsifted powdered
    sugar
1 teaspoon instant coffee granules
1 tablespoon vanilla extract
2 cups (280 g) all-purpose flour,
    plus more for dusting
Pinch of kosher salt

DULCE DE LECHE FILLING

1 (13.4-ounce/380 g) can store-
    bought dulce de leche, or about
    1⅔ cups homemade (page 281)
2 teaspoons freshly ground black
    pepper
Kosher salt

ICING (OPTIONAL)

½ cup (65 g) unsifted powdered
    sugar, plus more if needed
1 to 2 teaspoons whole milk, plus
    more if needed

This recipe is a play on an Italian jam cookie and the South American classic alfajores. I take a shortbread cookie, infuse it with the flavors of an espresso, and then fill it with dulce de leche—and black pepper. Sweet, buttery, and with a mellow heat that not only gives you complexity, but also prevents your palate from being overwhelmed with sweetness—we must avoid desserts that *empalagar* (make you sick because they're so cloying) at all costs!

MAKE THE SHORTBREAD: Preheat the oven to 350°F. Line a large baking sheet with parchment paper.

In the bowl of a stand mixer fitted with the paddle attachment (or using one of the alternate methods on page 25), beat the butter on medium-low speed until fluffy and pale yellow in color, 3 to 4 minutes. Reduce the mixer speed to low, then slowly add the powdered sugar and mix until combined. Scrape down the sides of the bowl.

In a medium bowl, combine the instant coffee and the vanilla and stir until the coffee dissolves. Add the espresso-vanilla mixture to the mixer bowl with the butter and mix on low until incorporated.

With the mixer running on low, slowly add the flour and salt and mix until the flour is incorporated and you're not afraid of making a giant mess, then increase the speed to medium and mix until the dough is slightly shiny, 3 to 5 minutes.

Turn the dough out onto a floured surface and roll it out into a rough rectangle the width and length of your baking sheet. Transfer the dough to the prepared baking sheet and press and flatten it into an even layer, about ½ inch thick. Using a paring knife, score the dough (making a mark but not cutting all the way through) into 3 rows of 12 cookies each.

Bake for 10 minutes; the cookies will still be very soft and pale. Leaving the cookies on the pan, use a knife or bench scraper to cut through the scored lines to detach the cookies from each other. Bake

for 4 to 6 minutes more, until lightly golden brown on the bottom. Remove from the oven and let cool completely before filling.

MAKE THE FILLING: In a medium bowl, combine the dulce de leche, pepper, and salt to taste and stir with a spoon until smooth.

MAKE THE ICING (IF USING): In a medium bowl, use a fork or whisk to stir together the powdered sugar and milk until the mixture is pourable—start with less milk and add more until you get the right consistency. If it's too thin, add more powdered sugar.

ASSEMBLE THE COOKIES: Place 18 of the cooled cookies on a serving tray. Spoon a nice dollop of the filling into the center of each cookie, then top with the remaining 18 cookies to sandwich the filling. Use a fork or spoon (or, if you wanna be fancy, a piping bag—it'll look fun either way) to drizzle icing over the top of each cookie. Let the icing set before serving.

Guava & Cheese Cookies

I was introduced to the joys of pulling a box of guava paste and some queso fresco out of the fridge very early on in life. It's an easy midday treat, or the perfect end to a meal when you want to linger. For me, it was occasionally even a breakfast.

Another extraordinary expression of the pairing is the pastelito de guayaba, a turnover with cream cheese coaxing the sweetness of the guava jam to heel. It's an iconic, iconic dessert, and I hope the Latin community doesn't mind me spinning the tradition into a cookie. I'm proud of this one.

Preheat the oven to 325°F. Line one large baking sheet or two small baking sheets with parchment paper.

In the bowl of a stand mixer fitted with the paddle attachment (or using one of the alternate methods on page 25), beat the butter on medium-low speed until fluffy and pale yellow in color, 3 to 4 minutes. Add the brown sugar and granulated sugar and mix on low until incorporated, light, and fluffy, about 3 minutes. Scrape down the sides and bottom of the bowl to make sure all the sugar and butter are combined and there are no visible clumps of either—do not skip this step.

With the mixer on low, add the egg and lemon extract and mix until incorporated.

In a medium bowl, whisk together the flour, baking soda, and salt. Add the dry ingredients to the mixer bowl with the butter mixture and pulse the mixer on and off, almost like you're trying to jump-start a car, so the flour gets gradually incorporated. Mix just until the flour is incorporated, about 1 minute. Add the guava and cheese and mix until incorporated—but be careful not to overmix! (If you mix the guava for too long, it can destabilize the dough. If you're nervous, just mix in the guava and cheese by hand, which is harder work but easier to control.)

Using a 2-ounce cookie scoop (or a large spoon—your portions should be ¼ cup), scoop the dough onto the prepared baking sheets, leaving at least 1½ to 2 inches between the cookies and ½ to 1 inch between the cookies and the edges of the pan. (If you don't want to bake them all at once, freeze some of the dough as directed on page 29.)

Bake for 14 to 16 minutes, until the edges are golden. Remove from the oven and transfer to a wire rack to cool before serving.

MAKES 12 COOKIES

1 cup (2 sticks/225 g) unsalted butter, softened

1 cup lightly packed (200 g) light brown sugar

¾ cup (150 g) granulated sugar

1 large egg

1 teaspoon imitation lemon extract (see page 20)

2½ cups plus 2 tablespoons (370 g) all-purpose flour

1 teaspoon baking soda

½ teaspoon kosher salt

½ cup (120 g) small-diced guava

½ cup (120 g) small-diced Queso Dominicano (see Note)

NOTE: *You can substitute Halloumi cheese for the Queso Dominicano, but reduce the salt to ¼ teaspoon.*

Bulla Snickerdoodles

DOUGH

1 cup (2 sticks/225 g) unsalted
    butter, softened
1½ cups (300 g) granulated sugar
¼ cup lightly packed (50 g) light
    brown sugar
2 large eggs
2¾ cups (385 g) all-purpose flour
2 tablespoons ground cinnamon
2 teaspoons cream of tartar
1 teaspoon baking soda
1 teaspoon ground ginger
½ teaspoon kosher salt
¼ teaspoon ground cloves
¼ teaspoon ground black pepper

BULLA ROLLING SUGAR

½ cup (100 g) granulated sugar
1 teaspoon ground cinnamon
1 teaspoon ground ginger
¼ teaspoon ground allspice
¼ teaspoon ground nutmeg
¼ teaspoon ground cloves

For this play on the snickerdoodle, I draw inspiration from a Jamaican school snack and lunchtime favorite: bulla, a delightful eggless cake that's packed with molasses and warming spices (cinnamon, ginger, allspice, and cloves). I've noticed that the amount and variety of spices varies from recipe to recipe. It should come as no surprise that mine goes pretty full-on in that department in both the dough and the sugar coating.

Preheat the oven to 400°F. Line two large baking sheets with parchment paper.

MAKE THE DOUGH: In the bowl of a stand mixer fitted with the paddle attachment (or using one of the alternate methods on page 25), beat the butter, granulated sugar, and brown sugar on high speed until light and pale, 8 to 10 minutes. Reduce the mixer speed to medium and add the eggs one at a time, mixing until combined and scraping down the sides and bottom of the bowl after each addition.

In a medium bowl, whisk together the flour, cinnamon, cream of tartar, baking soda, ginger, salt, cloves, and pepper to combine. Add the dry ingredients to the mixer bowl with the wet ingredients and pulse the mixer on and off, almost like you're trying to jump-start a car, so the flour gets gradually incorporated without flying all over your kitchen. When the dry ingredients are mostly combined, mix on low to incorporate them fully.

Using a 2-ounce cookie scoop (or a large spoon—your portions should be ¼ cup), scoop portions of the dough and place them on a plate.

MAKE THE ROLLING SUGAR: In a small bowl, combine the sugar, cinnamon, ginger, allspice, nutmeg, and cloves.

Roll the cookies in the sugar mixture to completely coat and place them on the prepared baking sheets, leaving at least 2 inches between the cookies and 1 inch between the cookies and the edges of the pan. (If you don't want to bake them all at once, freeze some of the dough as directed on page 29.)

Bake for 9 to 10 minutes, until golden. Remove from the oven and let cool on the pans for 3 minutes, then transfer to a wire rack to cool completely before serving.

Sunflower Rainbow Cookies

Almond paste is fundamental to so many desserts, and for good reason—it's delicious. But it's also expensive, and people with a tree-nut allergy can't enjoy any recipe that includes it. Can you imagine not being able to eat an Italian rainbow cookie? That doesn't seem fair. The solution had been staring at me in the bodega this whole time: sunflower seeds. I toast them and make them into a paste. (Really, you can make paste from any seed imaginable, so take this recipe and experiment until you find your paste of choice!)

These sunflower cookies feature tamarind strawberry jam as the filling, but go ahead and use any kind you want. Even store-bought, if you want to save yourself the time.

MAKE THE COOKIES: Preheat the oven to 325°F. Line three eighth sheet trays (roughly 6 by 9 inches) with parchment paper. Degrease the equipment you are going to use to whip your egg whites (see page 26).

In the bowl of a stand mixer fitted with the whisk attachment or in a large bowl using a hand mixer (or by hand, if you're stronger than I am), whip the egg whites on medium speed until foamy, 2 to 3 minutes. Gradually add half the sugar, then increase the mixer speed to high and whip until the egg whites are smooth, glossy, and doubled in volume and have formed stiff peaks, 3 to 4 minutes more. Transfer the mixture to a medium bowl and set aside. Replace the whisk attachment with the paddle.

I already made you degrease your equipment, so now I'm going to save you some work and say you don't have to clean the stand mixer bowl before this next step. That's compromise, baby! Combine the sunflower seed paste and the butter in the mixer bowl (or in a large bowl, if you're using a hand mixer) and beat on medium speed until soft and fluffy, 1 to 2 minutes. Add the remaining sugar and mix until pale and fluffy, 2 to 3 minutes. Scrape down the sides of the bowl to make sure all the sugar and butter are combined. With the mixer on high speed, add the egg yolks one at a time, mixing well after each addition. Add the vanilla

continues ▶

MAKES 27 COOKIES

ITALIAN RAINBOW COOKIES
4 large eggs, separated
1 cup (200 g) sugar
1 cup (200 g) Sunflower Seed Paste
   (page 218)
1½ cups (3 sticks/340 g) unsalted
   butter, softened
1 tablespoon vanilla extract
½ cup (120 mL) whole milk
1¾ cups plus 2 tablespoons (260 g)
   all-purpose flour
Pinch of kosher salt
4 drops purple food coloring
3 drops pink food coloring
2 drops yellow food coloring

TAMARIND SYRUP
¼ cup (50 g) sugar
3 tablespoons Tamarind Jam
   (page 280)

TAMARIND-STRAWBERRY FILLING
½ cup (160 g) strawberry jam
¼ cup (130 g) Tamarind Jam
   (page 280)
Pinch of citric acid
Pinch of kosher salt

CHOCOLATE TOPPING
2 tablespoons coconut oil
1 cup (170 g) dark chocolate chunks
   or fèves (60% cacao)

and mix until combined, making sure to scrape down the sides and bottom of the bowl to get every last bit of vanilla incorporated.

Reduce the mixer speed to low, pour in the milk, and mix until smooth, a minute or two. Turn off the mixer and add the flour and salt, then mix on low speed until the flour is no longer visible.

Divide the batter among three small bowls and tint one purple, one pink, and one yellow. Use a clean spatula to stir each batter so the color is evenly distributed.

Add a big spoonful of the whipped egg whites to each bowl and, using a rubber spatula, vigorously mix to loosen up the batter. It should drip off the spatula. Add one-third of the remaining egg whites to each bowl and very gently and carefully fold it in with the spatula. There should be some streaks of egg whites visible.

Pour each color of batter into one of the prepared baking sheets. Bake for 10 to 12 minutes, until the cookies are springy to the touch and their tops are firm but haven't browned. Remove from the oven and let cool in the pans.

MAKE THE SYRUP: In a small saucepan, combine the sugar and ½ cup (120 mL) water and heat over medium-high heat, gently stirring, just until the sugar has dissolved. Remove from the heat, add the tamarind jam, and whisk until smooth. Set aside.

MAKE THE FILLING: In a medium bowl, combine the strawberry jam, tamarind jam, citric acid, and salt and mix until smooth.

ASSEMBLE THE COOKIES: Brush the tops of the cooled cookies with the tamarind syrup and let soak for 5 minutes.

Using a spatula, spread half the filling over the purple sheet of cookie. Carefully flip the yellow sheet of cookie so it lands on top of the jam layer on the purple cookie, then peel away the parchment. Spread the remaining jam on top of the yellow layer, then carefully flip the pink cookie so it lands on top of the yellow and peel away the parchment. You should have a nice stack of cookies, with three layers of color and jam sandwiched between them. Place a sheet of parchment on top of the pink layer and place a baking sheet on top. Weigh it down with two heavy cans and refrigerate for 24 hours.

Remove the cookies from the fridge and let them come to room temperature.

MAKE THE TOPPING: Place the coconut oil and chocolate in a microwave-safe medium bowl. Microwave for 30 seconds on high, stopping to stir after 15 seconds, until the chocolate is melted. Stir until smooth.

Pour the chocolate topping over the pink cookie layer and use a spatula to spread it into a thin layer that covers the full rectangle. Wait for a few minutes for the chocolate to set a bit—but don't wait too long, or it will become *too* hard and crumble when you cut the cookies. Score the cookies into 1 by 2-inch rectangles, then cut into individual cookies.

Sorrel Snickerdoodles

MAKES 16 COOKIES

DOUGH

1 cup (2 sticks/225 g) unsalted butter, softened

1½ cups (300 g) granulated sugar

¼ cup lightly packed (50 g) light brown sugar

2 large eggs

1 teaspoon imitation lemon extract (see page 20)

2¾ cups (385 g) all-purpose flour

2 tablespoons ground cinnamon

2 teaspoons cream of tartar

1 teaspoon baking soda

½ teaspoon kosher salt

½ teaspoon ground ginger

4 drops pink food coloring

SORREL ROLLING SUGAR

½ cup (100 g) granulated sugar

1½ teaspoons ground cinnamon

¼ teaspoon ground cloves

⅛ teaspoon extra finely ground green peppercorns

2 tablespoons ground hibiscus leaves or hibiscus powder

Hibiscus (also known as sorrel) is a bright red, antioxidant-rich flower native to the tropics and subtropics. Most commonly used in drinks (think teas, agua frescas, or mixed drinks), hibiscus lends a beautiful color and almost cranberry-like sweetness to any dish. At some point I figured out that incorporating ground hibiscus into a sugar coating turns my snickerdoodle into a Sour Patch Kids snickerdoodle, and I never looked back.

Preheat the oven to 400°F. Line two large baking sheets with parchment paper.

MAKE THE DOUGH: In the bowl of a stand mixer fitted with the paddle attachment (or using one of the alternate methods on page 25), beat the butter, granulated sugar, and brown sugar on high speed until light and pale, 8 to 10 minutes. Reduce the mixer speed to medium and add the eggs one at a time, mixing until combined and scraping down the sides and bottom of the bowl after each addition. Add the lemon extract and mix until combined.

In a medium bowl, whisk together the flour, cinnamon, cream of tartar, baking soda, salt, and ginger to combine. Add the dry ingredients to the mixer bowl with the wet ingredients and pulse the mixer on and off, almost like you're trying to jump-start a car, so the flour gets gradually incorporated without flying all over your kitchen. When the dry ingredients are mostly combined, add the food coloring and mix on low to incorporate fully. The dough should be vibrant in color.

Using a 2-ounce cookie scoop (or a large spoon—your portions should be ¼ cup), scoop portions of the dough and put them on a plate.

MAKE THE ROLLING SUGAR: In a small bowl, combine the granulated sugar, cinnamon, cloves, green peppercorns, and ground hibiscus.

Roll the cookies in the sugar mixture to coat completely, then place them on the prepared baking sheets, leaving at least 2 inches between the cookies and 1 inch between the cookies and the edges of the pan. (If you don't want to bake them all at once, freeze some of the dough as directed on page 29.)

Bake for 9 to 10 minutes, until golden. Let the cookies cool on the pans for 3 minutes before transferring them to a wire rack to cool completely before serving.

Bodega Brownie Whoopie Pie

When I think of bodegas, the first things that pop into my head are honey buns, chopped cheese. . . . and Cosmic Brownies. I assumed that Cosmic Brownies were universal, that *everyone* knew the fudgy Little Debbie–brand treats. But apparently not everyone has a photographic memory for bodega snacks. Cosmic Brownies come individually wrapped in clear plastic and are studded with neon-colored candy-coated chocolate chips (which basically make them irresistible to ten-year-olds). My take is in the form of a whoopie pie—it's softer, more decadent, and, I think, even tastier.

MAKE THE WHOOPIE COOKIES: Preheat the oven to 375°F. Line several large baking sheets with parchment paper.

In the bowl of a stand mixer bowl fitted with the paddle attachment (or using one of the alternate methods on page 25), beat the butter on medium-low speed until fluffy and pale yellow in color, 3 to 4 minutes. Add the brown sugar and granulated sugar and mix on high speed until pale and creamy, 3 to 4 minutes. (Don't worry if you're still able to see some brown sugar. As long as it's coated by your butter, you should be A-OK.) Scrape down the sides and bottom of the bowl and mix on low speed to make sure all the sugar and butter are combined. Do not skip this step, and make sure no butter or sugar clumps are visible. Add the egg and mix on low until combined. Scrape down the bowl to get everything well integrated, then add the vanilla and mix on low until combined.

In a large bowl, whisk together the flour, cocoa powder, baking soda, and salt to combine. Add one-third of the flour mixture to the mixer bowl with the wet ingredients and mix on low speed for 1 minute. Scrape down the bowl, then add half the labneh and half the boiling water and mix on low until just incorporated. Add half of the remaining flour mixture and mix on low for 1 minute, then scrape down the bowl. Add the remaining labneh and boiling water and mix on low until just incorporated. Add the remaining flour mixture and mix on

continues ▶

MAKES 14 WHOOPIE PIES

WHOOPIE COOKIES
- ⅓ cup (⅔ stick/75 g) unsalted butter, softened
- ½ cup lightly packed (100 g) light brown sugar
- ½ cup (100 g) granulated sugar
- 1 large egg
- 1 teaspoon Dominican imitation vanilla extract
- 2 cups (280 g) all-purpose flour
- ¾ cup (75 g) black (noir) cocoa powder
- 1 teaspoon baking soda
- ½ teaspoon kosher salt
- ¾ cup (170 g) labneh or plain full-fat Greek yogurt
- ½ cup (120 ml) boiling water

FUDGY FILLING
- ½ cup (1 stick/115 g) unsalted butter, melted
- 1 cup (100 g) unsweetened Dutch-processed cocoa powder
- ⅓ cup (80 mL) heavy cream
- 3 tablespoons Dominican imitation vanilla extract
- Pinch of kosher salt
- 4 cups (500 g) unsifted powdered sugar

TO FINISH
- 1 ounce (30 g) dark chocolate (64% cacao)
- Vegetable oil cooking spray or a few drops of vegetable oil
- Rainbow candy-coated chocolate chips, for garnish

low for 1 minute, then scrape down the bowl and mix again until just incorporated.

Using a 1-ounce cookie scoop (or a spoon—your portions should be 2 tablespoons), scoop the dough onto the prepared baking sheets, leaving 2 inches between the cookies and 1 inch between the cookies and the edges of the pan. You should be able to fit between 8 and 12 cookies per pan, so depending on how many baking sheets you have, you might have to work in batches.

Bake for 8 to 10 minutes, until the cookies feel like a perfectly baked cake. Use a cake tester if you have one. (Psst, whoopie pies are cake masquerading as cookies.) Remove from the oven and let cool on a wire rack while you bake your next batch of cookies and make the filling.

MAKE THE FILLING: In the bowl of a stand mixer fitted with the whisk attachment (or, if you're a virtuoso, in a large bowl with a whisk), beat the melted butter and the cocoa powder on low speed until compact, about 3 minutes. Add the cream, vanilla, and salt and mix until smooth, about 1 minute. Reduce the mixer speed to low and add the powdered sugar. Mix until just combined and the risk is low that you'll spray powdered sugar everywhere, then kick the mixer into high gear and mix until glossy and fudgy, about 5 minutes more.

Now it's time to assemble your whoopie pies. Transfer the fudgy filling to a piping bag fitted with a medium round tip (or just use a cookie scoop or a spoon). Pipe a heaping 1-ounce (2-tablespoon) portion of the filling into the center of the flat side of a whoopie cookie, then sandwich the filling with a second whoopie cookie and place your assembled whoopie pie on a plate or tray. Repeat with the remaining cookies and filling.

MAKE THE CHOCOLATE DRIZZLE: In a small microwave-safe bowl, microwave the chocolate on high power in 15-second intervals, stirring after each, until the chocolate is melted and smooth. Add 2 or 3 spritzes of cooking spray and stir to mix.

Use a fork or spoon to drizzle the melted chocolate with gusto over the tops of your whoopie pies, then garnish with candy-coated chocolate chips and enjoy.

Moringa-Soursop Swirl Cookies

MAKES 18 COOKIES

1 cup (2 sticks/225 g) unsalted
  butter, softened
1½ cups (250 g) sugar, plus more
  for coating
1 large egg
1 tablespoon soursop puree
1 teaspoon vanilla bean paste or
  vanilla extract
2¼ cups (315 g) all-purpose flour
½ teaspoon baking powder
¼ teaspoon baking soda
¾ teaspoon kosher salt
3 tablespoons moringa powder

It feels like we can't get enough of matcha these days (see page 36). I love it, too, but allow me to introduce you to matcha's cooler cousin, moringa, the miracle fruit from the miracle tree. In powdered form, it tastes similar to matcha but delivers way more nutrients and far less caffeine. We should eat more of it. We should also eat more soursop, which we used to grow in my backyard in DR. Fresh from the tree, this tropical fruit tastes like an apple-banana hybrid and is creamy, pillowy soft, and absolutely delightful. You can find the frozen kind I call for at Asian and Latin American markets, as well as online.

In this visually stunning cookie, the herbaceous notes of the moringa and the banana-y taste of the soursop combine to create an unforgettable flavor bomb. No one I've given these cookies to has been anything less than thrilled. If you feel like playing around with other ingredients and flavors to make your own swirly delights, just use the same amount of powder and puree and go off.

Preheat the oven to 350°F. Line two large baking sheets with parchment paper.

In the bowl of a stand mixer fitted with the whisk attachment (or using one of the alternate methods on page 25), beat the butter and sugar on high speed until fluffy and pale, 8 to 10 minutes. Reduce the mixer speed to medium, add the egg, and mix until combined. Scrape down the sides and bottom of the bowl, then add the soursop puree and vanilla and mix until combined.

In a medium bowl, whisk together the flour, baking powder, baking soda, and salt to combine. Add the dry ingredients to the mixer bowl with the wet ingredients and pulse the mixer on and off, almost like you're trying to jump-start a car, so the flour gets gradually incorporated without flying all over your kitchen. When the dry ingredients are mostly combined, mix on low until the dough is smooth.

Remove the dough from the bowl and divide it into two equal portions. Return half the dough to the bowl and add the moringa powder. Mix on low until the powder is evenly incorporated and the dough is bright green, about 1 minute.

Using a 1-ounce cookie scoop (or a spoon—your portions should be 2 tablespoons), take a scoop of each flavor of dough and then slightly roll them together in between the palms of your hands to gently combine the two doughs until a swirl appears. Place the cookie on a plate and repeat with the remaining dough.

Pour some sugar into a small bowl. Roll the cookies in the sugar to coat completely, then place them on the prepared baking sheets, leaving at least 1½ to 2 inches between the cookies and 1 inch between the cookies and the edges of the pan. (If you don't want to bake them all at once, freeze some of the dough as directed on page 29.)

Bake for 10 to 12 minutes, until the edges and bottoms are golden. Remove from the oven and transfer to a wire rack to cool before serving.

GALLETAS PARA TODOS (COOKIES FOR ALL)

63

CCCC, aka Chocolate Chip Cookie Crisps

MAKES ABOUT 34 COOKIES

¾ cup (1½ sticks/170 g) unsalted butter, softened

1 cup lightly packed (200 g) light brown sugar

¼ cup (50 g) granulated sugar

2 large eggs

½ teaspoon vanilla bean paste or vanilla extract

1½ cups (210 g) all-purpose flour

¾ teaspoon Himalayan pink salt

¾ teaspoon baking soda

1 (10-ounce/285 g) bag mini chocolate chips

A one-stop, no-mixer master class on the quintessential American cookie, this one will speak to those who favor thin and crispy over chewy and gooey.

Preheat the oven to 375°F. Line two large baking sheet with parchment paper.

In a large bowl, use a spatula to beat the butter, brown sugar, and granulated sugar until fluffy. Add the eggs—I do it one at a time, but hey, it's your world and I'm just living in it. Do what you're gonna do. Add the vanilla and mix until incorporated. Add the flour, salt, baking soda, and chocolate chips and mix until the dough is smooth, about 2 minutes.

Using a 1-ounce cookie scoop (or a spoon—your portions should be 2 tablespoons), scoop the dough onto the prepared baking sheets. Wrap in plastic wrap and refrigerate for 30 minutes. (If you don't want to bake them all at once, freeze some of the dough as directed on page 29.)

Bake for 10 minutes, or until the edges and bottoms are golden. Remove from the oven and transfer to a wire rack to cool before serving.

Extra-Chewy Chocolate Chip Cookies

This cookie channels all the gooey parts of a brownie with a crunchy, crackly exterior. They are super easy to knock out and gluten-free—some of my finest work, if I may say so myself.

Preheat the oven to 375°F. Line two large baking sheets with parchment paper. Degrease the equipment you are going to use to whip your egg whites (see page 26).

In the bowl of a stand mixer fitted with the whisk attachment (or using one of the alternative methods on page 25), whip the egg whites on medium speed until stiff peaks form, 8 to 9 minutes.

Meanwhile, place the chocolate in a medium microwave-safe bowl. Microwave at full power in 15-second intervals, stirring after each, until the chocolate has melted. Set aside to cool slightly (to 96°F, to be precise), then stir in the rum.

With the mixer on medium-low speed, add the powdered sugar to the egg whites a couple of tablespoons at a time. Reduce the mixer speed to low, add the cocoa powder and salt, and mix until combined.

Remove the bowl from the stand mixer and add a couple of spoon-fuls of the egg white mixture to the melted chocolate. Mix vigorously with a rubber spatula until incorporated. Add the melted chocolate mixture to the bowl with the remaining egg whites and gently fold together with the spatula. The mixture should remain aerated.

Using a 1-ounce cookie scoop (or a large spoon—your portions should be 2 tablespoons), scoop the meringue onto the prepared baking sheets, leaving 1 to 1½ inches between each cookie and ½ to 1 inch between the cookies and the sides of the pan. (If you don't want to bake them all at once, freeze some of the dough as directed on page 29.)

Bake for 8 to 10 minutes, until glossy on the outside and gooey in the center. Remove from the oven and let cool on the baking sheet for a few minutes until set, then use a metal spatula to carefully transfer the cookies to a wire rack to cool completely.

MAKES 20 COOKIES

4 large egg whites

5 ounces (140 g) dark chocolate (60% cacao), chopped into chunks

1 teaspoon golden rum

2 cups (250 g) unsifted powdered sugar

¾ cup (75 g) unsweetened cocoa powder

½ teaspoon kosher salt

Rose Water & Coconut Macaroons

There's nothing wrong with regular old coconut flakes, but if you want to see what a huge difference hitting just the right texture can make in a dessert, try the super finely ground Baker's Angel Flake. Myriad bits of coconut disperse evenly throughout the batter, which is ideal for folks like me who have a very soft spot for coconut flavor—whether it's the coconut drops I ate as a kid or the fresh flesh I always loved digging into after a coconut fell from the tree in DR.

In these coffee-break favorites, rich coconut, bright lemon zest, and irresistibly floral rose water live in perfect harmony. And they're gluten-free, by the way.

Preheat the oven to 325°F. Line one large baking sheet or two small baking sheets with parchment paper. Degrease the equipment you are going to use to whip your egg whites (see page 26).

In the bowl of a stand mixer fitted with the whisk attachment or in a large bowl using a hand mixer (or, if you're crazy, by hand—but we don't have to live that way anymore!), whip the egg whites on high speed until they have doubled in volume and form stiff peaks (they should look like a fluffy cloud), 3 to 4 minutes.

In a large bowl, combine the coconut flakes, condensed milk, salt, vanilla, and rose water and use a rubber spatula to mix until a paste forms. Add one-third of the whipped egg whites and vigorously mix with the spatula until incorporated. Add the rest of the egg whites and use the spatula to gently fold them in. The mixture should remain aerated.

Using a 2-ounce cookie scoop (or a large spoon—your portions should be ¼ cup), scoop mounds of the mixture onto the prepared baking sheets, leaving 1½ to 2 inches between each macaroon and 1 inch between the macaroons and the edges of the pan.

Bake for about 25 minutes, until golden. Remove from the oven and let cool on the pan before serving.

MAKES 14 MACAROONS

2 large egg whites
5⅓ cups (14 ounces/395 g) unsweetened Baker's Angel Flake coconut flakes (see page 20)
1 (14-ounce/400 g) can sweetened condensed milk
1 teaspoon kosher salt
½ teaspoon vanilla bean paste
½ teaspoon rose water

Burnt Tahini Cookies

MAKES 32 COOKIES

2 tablespoons tahini

1 cup (225 g) Browned Butter (page 277)

½ cup (100 g) granulated sugar

1 cup lightly packed (200 g) light brown sugar

2 large eggs

2 teaspoons vanilla bean paste

2¾ cups (385 g) all-purpose flour

3 tablespoons instant espresso granules

1 teaspoon kosher salt

½ teaspoon baking powder

2¼ cups (285 g) chopped milk chocolate

Sesame seeds, for rolling

I found one little touch that makes tahini cookies even better: caramelizing the solids with brown butter. This simple step makes the flavors bloom—the whole thing becomes a deeper, richer, more savory symphony in your mouth. To give you an idea: I'm not a big snacker or grazer at all, which may surprise you. But when there's a batch of these hanging around, I can't walk by them without grabbing another. And then another. And hey, maybe one more after that.

Preheat the oven to 350°F. Line two large baking sheets with parchment paper.

In a small nonstick pan, cook the tahini over high heat, stirring frequently with a heat-resistant spatula, until it turns a golden brown color, 5 to 7 minutes. Transfer the tahini to the bowl of your stand mixer, add the browned butter, and stir by hand to combine.

Add the granulated sugar and brown sugar to the stand mixer bowl with the tahini-butter mixture, then beat on medium speed with the paddle attachment until incorporated. Scrape down the sides and bottom of the bowl, then mix on high speed until fluffy, 3 to 4 minutes. Reduce the mixer speed to medium and add the eggs one at a time, mixing until incorporated and scraping down the sides and bottom of the bowl after each addition. Add the vanilla and mix until incorporated.

In a large bowl, whisk together the flour, instant espresso, salt, and baking powder. Add the dry ingredients to the mixer bowl with the wet ingredients and pulse the mixer on and off, almost like you're trying to jump-start a car, so the flour gets gradually incorporated without flying all over your kitchen. When the dry ingredients are mostly combined, mix on low to incorporate them fully, but don't overmix. Add the chopped chocolate and mix on low until combined.

Using a 1-ounce cookie scoop (or a large spoon—your portions should be 2 tablespoons), scoop portions of the dough onto a plate. Place the sesame seeds in a small bowl and roll each cookie ball in the sesame seeds to coat completely. Arrange the cookies on the prepared baking sheets, leaving at least 1½ inches between the cookies and 1 inch between the cookies and the edges of the pan. (If you don't want to bake them all at once, freeze some of the dough as directed on page 29.)

Bake for 9 to 10 minutes, until the tops crack like crinkle cookies. Remove from the oven and let cool on a wire rack before serving.

Passion Fruit Half-Moon Cookies

I've been trying to tell y'all that baking an astounding cookie is not hard at all, and this recipe is more proof. Here, I'm embracing the classic black-and-white cookie, with a vanilla bean base and the obligatory chocolate ganache, but swapping in passion fruit for the traditional vanilla frosting. I sprinkle it with poppy seeds, hopefully giving every second-gen Latino kid like me—along with the rest of the world—the best of the city and the tropics in one bite.

MAKE THE COOKIES: Preheat the oven to 350°F. Line two rimmed half sheet pans (18 by 13 inches) with parchment paper.

In the bowl of a stand mixer fitted with the paddle attachment (or using one of the alternate methods on page 25), beat the sugar and butter on low speed until blended, about 3 minutes. Increase the speed to medium and beat until the mixture is pale yellow and fluffy, pausing to scrape down the bottom and sides of bowl once or twice, 2 to 5 minutes. Add the egg and mix until combined, then scrape down the bowl once more.

In a small bowl, whisk together the buttermilk and vanilla to combine. With the mixer on low speed, pour the buttermilk mixture into the butter mixture and mix until the batter resembles a thick pound cake batter, 2 to 3 minutes.

In a large bowl, whisk together the flour, baking soda, and salt to combine. Add the dry ingredients to the mixer bowl with the wet ingredients and pulse the mixer on and off, almost like you're trying to jump-start a car, so the flour gets gradually incorporated without flying all over your kitchen. When the dry ingredients are mostly combined, mix on low until the dough comes together. The dough will seem sticky, but that's how it's supposed to be!

Using a 1½-ounce cookie scoop (or a spoon—your portions should be about 3 tablespoons), scoop the dough onto the prepared baking sheets, leaving at least 1½ inches between the cookies and 1 inch between the cookies and the edges of the pan. (If you don't want

continues ▶

MAKES 8 TO 12 COOKIES

COOKIES
½ cup (100 g) granulated sugar
⅓ cup (⅔ stick/75 g) unsalted butter, softened
1 large egg
⅓ cup (80 mL) buttermilk
½ teaspoon vanilla extract
1½ cups (210 g) all-purpose flour
½ teaspoon baking soda
½ teaspoon kosher salt

GANACHE
3½ ounces (100 g) dark chocolate, chopped (½ cup)
1 tablespoon light corn syrup
Pinch of kosher salt
¼ cup (60 mL) heavy cream
¼ cup (60 mL) passion fruit puree

ICING
2 cups (250 g) unsifted powdered sugar
1 to 2 tablespoons passion fruit puree
3 drops yellow food coloring
Citric acid
Kosher salt

Poppy seeds, for garnish

to bake them all at once, freeze some of the dough as directed on page 29.)

Bake for 12 to 15 minutes, until the edges of the cookies are golden brown. Transfer to a wire rack to cool completely, at least 2 hours or up to overnight.

MAKE THE GANACHE: Place the dark chocolate, corn syrup, and salt in a medium heatproof bowl. In a small saucepan, heat the cream over medium heat until the moment just before it starts to simmer, 3 to 5 minutes. Pour the hot cream over the chocolate and let stand for 1 minute.

Meanwhile, wipe the saucepan clean, add the passion fruit puree, and bring to a simmer over medium heat, about 3 minutes. (Because of the acidity in the passion fruit, there's a chance of curdling the cream if they're heated up together!) Pour the puree over the cream and chocolate and whisk until the chocolate has melted and the ganache is well combined. Set the ganache aside to cool slightly until thickened enough to spread on the cookies, about 10 minutes. Transfer the ganache to a piping bag (or just use a spoon to spread it over the cookies).

MAKE THE ICING: Place the powdered sugar in a medium bowl and add the passion fruit puree 1 tablespoon at a time, whisking after each addition, until the consistency is malleable or pipeable. It should not be too thick or too runny—adjust with more sugar or puree to get it right. Add the food coloring and mix until bright and yellow. Add citric acid to taste (start with a pinch—I like to punch up the acidity because I grew up eating sour straws and candy from the bodega) and a pinch of salt (to bring balance to the sweetness). Transfer to a piping bag (but don't snip the tip yet) or just cover the bowl with plastic wrap and set aside until you're ready to decorate your cookies.

Flip all the cookies so their flat bottoms are facing up. Snip the tip off the piping bag and pipe ganache over half of each cookie to form a semicircle, then smooth the ganache with an offset spatula. Let the ganache set completely, about 20 minutes, before you pipe the passion fruit icing; otherwise, the two might run into each other. Nobody wants a blurry cookie! Snip the tip of the icing bag and outline the edge of half the cookie to make a half-moon shape. Then fill your border with more icing. Sprinkle poppy seeds on the passion fruit side of your cookie (they're supposed to resemble passion fruit seeds). Let the icing set for 15 to 20 minutes, then enjoy.

Brownies, Bars & Bites

Big Green Apple Bars

MAKES 12 BARS

APPLE PUREE

1½ cups (200 g) cubed peeled
    Granny Smith apples (½-inch
    cubes)
1 teaspoon fresh lime juice

CRUST

1 cup (2 sticks/225 g) unsalted
    butter, melted
½ cup (65 g) unsifted powdered
    sugar
¼ cup lightly packed (50 g) light
    brown sugar
1 teaspoon fresh lime juice
2½ cups (350 g) all-purpose flour
1 teaspoon kosher salt
¼ teaspoon baking soda
1 large egg

FILLING

2 cups (400 g) granulated sugar
1 tablespoon unsalted butter
2 tablespoons fresh lime juice
2 (3-ounce/90 mL) packs liquid
    pectin
2 teaspoons kosher salt
¼ teaspoon citric acid
½ cup (80 g) cubed unpeeled
    Granny Smith apple (¼-inch
    cubes), mixed with 1 tablespoon
    fresh lime juice immediately
    after cutting to prevent
    browning

As far as I know, no one has ever turned pâte de fruits, the flavor-packed French jelly candies, into an American-style bar cookie—but living in New York City taught me that wonderful things can happen when you thoughtfully meld the traditions that surround you. For example: the pastry techniques of Europe, the vibrant use of fruit in the Dominican Republic, and the wholesomeness of America's most iconic baked goods. I mean, it's also just hard to say no to soft, sweet apples; a fluffy, shortbread-y crust; and hints of acidity that keep you coming back for more. Serve these at every tea party!

Preheat the oven to 350°F. Line a 9 by 13-inch baking pan with aluminum foil and then parchment paper (see page 25).

MAKE THE APPLE PUREE: In a high-speed blender, combine the apple cubes, 1 cup (240 mL) water, and the lime juice. Blend on high until smooth, 4 to 5 minutes, making sure that you do not leave any chunks of apple visible. (No need to strain the puree—I like to leave the pulp in the puree because of the added pectin; pectin is what thickens fruit into purees, jam, pâte de fruits, etc.) Set aside.

MAKE THE CRUST: In the bowl of a stand mixer fitted with the paddle attachment (or using one of the alternate methods on page 25), beat together the butter, powdered sugar, and brown sugar on low speed until fully incorporated, 1 to 2 minutes. Add the lime juice and give it a good mix.

In a large bowl, whisk together the flour, salt, and baking soda to combine. Add the dry ingredients to the mixer bowl with the wet ingredients and pulse the mixer on and off, almost like you're trying to jump-start a car, so the flour gets gradually incorporated without flying all over your kitchen. When the dry ingredients are mostly combined, add the egg and mix on low for 1 to 2 minutes, until it all comes together and starts to look like cookie dough.

Transfer the dough to the prepared pan and spread it over the bottom until smooth. Bake for 15 minutes, or until the sides are lovely and golden. Remove from the oven and let cool completely while you make the filling.

MAKE THE FILLING: In a medium stainless-steel pot, combine 2 cups (480 mL) of the apple puree and the sugar and bring to a

rolling boil over medium-high heat, 5 to 8 minutes. Add the butter, increase the heat to high, and boil for 2 to 3 minutes more. Reduce the heat to medium and cook until the mixture reaches 225°F on a candy thermometer—this could take a good 15 minutes, so be patient, my loves! Add the lime juice, pectin, salt, and citric acid and return the mixture to a rolling boil. Cook until your thermometer reaches 225°F again, then remove the pot from the heat and quickly fold in the apple cubes.

Pour the filling into the crust. Gently cover the surface of the filling with plastic wrap, smooth out any bubbles, and let stand on the countertop overnight until fully set. The next day, cut into 3 by 4-inch squares and serve.

Carrot Cake Bars

Why does carrot cake always have to come in the form of a cake? That question inspired this bar, which for me is all about the spices. Some of them may seem a bit intense for a sweet like this, but the mace and the chile powder, for example, bring a savory heat that dazzles.

Preheat the oven to 350°F. Line a 9 by-13-inch baking pan with parchment paper (see page 25).

MAKE THE CREAM CHEESE SWIRL: In the bowl of a stand mixer fitted with the paddle attachment (or using one of the alternate methods on page 25), combine the cream cheese, buttermilk powder, salt, citric acid, and a sprinkle of sugar (if you have a real sweet tooth) and beat on low speed until combined, about 3 minutes. Set aside.

MAKE THE BATTER: In a food processor, pulse the carrots until finely pureed, adding a little bit of water if necessary (see Note).

In a medium bowl, whisk together the egg, granulated sugar, and brown sugar to combine. Add the melted butter, vanilla, and rum and whisk to combine. Fold in 1½ cups (340 g) of the carrot puree and the raisins.

In a large bowl, whisk together the flour, cinnamon, salt, nutmeg, ginger, baking powder, chile powder, and mace until well combined. Add the dry ingredients to the wet ingredients and fold with a spatula until the flour is no longer visible.

Pour the batter into the prepared pan and smooth the top with an offset spatula or the back of a spoon. Place 1-ounce (2-tablespoon) dollops of the cream cheese swirl on top of the batter, evenly spaced out. (You can leave them just like that or you can use a skewer to swirl the batter and cream cheese together—swirl just a bit, to keep the batter and cream cheese distinct.)

MAKE THE CRUNCHY TOPPING: In a medium bowl, stir together the rice cereal and walnuts to combine, then sprinkle the mixture over the batter.

Bake for 25 to 30 minutes, until the bars are golden brown and have a fluffy but gooey texture (a cake tester inserted into the center should come out a little bit damp). Remove from the oven and let cool completely, 2 to 4 hours, before cutting into eighteen 2 by-3-inch bars.

CREAM CHEESE SWIRL

8 ounces (225 g) cream cheese, at room temperature
1 teaspoon buttermilk powder
½ teaspoon kosher salt
⅛ teaspoon citric acid
Granulated sugar, to taste (optional)

BATTER

8 carrots (350 g), coarsely chopped
1 large egg
¼ cup (50 g) granulated sugar
1 cup lightly packed (200 g) light brown sugar
½ cup (1 stick/115 g) unsalted butter, melted
1 teaspoon vanilla extract
1 teaspoon dark rum
½ cup (115 g) dark raisins
¾ cup (105 g) all-purpose flour
2 teaspoons ground cinnamon
1 teaspoon kosher salt
1 teaspoon ground nutmeg
1 teaspoon ground ginger
¾ teaspoon baking powder
½ cup ground chile powder
⅛ teaspoon ground mace

CRUNCHY TOPPING

1½ cups (45 g) popped rice cereal
1 cup (115 g) chopped walnuts

NOTE: *You will need 1½ cups (340 g) of carrot puree for this recipe; store any extra in an airtight container in the refrigerator for up to 3 days or in zip-top bags in the freezer for up to 3 months.*

BROWNIES, BARS & BITES

Tropical Bark

¼ cup (40 g) assorted dried fruit
(see Note)

¼ cup (20 g) unsweetened
shredded coconut, toasted

¼ cup (35 g) assorted nuts and
seeds, such as toasted sunflower
seeds, pepitas, poppy seeds,
chopped almonds, chopped
cashews, or peanuts

20 ounces (565 g) good-quality
chocolate, such as dark
chocolate, white chocolate,
caramelized white chocolate
(such as Valrhona Dulcey), or
flavored chocolate (such as
Valrhona Inspiration Fraise),
chopped (if not using fèves or
discs)

This is a tropical spin on the Christmas bark you'll find at many
holiday tables and boutique chocolate shops. It's also a great introduction to chocolate work: You'll learn how to temper chocolate
(see page 29) so you can experience the magic of the bark, and gift
it as well. My only recommendation is that you use good-quality
chocolate. It won't really work if you opt for something that has a
high sugar content (like H******'s).

Line a large baking sheet with parchment paper.

In a large bowl, combine the dried fruit, toasted coconut, and assorted nuts and seeds; set aside.

TEMPER THE CHOCOLATE: Place 10 ounces (280 g) of the chocolate
in a microwave safe-bowl and microwave it on high in 15-second intervals, stirring occasionally to prevent the chocolate from overheat-
ing and burning in one spot. (If this does happen, do not mix!!! Fish
the burnt chocolate out with a clean dry spoon and remove it from
the bowl. Then use the residual heat to melt the rest of the chocolate.)
Continue until the chocolate is halfway melted, with unmelted pieces
of chocolate floating in a pool of liquid chocolate. Vigorously stir so
the residual heat will completely melt the rest of the chocolate. Check
the temperature of the melted chocolate—should reach 90° to 100°F,
but no hotter than this!

Add the remaining chocolate to the melted chocolate in batches
until the temperature drops to 80° to 82°F for dark chocolate, 75° to
77°F for milk chocolate, or 70° to 75°F for white chocolate or flavored
chocolate with a high cocoa butter percentage. The heat of the liquid
chocolate will not melt all the additional chocolate. Place the bowl
in the microwave and microwave on high in 5-second bursts, stirring
after each, until the temperature of the melted chocolate is 84°F for
dark chocolate, 81°F for milk chocolate, or 79°F for white chocolate/
flavored chocolate.

To test the chocolate, dip the tip of a paring knife or mini offset spatula into the melted chocolate and refrigerate the knife for 5 minutes
to set. If the chocolate is properly tempered once set, it should easily
pop off the knife and make a loud snapping noise when it does; it
should be shiny underneath where it came in contact with the metal
surface of the knife; and it should not bend when broken.

Working quickly, pour the chocolate over the prepared baking sheet and sprinkle the tropical fruit medley on top of the bark. Transfer the pan to the refrigerator and chill until set, 10 to 15 minutes. (Do not leave the chocolate in the fridge too long or condensation will form on the surface.)

Break the bark into large, irregular pieces and store in an airtight container in the refrigerator for up to 3 weeks, or package them in clear plastic bags to give as gifts.

NOTE: *For this recipe, pineapple, papaya, mango, apricot, banana, sour cherries, golden berries, cranberries, and/or goji berries would all be incredible. If you're working with larger fruit like mango, chop it into ¾-inch pieces before measuring.*

Cashew Brittle

SERVES 6

Vegetable oil cooking spray
1 cup (200 g) sugar
½ cup (65 g) crushed toasted
    unsalted cashews
½ teaspoon ground cinnamon
½ teaspoon flaky sea salt
½ teaspoon baking soda
4 ounces (115 g) dark chocolate
    (discs, fèves, or chopped from a
    bar; optional)

All the glory of honeycomb candy, plus the rich nuttiness of cashews. Why cashews? You can't spend an extended period of time in the Dominican Republic without encountering them. They're everywhere. You'll almost always find them at rest stops, or colmados, where folks sell bags filled with cashews harvested from their own backyards.

Line a large baking sheet with aluminum foil and spray with a little bit of cooking spray.

In a large saucepan, combine the sugar and ½ cup (120 mL) water and bring to a boil over medium-high heat. Reduce the heat to medium and cook until the caramel is a light amber color (what is commonly referred to as medium caramel); if you have a candy thermometer, the temperature should reach between 355° and 360°F. Immediately remove from the heat and stir in the cashews, cinnamon, and salt. Add the baking soda and stir lightly.

Carefully pour the mixture onto the prepared baking sheet without spreading it out. Let cool completely.

If desired, melt the chocolate (see page 29) and spread it over the back of the brittle. Break into pieces and enjoy!

Jalao de Coco

Jalao de Coco is a super-Caribbean delight with a satisfying gooey bite that may remind you of a chocolate truffle—but it features ginger, coconut, molasses, and everything nice. Best of all, it's a no-bake treat, so you don't even have to fire up your oven. You can freeze these guys for up to a month.

Oil a large baking sheet. Line a second large baking sheet or several plates with parchment paper.

In a food processor, grind the coconut into fine pieces and transfer to a large pot. Add the honey, brown sugar, ginger, molasses, salt, vanilla, and allspice and give it a good stir, then set the pot over medium heat. Bring the mixture to a gentle, bubbling simmer, stirring continuously to ensure the bottom doesn't burn and letting the brown sugar melt into the honey, then cook until the mixture has reduced by 50 to 60 percent and looks like a gooey paste, and the color is deeply caramelized (look for a deep brown, almost like molasses or tamarind paste!). The time will vary, but your candy thermometer should read 244°F. Remove from the heat and spread the mixture over the oiled baking sheet. Let cool to room temperature.

Using a ½-ounce cookie scoop or oiled hands, portion the mixture into 1-tablespoon balls and place them on the parchment-lined baking sheet or plates as you go. Let stand at room temperature for 2 to 3 hours, then store in an airtight container in the fridge for 5 to 7 days or in the freezer for up to 1 month. Thaw before enjoying.

NOTE: *Look for fresh coconuts at well-stocked supermarkets and grocery stores specializing in Asian (or Caribbean, naturally!!) ingredients. Alternatively, you can use frozen coconut chunks, which might be more readily available in the freezer aisle of your local store.*

SERVES 12

Olive oil, as needed

2 cups (about 6 ounces/170 g) grated fresh coconut without the skin (see Note)

1½ cups (360 mL) honey

½ cup lightly packed (100 g) light brown sugar

4 teaspoons grated fresh ginger

1½ teaspoons molasses

½ teaspoon flaky sea salt

¼ teaspoon vanilla extract

¼ teaspoon ground allspice

Guava Lemon Bars

Sour candies were my thing growing up. Nowadays I get that hit of acid and citrus mostly from fresh lemon and orange, and confections like this magical evocation of Sour Straws and fruit punch. If you really want to, you can make it without the lemon peel garnish, but I think it really hammers home that Sour Straw feeling.

MAKE THE SHORTBREAD CRUST: Preheat the oven to 350°F. Line a 9 by 13-inch baking pan with parchment paper (see page 25).

In the bowl of a stand mixer fitted with the paddle attachment (or using one of the alternate methods on page 25), beat the butter and powdered sugar on medium speed until pale, about 3 minutes. Add the egg and mix until smooth and shiny, 2 to 3 minutes, pausing as needed to scrape down the sides and bottom of the bowl.

In a large bowl, whisk together the flour, salt, and baking powder to combine. Add the dry ingredients to the mixer bowl with the wet ingredients and pulse the mixer on and off, almost like you're trying to jump-start a car, so the flour gets gradually incorporated without flying all over your kitchen. When the dry ingredients are mostly combined, mix on low to incorporate them fully.

Transfer the dough to the prepared pan and use your hands to press it into an even layer over the bottom, then use a spoon or offset spatula to smooth the surface of the dough until it is level. Dock the dough by pricking it all over with a fork, then bake for about 15 minutes, until the top is lightly golden.

MEANWHILE, MAKE THE FILLING: In a small saucepan, melt the guava paste over medium heat. Gradually stir the lemon juice into the melted guava paste—the paste is thick even when it's melted, so just keep mixing and eventually it will get where you need it to go.

In a large bowl, whisk together the eggs, egg yolks, and granulated sugar until pale and fluffy, about 5 minutes. Add the guava-lemon mixture and mix until well combined. (In French patisserie, adding hot sugar syrup to egg yolks is called a pâte à bombe, so I call this "guava e bomba," aka GEB.) Slowly pour the melted butter into the GEB and whisk until all the butter is incorporated.

continues ▶

MAKES 16 BARS

SHORTBREAD CRUST

1 cup (2 sticks/225 g) unsalted butter, softened

½ cup (65 g) unsifted powdered sugar

1 large egg

2 cups (280 g) all-purpose flour

½ teaspoon kosher salt

¼ teaspoon baking powder

FILLING

¾ cups (170 g) guava paste

Juice of 4 lemons (see Note)

6 large eggs

2 large egg yolks

1½ cups (150 g) granulated sugar

½ cup (1 stick/115 g) unsalted butter, melted

⅓ cup (45 g) all-purpose flour

2 teaspoons cornstarch

½ teaspoon kosher salt

Candied Lemon Peels (recipe follows), for garnish (optional)

In a medium bowl, whisk together the flour, cornstarch, and salt to combine. Add a little bit of the GEB and stir to make a slurry. Add the thickened flour mixture to the bowl with the rest of the GEB, fold to combine, and set aside until the crust is baked.

While the crust is still hot from the oven, pour in the filling and immediately return the pan to the oven. Bake for 30 minutes, until the filling is firm and set; if the bars are not set completely after 30 minutes, you may need to bake for 5 to 10 minutes more. Remove from the oven and let stand until the bars are cool to the touch, then place them in the fridge for an hour or two (this will help with the cutting process).

Using the overhanging parchment, lift the chilled bars out of the pan and place on a cutting board. Using a warm serrated knife, score the guava bars, then cut along the scored lines to make sixteen 2¼ by 3¼-inch bars.

Garnish with lemon candy peels before serving, if desired. Store in an airtight container in the fridge for 5 to 7 days or in the freezer for up to 2 months.

NOTE: *Reserve the peels from the juiced lemons to use in the Candied Lemon Peels (opposite), if desired.*

Candied Lemon Peels

Fill a nonreactive pot about halfway with water. Add the lemon peels and bring to a boil over medium-high heat. Drain the peels and fill the pot with water again. Repeat this step one more time until the peels are translucent and the pith is clear. Drain the peels and return them to the pot.

Add 2 cups (480 mL) water, 1 cup (200 g) of the sugar, and the cinnamon stick and bring to a boil over medium heat. Boil until the mixture looks thick, like corn syrup.

Drain the peels (save the syrup for something else—it makes a tasty lemonade!) and place them on a baking sheet, making sure they're separated so they can get good airflow and dry. Let stand until the peels turn translucent and are soft to the touch but feel sort of tacky, about 10 minutes.

Line a clean baking sheet with parchment paper.

Transfer the peels to a large bowl, add the remaining ½ cup (100 g) sugar and the citric acid, and toss to coat. Spread the peels over the prepared baking sheet and let sit at room temperature for at least 3 hours or up to overnight. After that, transfer them to an airtight container for longer storage—one trick is to add a marshmallow to the container to keep them fresh for longer.

Peels from 4 lemons,
    very thinly sliced
1½ cups (300 g) sugar
1 cinnamon stick
Pinch of citric acid

Pineapple "Gummy Bear" Bars

SHORTBREAD CRUST

½ cup (1 stick/115 g) unsalted
   butter, softened
1 cup (200 g) granulated sugar
2 large egg whites
1½ cups (210 g) all-purpose flour
1 teaspoon kosher salt

PINEAPPLE "GUMMY BEAR" FILLING

1 cup (240 mL) pineapple juice
2 (3-ounce/85 g) packages)
   pineapple-flavored gelatin
   powder, such as Jell-O
2 drops yellow food coloring
1 tablespoon fresh lime juice
½ teaspoon citric acid
¼ teaspoon kosher salt

GANACHE

2 cups (300 g) white chocolate
   pieces (discs, fèves, or chopped
   from a bar)
1 cup (240 mL) heavy cream
2 tablespoons corn syrup
¼ cup (60 g) prickly pear powder
1 teaspoon vanilla bean paste
½ teaspoon kosher salt
½ cup (1 stick/115 g) unsalted butter

NOTE: *Fun fact for all you science nerds—boiling the pineapple juice ensures that the enzymes in the juice that would otherwise eat the gelatin are neutralized.*

At last, here's your chance to DIY a gummy bear! Or, more specifically, a gummy bear–inspired filling on a shortbread crust. If you ask me, these bars don't *need* to be coated in chocolate, but they certainly *can* be—just check out the sidebar opposite.

MAKE THE SHORTBREAD CRUST: Preheat the oven to 325°F. Line a 9-inch square baking pan with parchment paper (see page 25), leaving a few inches overhanging two sides.

In the bowl of a stand mixer fitted with the paddle attachment (or using one of the alternate methods on page 25), beat the butter and granulated sugar on low speed until pale yellow, 3 to 4 minutes. Add the egg whites one at a time, mixing until incorporated and scraping down the sides and bottom of the bowl after each addition.

Turn off the mixer and add the flour and salt to the bowl. Pulse the mixer on and off, so the flour gets gradually incorporated without flying all over your kitchen. When the dry ingredients are mostly combined, mix on low to incorporate them fully.

Transfer the dough to the prepared pan and use your hands to press it into an even layer over the bottom, then use a spoon or offset spatula to smooth the surface of the dough until it is level. Dock the dough by pricking it all over with a fork, then bake for 10 to 15 minutes, until the top is lightly golden. Do not overbake or it will be difficult to cut later on. Remove from the oven and set aside to cool.

MAKE THE FILLING: In a nonreactive medium saucepan, bring the pineapple juice to a boil over medium-high heat (see Note). Remove from the heat. Add the gelatin and stir until it has dissolved. Add the food coloring and mix until well combined. Add the lime juice, citric acid, and salt and stir until the citric acid and salt have dissolved. Pour the filling over the baked shortbread crust and refrigerate, loosely covered with plastic wrap, for 2 to 4 hours, until firm and set.

MAKE THE GANACHE: Place the white chocolate in a large bowl.

In a medium pot, combine the cream and corn syrup and bring to a strong simmer over medium heat. Remove from the heat and add the prickly pear powder, vanilla, and salt. Whisk until all the ingredients are combined, then pour the cream mixture over the chocolate. Immediately whisk to melt the chocolate, then add the butter and whisk until smooth and well combined. Cover the ganache and let cool on your countertop until it's slightly above your body temp—you'll know because you'll touch it and it will still feel warm! It should still be runny and pourable, but if it's too stiff, microwave it for 10 to 15 seconds, until it has the consistency of sundae fudge.

Remove the shortbread from the fridge and pour the ganache over the gummy filling layer. Return the pan to the fridge and chill until the ganache layer is set, 3 to 5 hours, or preferably overnight.

Use the overhanging parchment to remove the whole candy bar from the pan and place it on a cutting board. Using a paring knife (and a ruler, if needed), score the dimensions of your candy bar and then use a warmed chef's knife to cut the bar into 1 by 3-inch rectangles. To coat the bars, see the sidebar below.

HOW TO MAKE A
Coated Candy Bar

Put your bars in a zip-top bag or airtight container and freeze overnight.

The next day, make your chocolate shell (see page 281). Line a baking sheet or plate with parchment paper. Remove a couple of candy bars from the freezer (leave the rest where they are to make sure they stay frozen as you work—cold bars are the key here). Balance a bar on a fork and dunk it into the melted chocolate shell to coat three sides. Flip the bar so the shortbread side is on the fork and lower it into the chocolate shell again; this time, you should only tap the surface of the chocolate, dipping the bar just far enough to coat the uncoated side. Repeat this two or three times, then scrape the underside of the chocolate-coated shortbread on the rim of the bowl to remove any excess chocolate and place it on the prepared baking sheet. Repeat to coat additional candy bars, only coating as many as you'll consume within the next few days.

Ultimate Chocolate Brownies

MAKES 12 BROWNIES

3¾ cups (750 g) granulated sugar
1 cup (2 sticks/225 g) unsalted
    butter, melted
2 teaspoons vanilla extract
4 large eggs
6 ounces (170 g) bittersweet choco-
    late (64% cacao), melted (see
    page 29)
1¼ cups (175 g) all-purpose flour
3 tablespoons plus ¼ teaspoon
    (20 g) black (noir) cocoa powder
1 teaspoon flaky sea salt
¼ teaspoon baking powder

This will be your ultimate brownie recipe: It's easy to follow and cleanup is a breeze. Did I mention you don't need to bring out any extra equipment to make these bad boys? All you need are a bowl, a spatula, and some noir cocoa powder (see page 21). That last ingredient is what gives these brownies that classic Oreo taste.

Preheat the oven to 350°F. Line a 9 by 13-inch baking pan with parchment paper (see page 25).

In a large bowl, whisk together the sugar, melted butter, and vanilla. Add the eggs one at a time, whisking until the egg is well incorporated after each addition. Add the melted chocolate and whisk until smooth. Using a spatula, stir in the flour, cocoa powder, salt, and baking powder until combined.

Pour the batter into the prepared pan and smooth out the top with the spatula. Bake for 40 to 50 minutes, until a cake tester inserted into the center comes out only slightly gooey. Remove from the oven and let cool in the pan for at least 30 minutes or up to an hour before cutting into squares. Store in an airtight container for 3 to 4 days, or in the freezer for up to a month.

NOTE: *To make Malty Brownies, add ¼ cup (37 g) malted milk powder with the flour. After transferring the batter to the prepared pan and smoothing the top, sprinkle with flaky salt and bake as directed. I know Ovaltine isn't for everyone, but for certain people, that malt flavor is absolutely everything, and anyone who inhales their box of Whoppers at the theater while they're still showing trailers will have trouble controlling themselves here, too.*

Summer Camp Milk Chocolate Brownies

My goal with these brownies is to give anyone who tries them a deep pang of nostalgia for their first day at summer camp, even if they never went to one. I'm imagining the long drive on the way to this intimidating and mysterious place, not knowing what to expect, struggling to imagine how you're going to survive there for more than a *month*. A couple of hours later, you're sticking marshmallows into a fire and hoping it'll never end. I guess that's why I go for some char on these.

Preheat the oven to 350°F. Line a 9 by 13-inch baking pan with parchment paper (see page 25). Line a baking sheet with aluminum foil.

Spread the cocoa powder over a small baking sheet and bake until a toasted aroma fills the air, 4 minutes or so. Remove from the oven and set aside.

Evenly spread the marshmallows over the foil-lined baking sheet and use a kitchen torch to heat them until golden. It's OK if some catch fire a bit. (If you don't have a kitchen torch, preheat the broiler and broil the marshmallows until golden, 1 to 2 minutes—keep a close eye on them, because they can go from perfectly toasty to burned really quickly!) Set aside.

In a large bowl, whisk together the sugar, melted butter, and vanilla. Add the eggs one at a time, whisking until well incorporated after each addition. Add the melted chocolate and whisk until smooth. Using a spatula, stir in the flour, toasted cocoa powder, malted milk powder, baking powder, and salt until combined. Set aside a handful or two of the graham cracker pieces and toasted marshmallows, then add the remainder to the batter and stir to combine. Add the graham cracker pieces and toasted marshmallows and stir to combine.

Scrape the batter into the prepared pan and smooth out the top with the spatula. Sprinkle the surface of the batter with the reserved graham crackers and toasted marshmallows. Bake for 40 to 50 minutes, until a cake tester inserted into the center comes out only slightly gooey. Remove from the oven and let cool in the pan for at least 30 minutes or up to 1 hour before cutting into squares. Store in an airtight container at room temperature for 3 to 4 days or in the freezer for up to a month.

MAKES 12 BROWNIES

3 tablespoons plus ¼ teaspoon (20 g) unsweetened Dutch-process cocoa powder

1 cup (100 g) mini marshmallows

3¾ cups (750 g) granulated sugar

1 cup (2 sticks/225 g) unsalted butter, melted

2 teaspoons vanilla extract

4 large eggs

6 ounces (170 g) milk chocolate, melted (see page 29)

1¼ cups (175 g) all-purpose flour

2 tablespoons malted milk powder

⅛ teaspoon baking powder

1 teaspoon fine sea salt

2 cups (170 g) roughly crushed graham cracker pieces

Mango & Brown Butter Blondies

MANGO JAM

3 mangoes, pitted, peeled, and
    diced (450 g), or 16 ounces
    (450 g) frozen diced mango
1½ cups (300 g) granulated sugar
½ teaspoon kosher salt
Juice of 1 lemon
2 tablespoons all-purpose flour

BLONDIE BATTER

¾ cup (170 g) Browned Butter
    (page 277), melted and cooled
    slightly
¾ cup lightly packed (150 g) light
    brown sugar
¼ cup (50 g) granulated sugar
3 large eggs
2 teaspoons vanilla extract
¾ cup (105 g) all-purpose flour
1½ teaspoons kosher salt
1 teaspoon baking powder
¼ teaspoon citric acid

Much like plantains, I wish I could put mangoes in every recipe. Make these blondies and you'll see what I mean. Seriously: Drop what you're doing and start making these right now if you can, since simply explaining how the fruit's signature gooeyness complements the rich notes of butter and caramel, or how it all just melts on the tongue, is never going to beat the pure comfort of eating one. Frozen mango and fresh ripe mango work equally well here. It's your call on this one.

Preheat the oven to 350°F. Line an 8-inch square baking pan with parchment paper (see page 25).

MAKE THE MANGO JAM: In a large saucepan, combine the mango, sugar, and salt and cook over medium heat until the mango is softened, about 10 minutes. Transfer the mango pieces to a blender, leaving the syrup in the pan. Cook the syrup until thick, about 5 minutes more. Remove from the heat.

Puree the mango chunks in the blender, adding as much of the syrup as you need to achieve a consistency like thick baby food. Add the lemon juice and blend for 1 minute. Add the flour and blend for 1 minute more.

MAKE THE BLONDIE BATTER: In the bowl of a stand mixer fitted with the paddle attachment, beat the browned butter, brown sugar, and granulated sugar on medium-low speed until aerated and paler in color, 4 to 5 minutes. With the mixer on medium-low speed, add the eggs one at a time, mixing until evenly combined and scraping down the sides and bottom of the bowl after each addition. Add the vanilla and mix to incorporate.

In a large bowl, whisk together the flour, salt, baking powder, and citric acid to combine. Add the dry ingredients to the mixer bowl with the wet ingredients and pulse the mixer on and off, almost like you're trying to jump-start a car, so the flour gets gradually incorporated without flying all over your kitchen. When the dry ingredients are mostly combined, mix on low for about 2 minutes, until the flour is no longer visible.

Pour half the blondie batter into the prepared pan and spread it evenly with an offset spatula or the back of a spoon. Spread the mango jam over the batter in an even layer, reserving a small amount for garnish. Pour the remaining blondie batter on top of the mango jam and spread it evenly. It will be a bit difficult, but move slowly and with intention! Add the last bit of mango jam on top of the batter and swirl with a wooden skewer.

Bake for 20 to 30 minutes, until golden brown. Remove from the oven and let stand until cool to the touch before cutting into 10 bars. Store in an airtight container in the fridge for a couple of days—that is, if you don't eat them all in one sitting . . . I won't judge.

Dulce de Leche en Tabla

Think of these as crumbly Dominican-style fudge candies that melt in your mouth. You can find the original version of these sweets everywhere in the Dominican Republic, from bakeries and drugstores to the rest stops you encounter driving down long winding roads and through mountainous terrain.

Line a 9-inch square baking dish with parchment paper (see page 25) and grease the parchment with cooking spray.

In a large nonstick pot, combine the milk, cream, vanilla, and cinnamon sticks and heat over medium heat until bubbles form around the edge of the pan and the mixture reaches 180°F. Turn off the heat, cover the pot, and let stand to infuse the milk with the cinnamon.

Fish out and discard the cinnamon, then add the granulated sugar, brown sugar, and salt. Bring the mixture to a boil over medium-high heat, then reduce the heat to medium-low and simmer, uncovered, stirring with a rubber spatula periodically to make sure the sugar doesn't burn, for 15 minutes. Check the consistency of the dulce: If it's thick but still very loose and viscous, cook, stirring with more frequency, until the dulce has thickened and reduced by 75 percent, anywhere from 15 to 30 minutes longer.

Continue cooking and stirring in 5-minute intervals until the dulce is thick and glossy and resembles pastry cream, 10 to 15 minutes; it should be slow moving and shouldn't ribbon off the spatula. Pour the dulce into the prepared baking dish. Spread evenly and tap the dish on the counter once to encourage any air bubbles to surface. Cover with a kitchen towel and let stand on the counter overnight.

The next day, touch the surface of the dulce to see if it has set. Remove the dulce from the baking dish and set it on a cutting board. Using a lightly oiled knife, score the dulce into 2 by 1-inch pieces, then cut along the scored lines to separate the candies; press firmly, applying even pressure on the knife. (If the dulce is too firm and isn't easily cut, break it with your hands.) Wrap the candies individually in parchment paper and store in an airtight container in a cool, dry place for up to 1 month.

MAKES 18 PIECES

Vegetable oil cooking spray, for greasing
4 cups (1 L) whole milk
¼ cup (60 mL) heavy cream
2 tablespoons vanilla bean paste
3 Ceylon cinnamon sticks, snapped into smaller pieces
2 cups (400 g) granulated sugar
½ cup lightly packed (100 g) light brown sugar
½ teaspoon kosher salt

Caipirinha Marshmallow

MAKES 20
MARSHMALLOWS

MARSHMALLOW BASE
6 (¼-ounce/7 g) packets unflavored
    gelatin powder
½ cup (120 mL) fresh lime juice
6 tablespoons (90 mL) cachaça
1 drop green food coloring

MARSHMALLOW SYRUP
3 cups (600 g) granulated sugar
2 cups (480 mL) corn syrup
1 teaspoon kosher salt

Vegetable oil cooking spray, for
    greasing
1 cup (125 g) unsifted powdered
    sugar, plus more for dusting

NOTE: *If you don't have a candy thermometer, you're looking for "soft ball stage." Fill a clear glass with ice water, and when the mixture starts to form large, slow bubbles on the surface, use a spoon to drizzle some of the syrup into the ice water, then touch the syrup to see if it can be rolled between your fingers into a ball. It should still be soft enough to flatten between your thumb and index finger.*

Infusing marshmallows seems like something you'd see at a frilly French bakery. My take on flavor-infused marshmallows leaves the snootiness behind, and hops a nonstop flight to Rio for Carnival with a touch of the popular Brazilian spirit cachaça. If you don't have cachaça, you can use another clear liquor like vodka. Or rum, now that I think about it—which would make this a mojito marshmallow. Not a bad idea.

MAKE THE MARSHMALLOW BASE: In the bowl of a stand mixer fitted with the whisk attachment (or in a large bowl, if you're not planning to use a stand mixer), combine the gelatin, lime juice, cachaça, and food coloring. Whisk by hand to combine, then let sit until the gelatin powder is fully hydrated, about 5 minutes.

MAKE THE MARSHMALLOW SYRUP: In a medium saucepan, combine the granulated sugar, corn syrup, salt, and ¾ cup (180 mL) water. Cook over medium heat until the mixture reaches 235°F on a candy thermometer (see Note).

With the mixer on medium speed, slowly stream the syrup into the gelatin mixture. When all the syrup is fully incorporated, increase the mixer speed high and whip until the mixture is glossy and thick and has cooled to room temperature, 5 to 8 minutes.

Meanwhile, line a 9 by 13-inch baking dish with parchment paper (see page 25) and grease the parchment with cooking spray.

Pour the marshmallow mixture into the prepared baking dish and spread it evenly with an oiled mini offset spatula or spoon. Dust with powdered sugar and let stand, uncovered, overnight.

The next day, the marshmallows should be firm to the touch. Place a cutting board over the baking dish and flip the block of marshmallows out onto the cutting board. With an oiled knife, cut the block into twenty 2¼ by 2½-inch marshmallows (you'll cut 4 rows and 5 columns). Cut one row at a time and work slowly, applying oil to the knife each time you cut. Pour the powdered sugar into a medium bowl and roll each cut marshmallow in the sugar to coat.

Let sit, uncovered, for 4 hours before placing them in an airtight container. They will keep at room temperature for up to 1 week.

Pies,
Tarts,

Cobblers
& Crumbles

Egg Tarts

These flan-esque "cupcakes" were born in Portugal, where they were made by nuns and became incredibly popular. Portuguese sailors brought egg tarts with them as they traveled all over the world, which is how they became a ubiquitous street food in Chinese port towns. I grew up eating Hong Kong–style egg tarts in Manhattan's Chinatown, where they cost only a dollar (and miraculously still do). You can infuse the egg filling with all kinds of flavors, from fruits to spirits, but I recommend going the traditional route so you can bask in the simple, pure beauty of a textbook custard.

9 ounces (255 g) Puff Pastry, homemade (page 277) or store-bought
1 cup (200 g) sugar
⅔ cup (160 mL) heavy cream
⅔ cup (160 mL) whole milk
⅔ cup (160 mL) evaporated milk
2 cinnamon sticks
6 large egg yolks, lightly beaten

If you're using homemade puff pastry, roll it out to ⅛ inch thick. Cut the pastry into 2-inch squares; if you're using store-bought dough, roll the squares out to stretch them a little bit. Place a puff pastry square in each cavity of two 6-cup cupcake tins (or work with one tin at a time, if you don't have two) and prick them with a fork, making tiny holes all over each square. Place the tins in the fridge or the freezer for at least 1 hour or up to overnight.

MEANWHILE, MAKE THE FILLING: In a medium pot, combine the sugar, cream, whole milk, evaporated milk, and cinnamon sticks and heat over medium heat until bubbles form around the edge of the pot and the mixture reaches 180°F.

Place the eggs yolks in a medium bowl. While whisking continuously, slowly add a ladleful of the hot cream mixture and whisk vigorously to incorporate. Pour the tempered egg mixture into the saucepan with the rest of the cream mixture. Remove from the heat and set aside to cool to room temperature.

Preheat the oven to 375°F.

Remove the prepared cupcake tins from the freezer and pour the filling into the puff pastry–lined cavities. Bake for 20 minutes, or until the tops are golden and slightly burnt. Remove from the oven and transfer to a wire rack to cool before serving.

Pineapple Empanadilla

FILLING

2 cups (330 g) small-diced
   pineapple
2 cups (400 g) granulated sugar
1 teaspoon lime zest
Pinch of kosher salt

DOUGH

2¼ cups (315 g) all-purpose flour,
   plus more for dusting
1 teaspoon kosher salt
Pinch of turmeric
½ cup (1 stick/115 g) very cold
   unsalted butter or shortening,
   cut into ½-inch pieces
1 large egg, lightly beaten, plus
   1 large egg, beaten, for egg wash
Vegetable oil cooking spray

2 cups (480 mL) vegetable oil, for
   frying

GLAZE

¾ cup (95 g) unsifted powdered
   sugar
A few drops yellow food coloring
1 to 2 tablespoons whole milk

When I visit my husband's family in Puerto Rico, this is one of my favorite things to eat. While their version uses ground beef filling, *this* version gives you the same layered flaky fluffiness of the best empanadas, along with the citrusy notes of pineapple, candied and translucent like the finest gummy bear.

MAKE THE FILLING: In a medium saucepan, combine the pineapple, granulated sugar, lime zest, and salt. Cook over medium heat without stirring until the pineapple softens and becomes translucent but still holds its shape and retains a bit of bite, about 12 minutes. Set aside to cool.

MEANWHILE, MAKE THE DOUGH: In a food processor, combine the flour, salt, and turmeric and blitz to combine. Add the butter and pulse until the butter is in pea-size bits. Add the egg and pulse to incorporate. With the motor running, gradually pour in up to ¼ cup (60 mL) cold water as needed until the dough is elastic and feels firm and smooth but not sticky. Scrape the dough onto a lightly floured surface and gather it into a ball. Flatten the dough into a disc, wrap in plastic wrap, and refrigerate for at least 1 hour or up to overnight.

Line a large baking sheet with parchment paper and spray it with cooking spray. On a lightly floured work surface using a lightly floured rolling pin, roll out the chilled dough to ⅛ inch thick. Using a 3½- to 4-inch paper circle as a guide (or the rim of a small bowl), cut out rounds of dough with a sharp paring knife, gathering the scraps and rolling them out again as needed until you have 12 dough rounds.

Place 1 tablespoon of the cooled filling in the center of a dough round and brush the edge of the dough very lightly with egg wash. Fold the dough in half around the filling to form a half-moon. Using the tines of a fork, crimp the edges to seal, ensuring that no gaps remain in the dough where the filling could escape. Transfer to the prepared baking sheet and repeat with the remaining dough and filling. Transfer the baking sheet to the refrigerator and chill the empanadillas until firm, about 1 hour.

In a medium saucepan, heat the oil over medium heat to 350°F. Line a baking sheet with paper towels. Working in batches of two, add the empanadillas to the hot oil and fry until golden brown on both sides, about 4 minutes total. Use a spider or a slotted spoon to transfer the

empanadillas to the paper towel–lined pan. Repeat with the remaining empanadillas, letting the oil return to 350°F between batches. If any filling escapes into the oil, use a skimmer to remove it from the oil to prevent it from burning. Let the empanadillas cool slightly before serving.

MAKE THE GLAZE: In a small bowl, stir together the powdered sugar and food coloring, then gradually whisk in enough milk to make a pourable glaze. (I used a piping bag in the photo above, but you can use a fork or spoon to drizzle the glaze over the empanadillas instead.) Serve warm.

Plantain Tarte Tatin

If you're anything like me and have so many plantains around that a good portion of them get too ripe, too soon, this is the perfect recipe. *Especially* when you've had enough of the sticky bun: this is your next plantain adventure.

Preheat the oven to 400°F.

In a large nonstick pot, melt the coconut oil and 1 tablespoon of the butter over medium heat. Place the plantains in the pot, cut-side down, and cook until lightly golden brown on both sides, about 2 minutes per side. Add 3 tablespoons of the coconut water and cover the pot. Cook for 3 to 4 minutes, until the plantains are completely soft, adding more coconut water as needed if the pot starts looking dry before the plantains have adequately softened. Once the plantains are soft, increase the heat to high to cook off any remaining coconut water. Reduce the heat to medium and add 1 tablespoon of the butter, the brown sugar, granulated sugar, cinnamon, nutmeg, allspice, and salt and lightly toss to coat the plantains.

Spread the rest of the butter evenly over the surface of a 10-inch oven-safe skillet (preferably cast iron). (Alternatively, spread the butter over a baking sheet in a circle where the tarte will go.) Sprinkle the brown sugar mixture over the butter and arrange the plantains on top of the circle of butter and sugar, packing them in tight to fill every nook and cranny.

If you're using homemade puff pastry, roll it out to ¼ inch thick and at least 11 inches square. Lay the pastry over the plantains, then trim it into a circle that extends 1 inch beyond the edges of the plantains (it will shrink as it bakes). Tuck the pastry in around the plantains, between them and the pan. Pierce the pastry once with a paring knife to create a vent for steam.

Bake for 30 to 40 minutes, until you see the pan caramel bubbling through the sides and the puff pastry is crispy, deep golden, and baked all the way through. Remove from the oven and let stand for 5 to 10 minutes.

Place a serving platter larger than the skillet over the tart and carefully flip the platter and the skillet together to remove the tart from the pan, being careful not to burn yourself with the pan caramel. Let cool slightly before serving.

2 tablespoons coconut oil
6 tablespoons (¾ stick/85 g) unsalted butter, softened
3 extra-ripe plantains, peeled and cut into 1½-inch-thick rounds
4 to 6 tablespoons (60 to 90 mL) coconut water
½ cup lightly packed (100 g) light brown sugar
3 tablespoons granulated sugar
½ teaspoon ground cinnamon
¼ teaspoon ground nutmeg
⅛ teaspoon ground allspice
Pinch of kosher salt
12 ounces (340 g) puff pastry, homemade (page 277) or store-bought (see Note)

NOTE: *If you're using store-bought pastry, you'll need one 14-ounce (400 g) sheet of frozen puff pastry dough (I recommend Dufour brand).*

Miso Dulce de Leche Mousse Pie

MAKES ONE 10-INCH PIE

CRUST
½ cup (1 stick/115 g) unsalted
    butter, softened, plus
    7 tablespoons (100 g), melted
½ cup lightly packed (100 g) light
    brown sugar
½ cup (50 g) unsweetened Dutch-
    process cocoa powder
¾ cup (105 g) all-purpose flour
¼ teaspoon baking powder
Pinch of kosher salt

FILLING
3⅓ cups (800 mL) heavy cream
1 (¼-ounce/7 g) packet unflavored
    gelatin powder
3 tablespoons white miso paste
¼ cup (75 g) dulce de leche, store-
    bought or homemade (page 281)
2 large egg yolks
8 ounces (225 g) unprocessed milk
    chocolate fèves or discs

TOPPING
1 cup (240 mL) heavy cream
¼ cup (30 g) unsifted powdered
    sugar
1 tablespoon vanilla bean paste
Pinch of kosher salt
Poppy seeds, for garnish

For me and many other cooks, miso is not an ingredient reserved for savory applications. Its salty umami flavor is incredible in desserts. In this recipe, it manages to enhance the decadence of dulce de leche while also taming its cloying sweetness.

Preheat the oven to 300°F. Line a large baking sheet with parchment paper.

MAKE THE CRUST: In the bowl of a stand mixer fitted with the paddle attachment (or using one of the alternate methods on page 25), combine the ½ cup (1 stick/115 g) softened butter with the brown sugar and cocoa powder and beat on low speed until the mixture forms a ball.

In a large bowl, whisk together the flour, baking powder, and salt to combine. Add the dry ingredients to the mixer bowl with the wet ingredients and pulse the mixer on and off, almost like you're trying to jump-start a car, so the flour gets gradually incorporated without flying all over your kitchen. When the dry ingredients are mostly combined, mix on low to incorporate them fully.

Spread the dough over the prepared baking sheet in a ¼-inch-thick layer and bake for 20 to 30 minutes, until golden and crispy. Remove from the oven and let the crust cool completely. Line a 10-inch pie dish with two layers of plastic wrap.

Transfer the cooled crust to a food processor and pulse until broken down into fine crumbs. With the motor running, drizzle in the remaining 7 tablespoons (100 g) melted butter and process until well combined.

Transfer the mixture to the prepared pie dish and press the crumbs firmly and evenly over the bottom and up the sides of the dish, using the flat bottom of a dry measuring cup to help press the crumbs neatly. Cover with plastic wrap and refrigerate while you make the filling.

MAKE THE FILLING: Pour ⅓ cup (80 mL) of the cream in a small bowl and sprinkle the gelatin evenly over the surface. Set aside for 5 minutes to bloom the gelatin.

In a medium pot, bring 1 cup (240 mL) of the cream to a light boil over medium heat. Add the miso and whisk vigorously.

In a medium bowl, whisk together the dulce de leche and the egg yolks until smooth. While whisking continuously, slowly add a ladleful of the warm miso cream and whisk vigorously to incorporate. Pour the tempered egg mixture into the saucepan with the rest of the miso cream. Increase the heat to medium and cook, whisking continuously to make sure the bottom doesn't scald or burn, until the mixture reaches 178°F. Remove the pan from the heat, add the bloomed gelatin, and whisk well to incorporate.

Put the milk chocolate in a clean, dry bowl and strain the miso-dulce mixture through a fine-mesh sieve into the bowl. Whisk until the chocolate has melted and the mixture is completely smooth and luscious. Cover with a kitchen towel and let stand until the ganache is cool to the touch.

Meanwhile, in the bowl of a stand mixer fitted with the whisk attachment or in a large bowl using a hand mixer or a stick blender, whip the remaining 2 cups (480 mL) heavy cream on medium speed until stiff peaks form, 5 to 6 minutes.

Whisk the ganache to loosen it, then add one-quarter of the whipped cream to the ganache and use a spatula to mix until you can no longer see white streaks and the mixture drips off the spatula. Add the remaining whipped cream and fold until completely incorporated.

Remove the prepared crust from the fridge and fill it with the mousse, spreading it evenly so it is nice and leveled. Cover lightly with plastic wrap and refrigerate overnight.

THE NEXT DAY, MAKE THE TOPPING: In the bowl of a stand mixer fitted with the whisk attachment or in a large bowl using a hand mixer or a stick blender, combine the cream, powdered sugar, vanilla, and salt and whip on medium speed until firm, 5 to 6 minutes. Transfer the whipped cream to a piping bag fitted with a large star tip.

Remove the pie from the fridge. Pipe whipped cream rosettes around the edge of the pie. Sprinkle poppy seeds over the top. Slice and enjoy!

Nasturtium Coconut Cream Pie

RITZ PIECRUST
2 sleeves Ritz crackers (about 60 crackers)
7 tablespoons (100 g) unsalted butter, melted

PIE FILLING
1 cup (25 g) nasturtium leaves (see Note)
1½ cups (360 mL) full-fat coconut milk
¾ cup (150 g) sugar
¼ cup (35 g) all-purpose flour
¼ teaspoon kosher salt
1½ cups (360 mL) whole milk
3 large eggs, beaten
2 tablespoons vanilla bean paste
1 tablespoon unsalted butter
½ teaspoon coconut extract

LEMON HONEY WHIPPED CREAM
2 cups (170 g) unsweetened shredded coconut, toasted
1½ cups (360 mL) heavy cream
3 tablespoons honey
Pinch of kosher salt
Zest of 1 lemon
½ teaspoon fresh lemon juice

I grow nasturtiums on my balcony at home. It takes a week or two for the seeds to sprout, giving you flowers with gorgeous colors for garnishes, and leaves with spicy herbaceous notes that bring balance to my recipes. It might sound weird to you, which I totally understand. But look, there was a time not too long ago when mint and basil were tough sells as dessert ingredients. Nasturtiums deserve the same embrace in the sweet kitchen.

MAKE THE CRUST: In a food processor, blitz the crackers into fine crumbs. Transfer them to a large bowl, add the melted butter, and stir to combine. Transfer the mixture to a 10-inch pie pan and press the crumbs firmly and evenly over the bottom and up the sides of the pan, using the flat bottom of a dry measuring cup to help press the crumbs neatly. Place the crust in the refrigerator to set while you make your filling.

MEANWHILE, MAKE THE FILLING: In a blender, combine the nasturtium leaves and coconut milk. Blend until the leaves are pureed and everything is bright green. Set aside.

In a medium saucepan, stir together the sugar, flour, and salt. Add the whole milk, then strain the nasturtium coconut milk into the pan (discard the solids). Bring to a boil over medium heat, stirring continuously, and cook until the mixture reaches 165°F and is thick like crème anglaise, about 10 minutes.

Place the eggs in a medium bowl. While whisking continuously, slowly add a ladleful of the hot milk mixture and whisk vigorously to incorporate. Pour the egg mixture into the saucepan with the rest of the milk mixture and whisk to combine. Increase the heat to medium-high, bring the mixture to a full boil and cook for 2 to 3 minutes, until large bubbles form on the surface and pop. Add the vanilla, butter, and coconut extract and stir to combine. Remove the filling from the heat and pour it into the baked crust. Cover with plastic wrap and refrigerate for at least 6 hours or up to overnight.

JUST BEFORE SERVING, MAKE THE WHIPPED CREAM: In a food processor, pulse 1 cup (85 g) of the toasted coconut into a powder. Reserve the remaining toasted coconut as a garnish.

In the bowl of a stand mixer fitted with the whisk attachment or in a large bowl using a hand mixer or a stick blender, combine the coconut powder, heavy cream, honey, salt, lemon zest, and lemon juice and whip until the mixture is soft and fluffy like a cloud, about 4 minutes.

Use the whipped cream to decorate the top of the pie and sprinkle the top with the remaining toasted coconut before serving.

NOTE: *You can swap out the nasturtiums for peppercress. Or try a different fresh herb entirely, like mint or basil!*

Guava & Cheese Turnover

MAKES 16

Puff Pastry, homemade (page 277)
    or store-bought
1 large egg, beaten, for egg wash
½ cup (115 g) whipped full-fat
    cream cheese
½ cup (160 g) guava paste
Sugar, for sprinkling (optional)

Puff pastry: two words that may strike fear into the hearts (and stomachs) of some of you reading this. But all it takes is one good, focused effort to master the technique and build a lifetime's worth of confidence and skill—and I want you to learn how to do it, since it's going to come in very handy (see the Plantain Tarte Tatin, page 105). Being able to make these turnovers filled with tangy cream cheese and guava paste is worth it alone. For a more muted alternative to the queso crema, try mozz instead.

Roll out the puff pastry to a 12-inch square that is about ⅛ inch thick, trimming the edges if needed. Cut the pastry into four 3-inch-wide strips, then cut each strip crosswise into 4 equal pieces to make sixteen 3-inch squares of pastry. Refrigerate the pastry squares until ready to assemble.

Line a large baking sheet with parchment paper.

To assemble the turnovers, brush the edges of 8 of the pastry squares with egg wash. Place 1 tablespoon of the cream cheese and 1 tablespoon of the guava paste in the center of each square. Top each square with one of the remaining pastry squares and press the edges together. Using the tines of a fork, press the edges firmly to seal. (If the fork sticks to the pastry, dip the tines in flour.) Using a small sharp knife, cut an X in the top of each pastry. Place on the prepared baking sheet, spacing them evenly apart. Cover and refrigerate for at least 2 hours or up to overnight. Cover and refrigerate the remaining egg wash as well.

Preheat the oven to 400°F.

Brush the pastries with the egg wash and sprinkle with sugar, if desired. Bake for about 25 minutes, until puffed, crispy, and golden brown, rotating the baking sheet halfway through. Remove from the oven and let cool for about 30 minutes before eating.

Carrot Buttermilk Pie

The American buttermilk pie is a Southern classic that I've been enamored with since my introduction to it at the Riverdale Diner in the Bronx. To me, a buttermilk pie is like a cross between a budin de pan and a Parisian tart, which is why I might be so obsessed with it. This rendition works in some carrot puree—a simple change that makes it even richer.

Preheat the oven to 350°F.

In a large bowl, whisk together the eggs, egg yolk, brown sugar, and granulated sugar until doubled in volume and glossy. Add the melted butter, lemon juice, vanilla, nutmeg, cinnamon, grains of paradise, and ¾ cup (180 mL) of the buttermilk and whisk with gusto. Add the carrot puree and mix again.

In a medium bowl, whisk together the flour, salt, and remaining ¼ cup (60 mL) buttermilk to make a slurry. Add the flour mixture to the carrot-buttermilk mixture and whisk until completely combined.

On a floured surface, roll out the pie dough to a 12-inch round and drape it over a 10-inch pie dish. Return the pie dough to the fridge until firm before continuing, at least 15 minutes.

Crimp the edge of the dough in wide petals: Gently pinch the edge between the thumb and index finger on your nondominant hand and gently press the index finger on your dominant hand forward until a petal forms. Dock the dough by pricking the bottom and sides all over with a fork. Cover the petaled edge with aluminum foil to prevent it from browning too much in the oven.

Pour the filling into the crust and bake for 45 to 60 minutes, until the crust is golden brown and the top of the pie is golden and caramelized. Remove from the oven and let cool in the fridge for 4 hours before serving. Top with powdered sugar, if desired.

MAKES ONE 10-INCH PIE

3 large eggs
1 large egg yolk
1 cup lightly packed (200 g) dark brown sugar
½ cup (100 g) granulated sugar
½ cup (1 stick/115 g) unsalted butter, melted
1 tablespoon fresh lemon juice
2 teaspoons vanilla extract
½ teaspoon ground nutmeg
½ teaspoon ground cinnamon
⅛ teaspoon grains of paradise (or freshly ground black pepper)
1 cup (240 mL) buttermilk
½ cup (125 g) carrot puree (from about 1 carrot)
¼ cup (35 g) all-purpose flour, plus more for dusting
½ teaspoon kosher salt
Lazy Girl Piecrust (page 278), chilled
Powdered sugar, for dusting (optional)

Peach, Cinnamon & Soursop Cobbler

MAKES ONE 9 BY 13-INCH
COBBLER

CRUST
Vegetable oil cooking spray
3 cups (420 g) all-purpose flour,
    plus more for dusting
1 tablespoon baking powder
¾ teaspoon kosher salt
½ cup (1 stick/115 g) unsalted
    butter, cubed and frozen
1 tablespoon granulated sugar
2 teaspoons honey
½ cup (120 mL) cold buttermilk
½ cup (120 mL) cold whole milk

FILLING
3 cups (460 g) sliced peaches (from
    3 or 4 peaches)
⅓ cup packed (80 g) light brown
    sugar
6 tablespoons (45 g) cornstarch
¼ cup (30 g) soursop puree
2 tablespoons unsalted butter,
    softened
1½ tablespoons ground cinnamon
Zest of 1 lemon
1 teaspoon kosher salt

TO FINISH
¼ cup (50 g) sanding sugar
Banana Dulce Sherbet (page 257;
    optional)
Powdered sugar (optional)

Peaches and soursop, one of my favorite ingredients (see page 62), are a wonderful match. This recipe will get you acquainted with soursop's distinct fruity-sour flavor—and teach you how to make fluffy biscuits along the way. Two birds, one cobbler.

MAKE THE CRUST: Preheat the oven to 400°F. Lightly grease a 9 by 13-inch baking dish with cooking spray.

In a food processor, combine the flour, baking powder, salt, and butter. Pulse until the butter has marbled into pea-size pieces. Add the granulated sugar and honey and blitz until just combined.

Transfer the flour mixture to a large bowl and make a well in the center. Add ¼ cup (60 mL) of the buttermilk and ¼ cup (60 mL) of the milk to the well and mix with a rubber spatula until all the liquid disappears. Add more milk and buttermilk a little bit at a time, mixing after each addition, until the dough is well hydrated and comes together. (You may not need all the dairy.)

Transfer the dough to a floured surface, then roll it out to ¼ inch thick. Cut the dough in half and stack one half over the other. Cut it in half again and stack the quarters on top of each other. Roll the stack of dough out to 1 inch thick and then cut it into 12 squares. Transfer to an airtight container and chill in the fridge or freezer while you make the filling.

MAKE THE FILLING: In a large bowl, combine the peaches, brown sugar, cornstarch, soursop puree, butter, cinnamon, lemon zest, and salt and give it a mix until a syrup develops from the cornstarch. (It's OK if the butter doesn't fully incorporate.)

Pour the filling into the prepared baking dish and add all the crust on top. The squares of dough will not completely cover the fruit. Brush the crust with any remaining milk or buttermilk and sprinkle sanding sugar over the top.

Bake the cobbler for 30 to 40 minutes, until the crust is golden and the filling is bubbling through the topping and looks jammy. Remove from the oven and let cool for 10 to 15 minutes before serving. If desired, serve with a scoop of sherbet and some powdered sugar.

Passion Fruit & Guava Mascarpone Tart

I love making this tart, because it has fruitiness, acidity, *and* creaminess. It also features three things you will always find in my house: guava paste, mascarpone, and frozen passion fruit. I'm not exaggerating—I am the same way with passion fruit as some people are with mixed berries. If I don't have fresh, I'm always going to have some frozen in my freezer. Some people might consider these ingredients "exotic," but to me, they are everyday essentials. I hope that by cooking through this book, you'll learn to feel the same way about guava and passion fruit, and start to keep them in your kitchen at all times, just like I do.

MAKE THE SHORTBREAD CRUST: Preheat the oven to 350°F. Very lightly spritz a 9-inch tart pan with a removable bottom with cooking spray or coat with butter.

In the bowl of a stand mixer fitted with the paddle attachment (or using one of the alternate methods on page 25), beat the butter, powdered sugar, and granulated sugar on low speed until creamy, 2 to 3 minutes. Reduce the mixer speed to medium and add the egg. Mix for 2 to 3 minutes, then scrape down the sides and bottom of the bowl.

Turn off the mixer and add the flour, cornstarch, and salt. Pulse the mixer on and off, almost like you're trying to jump-start a car, so the flour gets gradually incorporated without flying all over your kitchen. When the dry ingredients are mostly combined, turn the mixer on low speed and mix to incorporate them fully.

Transfer the dough to a floured surface and roll it out to a ¼-inch-thick square. Cut the dough into four sections and transfer each section to the tart pan, one by one, until the dough is covering the whole pan. Press lightly with your fingers to make sure the edges and nooks and crannies of the tart pan are evenly filled with dough. Dock the dough by pricking it all over with a fork, then trim the edges with a serrated knife—but make sure to leave a little overhang above the seam of the pan, as the dough will shrink when you bake it. Refrigerate the tart shell for 15 minutes, or until the dough is firm to the touch.

continues ▶

SHORTBREAD CRUST
Vegetable oil cooking spray (optional)

½ cup (1 stick/115 g) unsalted butter, softened, plus more for the pan (if not using cooking spray)

2 tablespoons powdered sugar

1 tablespoon granulated sugar

1 large egg

1¼ cups (175 g) all-purpose flour

2 tablespoons cornstarch

¼ teaspoon kosher salt

FILLING
¼ cup (60 mL) bottled or canned pineapple juice

1 (¼-ounce/7 g) packet unflavored gelatin powder

1½ cups (300 g) granulated sugar

1⅓ cups (300 g) unsalted butter

¼ cup (25 g) lemon zest

½ cup plus 1 tablespoon (110 g) thawed frozen passion fruit puree

Pinch of kosher salt

6 large eggs

8 large egg yolks

MASCARPONE TOPPING
1 cup (240 mL) heavy cream

¼ cup (75 g) guava paste

1 cup (240 g) mascarpone cheese

Pinch of kosher salt

¼ cup (30 g) unsifted powdered sugar

1 tablespoon cornstarch

Edible flowers, for garnish (optional)

Fresh passion fruit, for serving (optional)

Line the tart shell with parchment paper and fill it with dried beans or rice, or pie weights. Bake for 20 to 25 minutes, until the crust is golden all over, especially in the center. If the crust is not done after 25 minutes, reduce the oven temperature to 300°F and bake for 10 minutes more.

MEANWHILE, MAKE THE FILLING: Pour the pineapple juice into a small bowl. Sprinkle the gelatin evenly over the surface, stir to combine, and set aside for 1 to 2 minutes to bloom the gelatin.

In a nonreactive medium saucepan, combine the granulated sugar, butter, lemon zest, passion fruit puree, and salt. Heat over medium heat, stirring occasionally, until the butter melts and the mixture just starts to simmer (do not allow it to boil), about 6 minutes. Remove from the heat.

Meanwhile, in a medium bowl, whisk together the eggs and egg yolks. While whisking continuously, pour a ladleful of the hot sugar mixture into the bowl with the eggs and whisk until combined. Pour the tempered egg mixture into the saucepan and cook over medium heat, whisking continuously, until the curd becomes very thick and big, and slow bubbles begin to rise to the surface, 5 to 8 minutes. Immediately remove from the heat, add the bloomed gelatin mixture, and whisk until thoroughly combined.

Strain the filling through a fine-mesh sieve into another bowl, stirring the filling in the sieve to help it pass through (but do not press it through), then pour the filling into the baked crust. (You may not be able to fit all the filling into the crust. Cover and refrigerate any remaining filling to snack on or to use in layer cakes; it will keep for up to 1 week.) Refrigerate the pie until chilled, at least 4 hours or up to overnight.

MEANWHILE, MAKE THE TOPPING: In a small pot, combine ¼ cup (60 mL) of the cream and the guava paste and warm over medium heat, stirring gently once the cream starts bubbling, until the paste has dissolved. Remove from the heat and let cool to room temperature.

In the bowl of a stand mixer fitted with the whisk attachment (or using one of the alternate methods on page 25), combine the cooled guava mixture, mascarpone, and salt and mix on medium-low speed until combined.

In a small bowl, stir together the powdered sugar and cornstarch until well combined. Add the cornstarch mixture and the cream to the mascarpone mixture and mix on medium-low speed until stiff peaks form, 5 to 6 minutes. Be careful not to overmix, or the mascarpone will get grainy. Transfer the topping to a large piping bag fitted with a large rose tip.

Pipe a large swirl of the mascarpone mixture on top of the tart, starting from the center of the tart and spiraling all the way to the outer edge. When ready to serve, garnish the pie with edible flowers and fresh passion fruit pulp, if desired.

Ginger, Brown Butter & Apple Crumble

MAKES ONE 10-INCH
CRUMBLE

Vegetable oil cooking spray

CRUMBLE TOPPING
½ cup (1 stick/115 g) unsalted
    butter, softened
½ cup lightly packed (100 g) light
    brown sugar
¾ cup (105 g) all-purpose flour
½ cup (73 g) rolled oats, toasted
    (see Note), plus ¼ cup (36 g)
    rolled oats
1 teaspoon baking powder
Pinch of kosher salt

FILLING
4 cups (720 g) small-diced
    unpeeled Granny Smith
    apples (about 4 medium)
⅓ cup packed (80 g) brown sugar
¼ cup (30 g) cornstarch
3 tablespoons Browned Butter
    (page 277)
3 tablespoons grated fresh ginger
Zest of 1 lemon
1 teaspoon kosher salt

Sweet Plantain Gelato (page 273),
    for serving (optional)
Powdered sugar, for serving
    (optional)

NOTE: *To toast your oats, spread them in an even layer in a skillet and toast over medium heat, stirring frequently, until they smell nice and fragrant. It should take just a couple of minutes. Remove from the heat and let cool before using.*

Everyone should have a crumble recipe in their arsenal, so they can take fruit that is about to turn and create something magnificent. For this one, which features firm Granny Smiths, reserve a bit of the browned butter and pour it over the finished product, hot from the oven. Top with powdered sugar, and you're ready to . . . crumble.

Preheat the oven to 375°F. Lightly grease a 10-inch pie dish with butter or cooking spray.

MAKE THE CRUMBLE TOPPING: In the bowl of a stand mixer fitted with the paddle attachment (or using one of the alternate methods on page 25), beat the butter and brown sugar on medium-low speed until fluffy and aerated, 4 to 5 minutes.

In a large bowl, whisk together the flour, toasted and untoasted oats, baking powder, and salt to combine. Add the dry ingredients to the mixer bowl with the wet ingredients and pulse the mixer on and off, almost like you're trying to jump-start a car, so the flour gets gradually incorporated without flying all over your kitchen. When the dry ingredients are mostly combined, mix on low to incorporate them fully. Set aside while you make the filling.

MAKE THE FILLING: In a large bowl, combine the apples, brown sugar, cornstarch, browned butter, ginger, lemon zest, and salt. Mix until a syrup develops from the cornstarch, 1 to 2 minutes. (It's OK if the butter doesn't fully incorporate.)

Pour the apple filling into the prepared pie dish and then pour all the crumble on top. Spread the crumble over the filling to cover the surface, using your hands to break apart any pieces that seem larger than bite-size. Pat it down to make sure that any spaces are filled with topping. Cover the crumble with aluminum foil and cut a hole at the center of the foil to let steam escape.

Bake the crumble for 40 minutes, then remove the foil and bake for 10 minutes more, until the topping looks like a golden-baked sugar cookie and the filling is bubbling through the topping and looks jammy. Remove from the oven and let cool for 10 to 15 minutes before serving. Serve with a scoop of gelato and some powdered sugar on top, if desired.

No-Bake Spiced Plum & Tamarind Jelly Tart

MAKES ONE 9-INCH TART

PLUM JAM TOPPING

1 cup (150 g) diced plums
⅓ cup (65 g) granulated sugar
1½ ounces (45 mL) liquid pectin
    (half of a 3-ounce/90 mL packet)
Pinch of citric acid

CRUST

14 ounces (400 g) graham crackers
    (about 25 sheets of graham
    crackers)
Pinch of kosher salt
7 tablespoons (100 g) unsalted
    butter, melted

TAMARIND JELLY FILLING

3 cups (720 mL) tamarind juice or
    Tamarind Jam (page 280)
½ cup (100 g) granulated sugar
½ cup (120 mL) fresh lemon juice
4 (¼-ounce/7 g) packets unflavored
    gelatin powder
Pinch of citric acid

2 cups (300 g) sliced plums

Edible flowers, for serving
Fresh plums, for serving

Of the numerous no-bake recipes in this book, this might be the most no-bakey of them all. Plum and tamarind are a match made in heaven. In this recipe, I turn the plums into a kind of chutney, which I scoop onto a graham cracker tart filled with a tamarind jelly that holds its shape just right.

MAKE THE PLUM JAM: In a small nonreactive pot, combine the diced plums, granulated sugar, and pectin and bring to a boil over medium-high heat. Cook until the mixture is thick and bubbling, 4 to 5 minutes.

To test if the jam is done, you'll need two metal bowls. Fill one of the bowls with ice. Ladle a small amount of jam into the second bowl and set it over the bowl of ice to cool it rapidly. The cooled jam should have the consistency of store-bought jam: thick, chunky, spreadable on toast. When the jam is ready, stir in the citric acid, then cool down all the jam with the same double bowl method. (If you'd like, you can make the jam in advance and store it in an airtight container in the fridge for 3 to 4 days.)

MAKE THE CRUST: Line a 9-inch pie dish with two layers of plastic wrap.

In a food processor, blitz the graham crackers into fine crumbs. (You should have about 3⅔ cups of crumbs.) Add the salt. With the motor running, drizzle in the melted butter and process until well combined. Transfer the crumb mixture to the prepared pie dish and press it firmly and evenly over the bottom and up the sides of the prepared dish, using the flat bottom of a dry measuring cup to help press the crumbs neatly. Cover with plastic wrap and refrigerate while you make the filling.

MAKE THE FILLING: In a medium pot, combine the tamarind juice and granulated sugar and bring to a boil over medium-high heat.

Place the lemon juice in a small bowl. Sprinkle the gelatin evenly over the surface, stir to combine, and set aside for 1 to 2 minutes to bloom the gelatin.

Add the bloomed gelatin and the citric acid to the tamarind mixture.

Place the tart shell on a baking sheet so it's easier to carry. Arrange the sliced plums in the tart shell in a pretty spiral shape and then pour the tamarind jelly on top, filling the tart shell almost to the top. The plums will rise to the top, so the whole thing will be a little wobbly . . . carefully transfer the tart to the fridge and refrigerate overnight.

To finish, remove the pie from the fridge, scoop dollops of the plum jam onto the pie, and decorate with edible flowers and fresh plums. Slice and enjoy!

Gooseberry-Strawberry Crostata

2 cups (400 g) quartered
  strawberries

1 cup (150 g) gooseberries, halved
  if large

¼ cup (30 g) cornstarch

⅓ cup packed (80 g) dark brown
  sugar

Zest of 1 lemon

1 teaspoon kosher salt

All-purpose flour, for dusting

1 recipe Lazy Girl Piecrust
  (page 278)

1 large egg white, beaten

¼ cup (50 g) muscovado sugar

Creamy Vanilla Gelato (page 269),
  for serving (optional)

Powdered sugar, for serving
  (optional)

The cool thing about crostatas—or, I should say, *one* of the cool things about crostatas—is that you can make them as ugly as you want and it'll look like you did it that way on purpose. Because it's a crostata. This particularly summer-y crostata celebrates the gooseberry, which looks like a cross between a yellow grape and a tomato, and has a very elegant sweetness that mellows out the strawberries perfectly.

Some guests may not be familiar with gooseberries. Nobody will say no to a crostata, though, so put a little in there and maybe don't say anything about it. Tell them it's a strawberry dessert. They will find it more complex than they expected. They will ask, *How did you make this?* And you will answer, *gooseberries.* What a fun word to say.

Preheat the oven to 400°F. Line a 13 by 18-inch sheet pan with parchment paper.

In a large bowl, combine the strawberries, gooseberries, cornstarch, brown sugar, lemon zest, and salt. Mix until a syrup develops from the cornstarch.

On a floured surface, roll out the pie dough to a little thicker than ⅛ inch. Dock the dough by pricking it all over with a fork and transfer it to the prepared baking sheet.

Brush the outer edge of the dough with the egg white, then blot it dry with a paper towel (it should feel sticky like glue). Use a slotted spoon to add the filling to the center of the dough (just the solids—you can leave behind most of the liquid), leaving 2 inches uncovered around the edge. Fold the exposed dough up over the filling very organically to "seal" the crostata, overlapping the edges and leaving the filling exposed in the center.

Brush the dough with the egg white and then sprinkle with muscovado sugar. Bake for 55 to 65 minutes, until the crust looks deep golden with a few specks of darker spots and the filling is bubbling and jammy. Remove from the oven and let cool for 10 to 15 minutes before slicing with a serrated knife. If desired, serve with a scoop of creamy vanilla gelato and some powdered sugar.

Tamarind Pecan Pie

Not to flex too much, but I made this for an event at the Culinary Institute of America in Napa and I almost had to call security because so many people came up to ask me for the recipe. To be clear: I don't think pecan pie needs any help, but just a little tamarind and a lot less corn syrup will punch up the flavors beyond belief. It's the best damn pecan pie I've ever had.

Preheat the oven to 350°F.

In the bowl of a stand mixer fitted with the paddle attachment (or using one of the alternate methods on page 25), beat the eggs and sugar on medium speed until pale and fluffy, 3 to 4 minutes. Stream in the corn syrup and vanilla and mix until incorporated. Scrape down the sides of the bowl, then add the tamarind jam and salt and mix until incorporated.

With the mixer on low speed, stream in the melted butter and mix until homogeneous, about 2 minutes. Turn off your mixer, then fold in the pecans with a rubber spatula.

On a floured surface, roll out the pie dough to a 12-inch round and drape it over a 10-inch pie dish. Return the pie dough to the fridge until firm before continuing, at least 15 minutes.

Crimp the edge of the dough in wide petals: Gently pinch the edge between the thumb and index finger of your nondominant hand and gently press the index finger of your dominant hand forward until a petal forms. Dock the dough by pricking the bottom and sides all over with a fork. Cover the petaled edge with aluminum foil to prevent it from browning too much in the oven.

Pour the filling into the crust and bake for 40 to 50 minutes, until the crust is golden brown and amazing and the top of the pie is slightly golden and glossy. Remove from the oven and let cool for 3 to 4 hours before serving. Top with powdered sugar, if desired.

MAKES ONE 10-INCH PIE

3 large eggs
1 cup (200 g) sugar
½ cup (120 mL) corn syrup
1 teaspoon vanilla extract
½ cup (160 g) Tamarind Jam (page 280)
¾ teaspoon kosher salt
2 tablespoons unsalted butter, melted
1 cup (145 g) chopped pecans
All-purpose flour, for dusting
Lazy Girl Piecrust (page 278), chilled
Powdered sugar, for dusting (optional)

Bizcochitos

& Other Cakes You'll Like

A Beginner's Guide to Dominican Cake

If, like me, you currently reside in a place where it's hard to find Dominican cake, don't fret—I'll show you how to make your own. But if you live within reach of a Dominican bakery (especially if it's Bizcocho de Colores at 241 Sherman Avenue in Inwood), stop what you're doing and pay them a visit.

I want to tell you about Daisy Lebron. She is the owner of Bizcocho de Colores, which she opened in 1982 after immigrating to New York from the Dominican Republic. She has been a staple of my life since I was a toddler . . . maybe even before I was that age. I feel like many people who grew up in Inwood, Kingsbridge, and the Van Cortlandt Park areas of New York City feel the same way I feel about Bizcocho de Colores. If you are a New Yorker of Dominican descent and need some sweets for a family function, you always go to see Miss Daisy. The last birthday cake Hector's grandmother enjoyed before she passed at 101 years old was made by Miss Daisy.

She introduced me to the beauty of baking—tres leches, estrellas de guayaba, pan de agua, pan dulce, all sorts of puff pastry desserts. I loved her work so much that I was banned from getting too close to the cakes at family celebrations, because I had a habit of sticking my hand, face, and whole body in the delightful layers of a bizcocho Dominicano. There's a photo of me at three years old after doing this, with my mother looking on in bemusement.

When I told her about the book, Miss Daisy was beaming with joy. "The fruits of what I have done," she told me. I hope to make her proud, starting with this cake and the breathtaking suspiro (that's the meringue) that I will always associate with Miss Daisy and the area I call home.

Preheat the oven to 350°F. Spray three 8-inch round cake pans with cooking spray and line them with parchment paper.

Divide the cake batter evenly among the prepared pans and bake for 15 to 20 minutes, until the cakes are springy to the touch and a cake

continues ▶

MAKES ONE 3-TIERED 8-INCH CAKE

Vegetable oil cooking spray
1 recipe Dominican Cake Batter (page 278)
¼ cup (50 g) granulated sugar
½ cup (120 mL) half-and-half
1 (13.4-ounce/380 g) can store-bought dulce de leche, about 1⅔ cups homemade Dulce de Leche (page 281), or 1 (14-ounce/400 g) pack guava paste
1 recipe Suspiro, aka Dominican Meringue (page 279; see Note)

NOTES: *Wait until the cake layers are baked and cooled and your filling is prepared before you make your suspiro.*

If you're having trouble with your suspiro keeping its shape, then you should whip your meringue for longer. It'll take a while, maybe 10 to 15 minutes (or more!), but it should be completely cool to the touch by the time you're done.

In the photo on page 130, I divided the suspiro into three batches, then dyed one with a few drops of pink food coloring and another with a few drops of orange food coloring. This step is totally optional . . . do you!

tester inserted into the center of each comes out clean. Do not over-bake! Remove from the oven and let cool completely.

In a small bowl, whisk together the sugar and half-and-half until dissolved. Pour the soak over the cooled cakes so they get nice and moist.

In the bowl of a stand mixer fitted with the paddle attachment or in a large bowl using a hand mixer, beat the guava paste until smooth and spreadable, 3 to 4 minutes. (If you're using dulce de leche, you can skip this step since it's already spreadable.)

Make your suspiro and scoop it into a piping bag fitted with a large round tip. Pipe a ring of suspiro around the edge of two of the cake layers, aiming for just inside the edge. Divide the dulce de leche between the two cake layers and spread it evenly, avoiding the suspiro at the edge. Stack the filled layers on top of one another, then set the naked cake layer on top. Cover the top and sides of the cake with a thin layer of suspiro, using an offset spatula or the back of a spoon to lock in the crumbs. If you don't want to decorate the cake using a piping tip and a piping bag, simply add a large mound of suspiro to the top of the cake, then decorate it organically: Let some of the suspiro spill over the edge and freeform the sides like you did for the top of your cake.

To decorate the bizcocho as it's pictured on page 130, outfit your pastry bag with an icer piping tip (Ateco 789 or 790), then fill it with 1 to 3 scoops of suspiro (depending on the size of the bag—you can always add more suspiro along the way as needed). Pipe the suspiro in half-moons or squiggles with the serrated edge facing toward you for a detailed ridged design.

Nutcracker Cupcakes

The Nutcracker is an infamous, rum-forward alcoholic beverage sold (surreptitiously) in and around bodegas that is so tasty, you can easily forget that a few too many sips spells trouble. The flavors work so well as the filling for these little cupcakes adapted from my Dominican cake. Don't worry about getting drunk: I've pulled back on the booze in the soak.

MAKE THE CUPCAKES: Preheat the oven to 350°F. Line a 12-cup muffin tin with paper or foil liners and spray the liners with cooking spray.

In the bowl of a stand mixer fitted with the paddle attachment (or using one of the alternate methods on page 25), combine the granulated sugar, brown sugar, butter, oil, and shortening and beat on medium speed until fluffy and pale, about 8 minutes.

Reduce the mixer speed to medium and add the eggs one at a time, mixing until incorporated and scraping down the sides and bottom of the bowl with a rubber spatula after each addition. Beat until glossy and well combined, 5 to 8 minutes.

In a medium bowl, whisk together the flour, cornstarch, baking powder, and salt to combine. Add half the dry ingredients to the mixer bowl with the wet ingredients and pulse the mixer on and off, almost like you're trying to jump-start a car, so the flour gets gradually incorporated without flying all over your kitchen. When the dry ingredients are mostly combined, mix on low to incorporate them fully, about 3 minutes.

Pour in the evaporated milk and mix until just incorporated. Repeat with the vanilla and then the vinegar. Scrape down the bowl. Add the remaining flour mixture and mix on low speed for 3 minutes, then increase the speed to medium and mix until smooth, 2 to 3 minutes more.

Pour the batter into the prepared muffin tin, filling each cup about three-quarters of the way. Bake for 10 to 15 minutes, until a cake tester inserted into the center comes out clean. The tops should just be light

continues ▶

MAKES 12 CUPCAKES

CUPCAKES
Vegetable oil cooking spray
1¼ cups (125 g) granulated sugar
2½ tablespoons light brown sugar
2½ tablespoons unsalted butter
2½ tablespoons vegetable oil
2½ tablespoons vegetable shortening
4 large eggs
1 cup plus 3 tablespoons (170 g) all-purpose flour
3 tablespoons (30 g) cornstarch
1¼ teaspoons baking powder
¼ teaspoon kosher salt
⅔ cup (160 mL) evaporated milk
2 teaspoons Dominican imitation vanilla extract
1½ teaspoons apple cider vinegar

SOAK
½ cup (120 mL) elderflower liqueur
1 tablespoon Everclear or white rum

FILLING
1½ tablespoons (30 g) grape jelly
1½ tablespoons (30 g) strawberry jelly
2 ounces (115 g) guava paste
1½ teaspoons fresh lemon juice
1½ teaspoons dark rum
Pinch of citric acid
Pinch of kosher salt
¼ teaspoon vanilla bean paste
1 recipe Suspiro, aka Dominican Meringue (page 279; see Note)

golden brown; any browner than that and the cupcakes will be dry. Remove from the oven and let cool completely.

Use an apple corer (or go surgical with a knife!) to core out a 1½-inch cylinder from the center of each cooled cupcake (do not go all the way through—keep the bottom of the cupcake intact). You can eat the cylinders as a snack!

MAKE THE SOAK: In a small bowl, mix together the elderflower liqueur and Everclear. Spoon the soak over the cupcakes so they get nice and moist.

MAKE THE FILLING: In a medium bowl, mix together both types of jelly, the guava paste, lemon juice, rum, citric acid, salt, and vanilla. Use a spoon to scoop the filling into the divots in the cupcakes.

Make your suspiro and transfer it to a piping bag fitted with a large round tip (or just use a spoon to spread it). Frost the tops of the cupcakes with the suspiro. From here, you have two choices: You can enjoy the cupcakes as is, or use a kitchen blowtorch to brown the suspiro. I have a blowtorch and am always looking for excuses to use it, so you know what I'm gonna do. (FYI, I do not recommend toasting these under the broiler, since there's a chance the cupcake wrappers will catch fire.)

NOTE: *Wait until the cupcakes are baked, cooled, and filled before making your suspiro.*

Ginger Tea & Lime Cake

MAKES ONE 3-TIERED
8-INCH CAKE

Vegetable oil cooking spray
1 recipe Dominican Cake Batter
(page 278), made with
1 teaspoon ground ginger
mixed into the flour mixture

SOAK
2 ounces (60 g) fresh ginger, peeled
and sliced into coins
¼ cup lightly packed (50 g) dark
brown sugar

FILLING
¾ cup (180 mL) whole milk
¼ cup (60 mL) heavy cream
¼ cup (50 g) canned creamed
corn, pureed in a blender until
smooth
¼ cup plus 2 tablespoons (75 g)
granulated sugar
1 teaspoon vanilla bean paste
3 large egg yolks
2 tablespoons cornstarch
4 tablespoons (½ stick/55 g)
unsalted butter, softened

1 recipe Suspiro, aka Dominican
Meringue (page 279; see Note)

This cake features a little touch of vinegar in the batter and fresh ginger in the soak, resulting in a really fun Dominican meringue infused with lime juice and lime zest.

Preheat the oven to 350°F. Spray three 8-inch round cake pans with cooking spray and line them with parchment paper.

Divide the cake batter evenly among the prepared pans and bake for 15 to 20 minutes, until the cakes are springy to the touch and a cake tester inserted into the center of each comes out clean. Do not over-bake! Remove from the oven and let cool completely.

MEANWHILE, MAKE THE SOAK: In a small saucepan, combine the ginger, brown sugar, and ½ cup (120 mL) water and bring to a boil over medium-high heat. Cook, stirring, until the ginger is fragrant and the sugar has dissolved. Let cool completely, then strain and discard the ginger. Pour the soak over the cooled cakes so the cakes get nice and moist.

MAKE THE FILLING: In a medium saucepan, combine ½ cup plus 1 tablespoon (135 mL) of the milk, the cream, creamed corn, granulated sugar, and vanilla and heat over medium heat just until bubbles form around the edge of the pan.

In a medium bowl, whisk together the egg yolks, cornstarch, and remaining 3 tablespoons (45 mL) milk until smooth. While whisking continuously, slowly pour a thin stream of the hot milk mixture into the bowl with the egg mixture and continue until you've added about half the milk mixture. Whisk until combined, then pour the egg mixture into the saucepan with the remaining milk mixture and whisk to combine. Cook over medium heat, whisking continuously, until the mixture thickens, starts to bubble, and reaches 185°F on a digital ther-mometer, about 8 minutes. Remove from the heat and immediately strain the custard through a fine-mesh sieve into a bowl, using a rub-ber spatula to push it through. Add the butter and stir until smooth. Cover the custard with a piece of parchment or plastic wrap pressed directly against the surface and refrigerate until completely cool, at least 2 hours or up to overnight.

When you're ready to assemble the cake, make the suspiro and transfer it to a piping bag fitted with a large round tip. Pipe a ring of suspiro around the edge of two of the cake layers, aiming for just inside the outer edge. Divide the filling between the two cake layers and spread it evenly, avoiding the suspiro at the edge. Stack the filled layers on top of one another, then set the naked cake layer on top. Cover the top and sides of the cake with suspiro, using an offset spatula or the back of a spoon to spread it evenly. Add a large mound of suspiro to the top of the cake, decorating organically but not letting it spill over the edge.

NOTE: *Wait until the cake is baked and cooled and the filling is prepared before you make your suspiro.*

Maria Cookie Tres Leches Cake

Tres leches is a delicious, iconic, and often too sweet (my opinion) soaked sponge cake dessert. My take on this classic highlights a bodega staple and one of the world's great cookies—galletas de Maria. The addition of salt and the omission of evaporated milk lead to the tres leches I wish had existed when I was growing up.

MAKE THE CAKE: Preheat the oven to 350°F. Line a 9 by 13-inch baking pan with parchment paper (see page 25) and spray it with cooking spray.

In the bowl of a stand mixer fitted with the paddle attachment (or using one of the alternate methods on page 25), beat the sugar and eggs on medium speed until fluffy and pale, about 8 minutes. Reduce the mixer speed to low and add the oil in a thin stream. Mix until glossy and combined. Gradually pour in the milk and mix until combined. Scrape down the sides and bottom of the bowl with a rubber spatula.

In a medium bowl, whisk together the flour, baking powder, baking soda, and salt. Add the dry ingredients to the mixer bowl with the wet ingredients and pulse the mixer on and off, almost like you're trying to jump-start a car, so the flour gets gradually incorporated without flying all over your kitchen. When the dry ingredients are mostly combined, mix on low to incorporate them fully, about 3 minutes. Increase the speed to medium and mix until smooth, 2 to 3 minutes more. Turn off the mixer and use a rubber spatula to fold the crushed Maria cookies into the batter.

Pour the batter into the prepared cake pan and bake for 30 to 40 minutes, until the cake is springy to the touch and a cake tester inserted into the center comes out clean. Remove from the oven and use a skewer or the tines of a fork to poke the cake all over to help it absorb the soak later (give it 30 to 40 pokes—but if the cake looks like it's

continues ▶

MAKES ONE
9 BY 13-INCH CAKE

CAKE
Vegetable oil cooking spray
1¾ cups (350 g) sugar
3 large eggs
1¼ cups (300 mL) vegetable oil
1¼ cups (300 mL) whole milk
2½ cups (350 g) all-purpose flour
½ teaspoon baking powder
½ teaspoon baking soda
2 teaspoons kosher salt
⅓ cup (65 g) crushed Maria cookies

SOAK
1 cup (240 mL) heavy cream
1 (14-ounce/400 g) can sweetened
    condensed milk
½ cup (120 mL) half-and-half
1 tablespoon vanilla bean paste
1 teaspoon kosher salt

TOPPING
2 cups (480 mL) heavy cream
½ cup (100 g) sugar
Maria cookies, broken into pieces,
    for garnish
Edible flowers, for garnish
    (optional)

going to start falling apart, stop before you've gone too far!). Let cool completely.

MEANWHILE, MAKE THE SOAK: In a medium bowl, whisk together the cream and condensed milk to combine. Add the half-and-half, vanilla, and salt and whisk to combine.

With the cake still in the pan, cut it into twelve 3 by 4-inch pieces. Pour half the soak over the cake, then refrigerate for 10 minutes, adding more soak if the cake absorbs it all. Reserve any remaining soak for serving.

MAKE THE TOPPING: In the bowl of a stand mixer fitted with the whisk attachment or in a large bowl using a hand mixer or a stick blender, whip the cream and sugar until medium peaks form, about 7 minutes.

Spoon the whipped cream over the cake while it's still in the pan or plate each piece and top individually with a dollop of cream. Add some crumbled Maria cookie to each serving and top with edible flowers, if desired. Drizzle any remaining soak over the cake, if you like, and serve.

Morir Soñando Tres Leches Cake

Morir soñando, which is the inspiration for the soak in this cake, is a Dominican drink made with orange juice, sweetened condensed milk, and evaporated milk. I'd describe it as next-level Creamsicle, because everything that condensed milk touches turns to gold.

MAKE THE CAKE: Preheat the oven to 350°F. Line a 9 by 13-inch baking pan with parchment paper (see page 25) and spray it with cooking spray.

In the bowl of a stand mixer fitted with the paddle attachment (or using one of the alternate methods on page 25), beat the sugar and eggs on medium speed until fluffy and pale, about 8 minutes. Add the orange zest and orange extract and mix until combined. Reduce the mixer speed to low and add the oil in a thin stream. Mix until glossy and combined. Gradually pour in the milk and mix until combined. Scrape down the sides and bottom of the bowl with a rubber spatula.

In a medium bowl, whisk together the flour, salt, baking powder, and baking soda. Add the dry ingredients to the mixer bowl with the wet ingredients and pulse the mixer on and off, almost like you're trying to jump-start a car, so the flour gets gradually incorporated without flying all over your kitchen. When the dry ingredients are mostly combined, mix on low to incorporate them fully, about 3 minutes. Increase the speed to medium and mix until smooth, 2 to 3 minutes more.

Pour the batter into the prepared pan and bake for 30 to 40 minutes, until the cake is springy to the touch and a cake tester inserted into the center comes out clean. Remove from the oven and use a skewer or the tines of a fork to poke the cake all over to help it absorb the soak later (give it 30 to 40 pokes—but if the cake looks like it's going to start falling apart, stop before you've gone too far!). Let cool completely.

MAKES ONE 9 BY 13-INCH CAKE

CAKE
Vegetable oil cooking spray
1¾ cups (350 g) sugar
3 large eggs
3 tablespoons orange zest
1 teaspoon orange extract
1¼ cups (300 mL) vegetable oil
1¼ cups (300 mL) whole milk
2½ cups (350 g) all-purpose flour
2 teaspoons kosher salt
½ teaspoon baking powder
½ teaspoon baking soda

SOAK
1¼ cups (300 mL) heavy cream
1 (14-ounce/400 g) can sweetened
    condensed milk
¼ cup (60 mL) orange juice
1 tablespoon vanilla bean paste
1 teaspoon kosher salt

TOPPING
2 cups (480 mL) heavy cream
½ cup (100 g) sugar
Orange slices, for garnish

continues ▶

MEANWHILE, MAKE THE SOAK: In a medium bowl, whisk together the cream and condensed milk to combine. Add the orange juice, vanilla, and salt and whisk to combine.

With the cake still in the pan, cut it into twelve 3 by 4-inch pieces. Pour half the soak over the cake, then refrigerate for 10 minutes, adding more soak if the cake absorbs it all. Reserve any remaining soak for serving.

MAKE THE TOPPING: In the bowl of a stand mixer fitted with the whisk attachment or in a large bowl using a hand mixer or a stick blender, whip the cream and sugar until medium peaks form, about 7 minutes.

Spoon the whipped cream over the cake while it's still in the pan or plate each piece and top individually with a dollop of cream. Add an orange slice to each serving. Drizzle any remaining soak over the cake, if you like, and serve.

Torta de Limón

A lighter approach to lemon olive oil cake, my version leans on avocado oil, a hint of black pepper, and a pinch of citric acid to take this moist and lemony treat to the next level.

MAKE THE CAKE: Preheat the oven to 350°F. Line a 10-inch round cake pan with parchment paper and spray it with cooking spray.

In the bowl of a stand mixer fitted with the paddle attachment (or using one of the alternate methods on page 25), beat the granulated sugar and eggs on medium speed until fluffy and pale, about 8 minutes. Reduce the mixer speed to low and add the olive oil and avocado oil in a thin stream. Mix until glossy and combined. Scrape down the sides and bottom of the bowl with a rubber spatula.

In a medium bowl, whisk together the flour, baking powder, baking soda, salt, and pepper. Add half the dry ingredients to the mixer bowl with the wet ingredients and pulse the mixer on and off, almost like you're trying to jump-start a car, so the flour gets gradually incorporated without flying all over your kitchen. When the dry ingredients are mostly combined, mix on low to incorporate them fully, about 3 minutes.

Gradually pour in the milk and mix until combined. Scrape down the bowl, then add the remaining flour mixture and mix until smooth, 2 to 3 minutes more.

Pour the batter into the prepared cake pan and bake for 30 to 40 minutes, until the cake is springy to the touch and a cake tester inserted into the center comes out clean. Remove from the oven and let cool slightly in the pan, then flip the cake onto a parchment-lined work surface and let cool completely.

MEANWHILE, MAKE THE ICING: In a medium bowl, whisk together the powdered sugar, lemon juice, salt, and citric acid until smooth.

Pour the icing over the cooled cake and garnish with lemon wedges.

CAKE
Vegetable oil cooking spray
1¾ cups (350 g) granulated sugar
3 large eggs
1 cup (240 mL) olive oil
½ cup (120 mL) avocado oil
2 cups (280 g) all-purpose flour
½ teaspoon baking powder
½ teaspoon baking soda
1½ teaspoons kosher salt
¼ teaspoon finely ground black pepper
1¼ cups (300 mL) whole milk

ICING
2 cups (250 g) unsifted powdered sugar
Juice of 1 lemon
Pinch of kosher salt
Pinch of citric acid

Lemon wedges, for garnish

Golden Rum Cake

MAKES ONE 10-INCH CAKE

½ cup (120 mL) golden rum
4 tablespoons (½ stick/55 g)
    unsalted butter
1 cup (200 g) sugar
1 teaspoon vanilla extract
1 cinnamon stick
¾ teaspoon kosher salt
1 recipe The Only Rum Cake Recipe
    You'll Ever Need (page 279)
Edible flowers, for garnish
    (optional)

A while back, I started selling this cake by mail-order during the holiday season. People couldn't live without it, so it became a year-round thing, just like that. I can't say I was surprised: rummy pound cake is pure nostalgia, no matter where you come from—even if you didn't grow up eating anything like it. Fair warning to the expectant mothers and readers who do not drink alcohol: I'm not shy with the rum soak.

In a medium saucepan, combine all but 1 tablespoon of the rum, ¼ cup (60 mL) water, the butter, sugar, vanilla, cinnamon, and salt and bring to a boil over medium-high heat. Cook until the butter melts completely and the sugar has dissolved. Remove from the heat and stir in the remaining 1 tablespoon rum.

Remove the cake from the baking pan and use a skewer or cake tester to poke it all over—top, bottom, sides—then place it back in the pan.

If the rum soak has cooled, warm it up in the saucepan over low heat. Strain the warm soak through a fine-mesh sieve over the cake, a little at a time, until it has been fully absorbed. (You may not need the full amount of soak; it will depend on the temperature and humidity in your region.) Cut the cake into pieces and serve, garnished with edible flowers, if desired.

Chocolate Rum Cake

I wasn't about to pass up another chance to display the beauty of my Paola Spices™, please all the chocolate lovers, and deliver a rum cake recipe for those among us who might really like rum but don't necessarily want to drown in it, like me. This is an extremely easy riff to pull off and definitely a crowd-pleaser.

In a medium saucepan, combine all but 1 tablespoon of the rum, ¼ cup (60 mL) water, the butter, sugar, vanilla, cinnamon, allspice, cloves, and salt and bring to a boil over medium-high heat. Cook until the butter melts completely and the sugar has dissolved. Remove from the heat and stir in the remaining 1 tablespoon rum.

Remove the cake from the baking pan and use a skewer or cake tester to poke it all over—top, bottom, sides—then place it back in the pan.

If the rum soak has cooled, warm it up in the saucepan over low heat. Strain the warm soak through a fine-mesh sieve over the cake, a little at a time, until it has been fully absorbed. (You may not need the full amount of soak; it will depend on the temperature and humidity in your region.) Cut the cake into pieces and serve.

MAKES ONE 10-INCH CAKE

½ cup (120 mL) golden rum

4 tablespoons (½ stick/55 g) unsalted butter

1 cup (200 g) sugar

1 teaspoon vanilla extract

1 cinnamon stick

5 allspice berries

4 whole cloves

¾ teaspoon kosher salt

1 recipe The Only Rum Cake Recipe You'll Ever Need (page 279), made with ½ cup (50 g) unsweetened Dutch-processed cocoa powder added with the flour

Rum Punch Cake

MAKES ONE 10-INCH CAKE

½ cup (120 mL) golden rum
¼ cup (60 mL) pineapple juice
4 tablespoons (½ stick/55 g)
    unsalted butter
1 cup (200 g) sugar
3 tablespoons ground hibiscus
    leaves or hibiscus powder
2 tablespoons diced mango
1 teaspoon vanilla extract
4 cinnamon sticks
¾ teaspoon kosher salt
½ teaspoon citric acid
1 recipe The Only Rum Cake Recipe
    You'll Ever Need (page 279)
Edible flowers, for garnish
    (optional)

The first time I took one of these out of the oven, I felt like Dorothy stepping out of her sepia-toned existence and into a wonderful world of tart, Technicolor fruitiness. All credit goes to Jamaica for this amazing creation.

In a medium saucepan, combine all but 1 tablespoon of the rum, ¼ cup (60 mL) water, the pineapple juice, butter, sugar, hibiscus leaf, mango, vanilla, cinnamon, and salt and bring to a boil over medium-high heat. Cook until the butter melts completely and the sugar has dissolved. Remove from the heat and stir in the remaining 1 tablespoon rum and the citric acid.

Remove the cake from the baking pan and use a skewer or cake tester to poke it all over—top, bottom, sides—then place it back in the pan.

If the rum soak has cooled, warm it up in the saucepan over low heat. Strain the warm soak through a fine-mesh sieve over the cake, a little at a time, until it has been fully absorbed. (You may not need the full amount of soak; it will depend on the temperature and humidity in your region.) Cut the cake into pieces and serve, garnished with edible flowers, if desired.

Maria Cookie Icebox Cake

This is one of those set-it-and-forget-it-type cakes that I love so much. It's a perfect summertime dessert because you literally don't have to turn on your oven (but that shouldn't stop you from making it year-round). I go for warming spices in the whipped cream here, but feel free to modify this by adding whatever flavorings feel right to you. You can also swap out the dulce de leche topping for something else—ganache, jam, it all works.

Lightly coat a 9-inch springform pan with cooking spray. Line the pan with a large piece of plastic wrap, covering the bottom and coming up the sides. Rotate the pan 90 degrees and add a second layer of plastic wrap perpendicular to the first so that all sides of the pan are evenly covered.

In a food processor, process 10 of the Maria cookies until broken down into coarse crumbs.

In a large bowl using a stick blender or a hand mixer, combine the cream, powdered sugar, vanilla, salt, cinnamon, cloves, and nutmeg and whip until the cream holds medium-soft peaks, about 4 minutes. (Or you can do this in the bowl of a stand mixer fitted with the whisk attachment. Do you, baby.)

Layer whole Maria cookies over the bottom of the pan, arranging them with their embossed sides down and covering the bottom as much as possible (there will be some gaps, though). Spoon about 1½ cups (360 mL) of the whipped cream mixture over the cookies and smooth the top with a spatula. Sprinkle some of the cookie crumbs over the cream. Repeat the process 5 times more, ending with a final layer of whole cookies. Cover loosely with plastic wrap or a kitchen towel and refrigerate for at least 6 hours or up to overnight to allow the cookies to soften.

When ready to serve, invert the pan onto a serving plate, then remove the springform ring and lift off the pan bottom. Carefully peel away the plastic wrap and spread dulce de leche over the top of the cake, leaving the outer perimeter of the cookies exposed. Garnish the cake with strawberries and edible flowers, if desired, and serve.

MAKES ONE 9-INCH CAKE

Vegetable oil cooking spray
2 (7-ounce/200 g) sleeves Maria cookies (about 60 cookies)
4 cups (1 L) heavy cream
1 cup (125 g) unsifted powdered sugar
2 teaspoons vanilla extract
1 teaspoon kosher salt
½ teaspoon ground cinnamon
⅛ teaspoon ground cloves
⅛ teaspoon ground nutmeg
Dulce de leche, homemade (page 281) or store-bought, for garnish
Whole and halved strawberries, for garnish
Edible flowers, for garnish (optional)

Burnt Tahini & Concord Grape Cake

MAKES ONE 10-INCH CAKE

CAKE
Vegetable oil cooking spray
¼ cup (70 g) tahini
1¾ cups (350 g) granulated sugar
3 large eggs
1 cup (240 mL) olive oil
½ cup (120 mL) avocado oil
2 cups (280 g) all-purpose flour
¼ cup (40 g) sesame seeds
1½ teaspoons kosher salt
½ teaspoon baking powder
½ teaspoon baking soda
¼ teaspoon finely ground black
   pepper
1¼ cups (300 mL) whole milk
¼ cup (75 g) grape jelly

ICING
2 cups (250 g) unsifted powdered
   sugar
2 tablespoons grape juice
1 tablespoon vanilla bean paste
1½ teaspoons fresh lemon juice
Pinch of kosher salt
Pinch of citric acid

Sesame seeds, for garnish
Seedless grapes (preferably still on
   their stems), for garnish

I bet you could walk into any bodega and find all the ingredients you need to make this cake, which seizes on the same caramelly notes in the Burnt Tahini Cookies (page 68) and celebrates the grape jelly I ate for years without knowing it was made with Concord grapes. When I tasted the "real" thing for the first time—more seeds than flesh and skin—I went straight back to the jar.

MAKE THE CAKE: Preheat the oven to 350°F. Line a 10-inch round cake pan with parchment paper and spray it with cooking spray.

In a small nonstick pan, cook the tahini over medium-low heat, stirring frequently with a heat-resistant spatula, until the moisture of the tahini evaporates and it turns a golden brown color, 5 to 7 minutes. Scrape the tahini into a small bowl and let cool.

In the bowl of a stand mixer fitted with the paddle attachment (or using one of the alternate methods on page 25), beat the granulated sugar and eggs on medium speed until fluffy and pale, about 8 minutes. Reduce the mixer speed to low and add the olive oil and avocado oil in a thin stream. Mix until glossy and combined. Add the tahini and mix until combined. Scrape down the sides and bottom of the bowl with a rubber spatula.

In a medium bowl, whisk together the flour, half the sesame seeds, the salt, baking powder, baking soda, and pepper. Add half the dry ingredients to the mixer bowl with the wet ingredients and pulse the mixer on and off, almost like you're trying to jump-start a car, so the flour gets gradually incorporated without flying all over your kitchen. When the dry ingredients are mostly combined, mix on low to incorporate them fully, about 3 minutes.

Gradually pour in the milk and mix until combined. Scrape down the bowl, then add the remaining flour mixture and mix until smooth, 2 to 3 minutes more.

Pour the batter into the prepared cake pan and sprinkle with the remaining sesame seeds. Gently spread the jelly in a thin layer over the top. Bake for 30 to 40 minutes, until the cake is springy to the touch

and a cake tester inserted into the center comes out clean. Remove from the oven and let cool slightly in the pan, then flip the cake onto a parchment-lined work surface and let cool completely.

MEANWHILE, MAKE THE ICING: In a medium bowl, whisk together the powdered sugar, grape juice, vanilla, lemon juice, salt, and citric acid until smooth.

Pour the icing over the cooled cake, garnish with sesame seeds and grapes, and serve.

Mojito Rum Cake

½ cup (120 mL) dark rum

4 tablespoons (½ stick/55 g)
   unsalted butter

1 cup (200 g) sugar

1 teaspoon vanilla extract

1 cinnamon stick

¼ teaspoon mint extract

¾ teaspoon kosher salt

1 fresh mint sprig

1 recipe The Only Rum Cake Recipe
   You'll Ever Need (page 279)

Add a little mint to the soak, swap white rum in for dark, and boom: you've got yourself a ticket to Havana. By far, this is the lightest of the rum cakes in the PV collection. A summertime treat fit for any backyard gathering.

In a medium saucepan, combine all but 1 tablespoon of the rum, ¼ cup (60 mL) water, the butter, sugar, vanilla, cinnamon, mint extract, and salt and bring to a boil over medium-high heat. Cook until the butter melts completely and the sugar has dissolved. Remove from the heat and stir in the remaining 1 tablespoon rum and the mint sprig.

Remove the cake from the baking pan and use a skewer or cake tester to poke it all over—top, bottom, sides—then place it back in the pan.

If the rum soak has cooled, warm it up in the saucepan over low heat. Strain the warm soak through a fine-mesh sieve over the cake, a little at a time, until it has been fully absorbed. (You may not need the full amount of soak; it will depend on the temperature and humidity in your region.) Cut the cake into pieces and serve.

Dominican Sweet Potato Bread

What we've got here is zucchini bread with the added richness from Japanese sweet potatoes. It's a homely looking bake inspired by the roasted sweet potatoes you find at roadside stalls all over the DR. I know when some of you slice into it, you're gonna be like, "I don't know about this one." Trust the process. I guarantee you will fall in love.

Preheat the oven to 450°F.

Using a fork, generously poke the sweet potatoes all over. Wrap them tightly in alumium foil and roast directly on the oven rack for 30 to 40 minutes, until soft, tender, and with visible steam coming out. (The texture of the sweet potato flesh after mashing should be silky and soft, so when in doubt, err on the side of more cook time, since you want to release enough sweetness and make sure that the starch is fully cooked out.) Remove from the oven and let cool. Reduce the oven temperature to 350°F. Line a loaf pan with parchment paper and spray it with cooking spray.

When the sweet potatoes are cool enough to handle, halve them and scoop the flesh into a bowl. Use a fork to lightly mash the flesh. Set aside 2 cups (400 grams) of the mashed sweet potatoes (reserve the rest for another use).

In a medium bowl, whisk together the flour, cinnamon, ginger, salt, baking soda, baking powder, and cloves until well combined.

In a separate medium bowl, whisk together the eggs, sugar, oil, 2 cups (400 g) mashed sweet potatoes, and ⅔ cup (150 mL) water until combined. Add the dry ingredients to the wet and stir vigorously to combine.

Pour the mixture into the prepared loaf pan and bake for 1 hour, or until a cake tester comes out clean. Let cool in the pan for a few minutes, then transfer to a wire rack to cool completely. Store any leftovers in an airtight container with a marshmallow inside it (this keeps the bread fresher for longer). Or slice it into pieces, wrap them individually, and freeze for up to 3 months (microwave for 30 seconds to defrost).

MAKES 1 LOAF

1 pound (455 grams) sweet potatoes (about 3 medium)
Vegetable oil cooking spray
2¾ cups (385 grams) all-purpose flour
2 teaspoons ground cinnamon
2 teaspoons ground ginger
1½ teaspoons kosher salt
1 teaspoon baking soda
½ teaspoon baking powder
½ teaspoon ground cloves
4 large eggs
2⅔ cups (530 grams) granulated sugar
¾ cup plus 3 tablespoons (225 mL) vegetable oil

Coquito Cheesecake

If you're a fan of the Ponche Babka (page 199), then boy, do I have a cheesecake for you. Coquito is basically Puerto Rican eggnog, a drink that feels like dessert that I have decided to turn into a dessert that feels like a drink. By the way, it's the addition of coconut and lack of eggs that generally that makes coquito distinct from your typical eggnog.

MAKE THE CRUST: Preheat the oven to 325°F. Wrap the exterior (bottom and sides) of a 10-inch springform pan with a single sheet of aluminum foil (this will protect it in the water bath later).

Combine the cookies and salt in a food processor and process until broken down into fine crumbs. With the processor running, stream in the melted butter and process until combined. The mixture should look like wet sand.

Using your hands, press the crumb mixture evenly over the bottom and up the sides of the prepared pan, then use the flat bottom of a dry measuring cup to press the crumbs neatly.

MAKE THE FILLING: In a medium bowl, whisk to combine the sugar, nutmeg, and salt. In the bowl of a stand mixer fitted with the paddle attachment (or using one of the alternate methods on page 25), beat the cream cheese and sugar-spice mixture on medium-high speed until fluffy, about 4 minutes. Add the eggs and egg yolks one at a time, mixing until incorporated and scraping down the sides and bottom of the bowl with a rubber spatula after each addition. Add the coconut extract, rum, and vanilla and mix until combined. Add the labneh and coconut cream and mix until combined as well.

Pour the filling into the crust. Set the springform pan in a roasting pan. Run water from the tap until the water is very hot. Add enough hot water to the roasting pan to come halfway up the sides of the springform pan, being careful not to get any water in the springform pan. The springform pan should not be floating.

Carefully transfer the roasting pan to the oven and bake the cheesecake for 45 minutes to 1 hour, until the middle is just set, the top is slightly golden, and a cake tester inserted into the center comes out clean. Remove from the oven, remove the cake pan from the roasting pan, and let cool to room temperature. Cover and refrigerate overnight.

Remove the sides of the pan, slice the cheesecake, and serve.

MAKES ONE 10-INCH CAKE

CRUST

1 (7-ounce/200 g) sleeve Maria cookies (about 20 cookies)

¼ teaspoon kosher salt

7 tablespoons (100 g) unsalted butter, melted

FILLING

¾ cup (150 g) sugar

2 teaspoons ground nutmeg

½ teaspoon kosher salt

2 (8-ounce/225-gram) packages cream cheese, at room temperature

2 large eggs

3 large egg yolks

1 tablespoon coconut extract

2 teaspoons dark rum

1 teaspoon vanilla bean paste

½ cup (120 mL) labneh or plain full-fat Greek yogurt

½ cup (120 mL) unsweetened coconut cream

Roasted Apple & Apple Cider Vinegar Cake

MAKES ONE 10-INCH CAKE

Vegetable oil cooking spray

APPLES

3 cups (540 g) diced peeled
    Honeycrisp or Granny Smith
    apples (about 3 medium)
½ cup lightly packed (100 g) light
    brown sugar
1 tablespoon ground cinnamon
1 teaspoon ground ginger
¼ teaspoon ground cloves
2 tablespoons fresh lemon juice
1 tablespoon light corn syrup
4 tablespoons (½ stick/55 g)
    unsalted butter, cubed

CAKE

1½ cups (300 g) granulated sugar
3 large eggs
1 cup (240 mL) olive oil
½ cup (120 mL) avocado oil
2 cups (280 g) all-purpose flour
1½ teaspoons kosher salt
½ teaspoon baking powder
½ teaspoon baking soda
1 cup (240 mL) evaporated milk
¼ cup (60 mL) apple cider vinegar

TOPPING

2 cups (480 mL) heavy cream
2 tablespoons honey
Pinch of kosher salt

Here you have a spin on an olive oil cake that is super simple to make and super fun to eat: you get all the best notes of apple cider vinegar, minus the powerful punch, and it's just gorgeous to see the juices from the apples drip down the sides.

Preheat the oven to 425°F. Line a large baking sheet with aluminum foil. Line a 10-inch round cake pan with parchment paper and spray it with cooking spray.

PREPARE THE APPLES: In a large bowl, combine the apples, brown sugar, cinnamon, ginger, cloves, lemon juice, and corn syrup and toss to combine. Transfer the apples to the prepared baking sheet and scatter the butter cubes over the top. Roast for 25 to 30 minutes, until the apples are golden and the edges have caramelized. Remove from the oven and let cool completely. Reduce the oven temperature to 350°F.

MAKE THE CAKE: In the bowl of a stand mixer fitted with the paddle attachment (or using one of the alternate methods on page 25), beat the granulated sugar and eggs on medium speed until fluffy and pale, about 8 minutes. Reduce the mixer speed to low and add the olive oil and avocado oil in a thin stream. Mix until glossy and combined. Scrape down the sides and bottom of the bowl with a rubber spatula.

In a medium bowl, whisk together the flour, salt, baking powder, and baking soda. Add half the dry ingredients to the mixer bowl with the wet ingredients and pulse the mixer on and off, almost like you're trying to jump-start a car, so the flour gets gradually incorporated without flying all over your kitchen. When the dry ingredients are mostly combined, mix on low to incorporate them fully, about 3 minutes.

Gradually pour in the evaporated milk and mix until combined. Add the vinegar and mix until combined, pausing to scrape down the bowl. Add the remaining flour mixture and mix until smooth, 2 to 3 minutes more.

Pour the batter into the prepared cake pan. Bake for 30 to 40 minutes, until the cake is springy to the touch and a cake tester inserted

into the center comes out clean. Remove from the oven and let cool slightly, then flip the cake onto a parchment-lined work surface and let cool completely.

MEANWHILE, MAKE THE TOPPING: In the bowl of a stand mixer fitted with the whisk attachment or in a large bowl using a hand mixer or a stick blender, whip the cream, honey, and salt until firm peaks form, about 10 minutes.

Spoon the whipped cream over the cake, then use the back of your spoon to make a well in the center of the whipped cream. Spoon the apples into the well, then serve.

Pineapple Sumac Upside-Down Cake

CARAMEL

Vegetable oil cooking spray

½ cup packed (120 g) light brown sugar

½ cup (1 stick/115 g) unsalted butter, plus more for greasing

1 tablespoon light corn syrup

¾ teaspoon kosher salt

¼ teaspoon ground nutmeg

¼ teaspoon ground cinnamon

¼ teaspoon vanilla extract

1 (20-ounce/570 g) can pineapple chunks in juice, drained and patted dry

CAKE

1¾ cups (350 g) granulated sugar

3 large eggs

1 cup (240 mL) olive oil

½ cup (120 mL) avocado oil

2 cups (280 g) all-purpose flour

1 tablespoon ground sumac

1½ teaspoons kosher salt

½ teaspoon baking powder

½ teaspoon baking soda

1¼ cups (300 mL) whole milk

The edible sumac berry is a bright red superfood that's super popular in Middle Eastern cuisine and, with its floral, acidic taste, one of my favorite pantry ingredients. I wanted to include it in this book because it's a great example of the Levantine influence on Dominican cuisine, which I have a feeling may come as a surprise to some folks. Sumac gives a pleasant twist to classic pineapple upside-down cake, not that it needed my help to be awesome!

MAKE THE CARAMEL: Preheat the oven to 350°F. Spray a 10-inch round cake pan with cooking spray.

In a medium saucepan, combine the brown sugar, butter, corn syrup, salt, nutmeg, cinnamon, and vanilla. Cook over medium heat, stirring occasionally, until the butter has melted, about 2 minutes (the sugar should not be fully dissolved at this point). Remove from the heat. Stir the caramel, then pour it into the prepared cake pan and spread it evenly with a spatula. Scatter the pineapple chunks over the caramel.

MAKE THE CAKE: In the bowl of a stand mixer fitted with the paddle attachment (or using one of the alternate methods on page 25), beat the granulated sugar and eggs on medium speed until fluffy and pale, about 8 minutes. Reduce the mixer speed to low and add the olive oil and avocado oil in a thin stream. Mix until glossy and combined. Scrape down the sides and bottom of the bowl with a rubber spatula.

In a medium bowl, whisk together the flour, sumac, salt, baking powder, and baking soda. Add half the dry ingredients to the mixer bowl with the wet ingredients and pulse the mixer on and off, almost like you're trying to jump-start a car, so the flour gets gradually incorporated without flying all over your kitchen. When the dry ingredients are mostly combined, mix on low to incorporate them fully, about 3 minutes.

Gradually pour in the milk and mix until combined. Scrape down the bowl, then add the remaining flour mixture and mix until smooth, 2 to 3 minutes more.

Pour the batter over the pineapple in the cake pan. Bake for 30 to 40 minutes, until the cake is springy to the touch and a cake tester inserted into the center comes out clean. Remove from the oven and let cool slightly, then flip the cake onto a serving platter and let cool completely before serving.

Chocolate Malta Cake

MAKES ONE 10-INCH CAKE

CAKE
Vegetable oil cooking spray
1½ cups (300 g) granulated sugar
3 large eggs
2 tablespoons molasses
1 teaspoon vanilla extract
¼ teaspoon dark rum
1 cup (240 mL) olive oil
½ cup (120 mL) avocado oil
2 cups (280 g) all-purpose flour
1½ teaspoons kosher salt
½ teaspoon baking powder
½ teaspoon baking soda
1 cup (240 mL) malta beverage
¼ cup (60 mL) whole milk

ICING
2 cups (250 g) unsifted powdered
  sugar
¼ cup (25 g) unsweetened Dutch-
  processed cocoa powder, plus
  more for dusting
2 to 4 tablespoons malta beverage,
  as needed
1 tablespoon vanilla bean paste
Pinch of kosher salt

We've all seen our fair share of chocolate sweets and bakes infused with coffee. But have you ever heard about, let alone taste, what happens when you give malta a try instead? Bitter, sweet, rich, hoppy, and amazingly elevated.

MAKE THE CAKE: Preheat the oven to 350°F. Line a 10-inch round cake pan with parchment paper and spray it with cooking spray.

In the bowl of a stand mixer fitted with the paddle attachment (or using one of the alternate methods on page 25), beat the granulated sugar and eggs on medium speed until fluffy and pale, about 8 minutes. Add the molasses, vanilla extract, and rum and mix until combined. Reduce the mixer speed to low and add the olive oil and avocado oil in a thin stream. Mix until glossy and combined. Scrape down the sides and bottom of the bowl with a rubber spatula.

In a medium bowl, whisk together the flour, salt, baking powder, and baking soda. Add half the dry ingredients to the mixer bowl with the wet ingredients and pulse the mixer on and off, almost like you're trying to jump-start a car, so the flour gets gradually incorporated without flying all over your kitchen. When the dry ingredients are mostly combined, mix on low to incorporate them fully, about 3 minutes.

Gradually pour in the malta and mix until combined. Gradually pour in the milk and mix until combined, pausing to scrape down the bowl. Add the remaining flour mixture and mix until smooth, 2 to 3 minutes more.

Pour the batter into the prepared cake pan. Bake for 30 to 40 minutes, until the cake is springy to the touch and a cake tester inserted into the center comes out clean. Remove from the oven and let cool slightly, then flip the cake onto a parchment-lined work surface and let cool completely.

MEANWHILE, MAKE THE ICING: In a medium bowl, whisk together the powdered sugar, cocoa powder, 2 tablespoons of the malta, the vanilla paste, and the salt until smooth. If you want a thinner icing, add up to 2 tablespoons additional malta.

Pour the icing over the cooled cake and let it set before serving. Garnish with a dusting of cocoa powder.

Doña Dona

Baked & Fried Delights

Plantain Sticky Buns

Like many kids with roots in the Caribbean, I grew up eating plantains all the time. They are central to who I am as an eater and a cook. So are Little Debbie's Honey Buns, which I discovered one day at the bodega after school when I was trying to make the best of the two bucks my mom gave me every morning for snacks. I figured I'd give them a shot—and my life has never been the same since I first sampled that sticky, slightly sweet, all-around awesome creation. Fast-forward to a few years ago when my mom and I were watching Guy Fieri on "Triple D," as we called it. Guy—I think we're on a first-name basis now—highlighted a spot that is famous for its Philadelphia-style sticky buns, covered in pecans. Mom urged me to make my own.

I came up with the idea of crossing a honey bun with the Philly version to create a pastry that is delicate yet completely indulgent. I realized that, when you swap in plantains that have been cooked down with a little brown sugar and a bunch of spices for the traditional filling, you get something far gooier and extraordinary.

The key is getting your hands on very overripe plantains; that particular sweetness is impossible to replicate. And don't worry if the caramel doesn't look smooth when you first pour it into the pan; the heat will magically transform it into a smooth, silky texture as it bakes.

MAKE THE FILLING: In a small saucepan, combine the plantain, brown sugar, ½ cup (120 ml) water, the cinnamon, vanilla, ginger, salt, pepper, allspice, and nutmeg. Cook over medium heat, stirring occasionally, until the plantain softens, the liquid starts to thicken, and the whole mixture becomes very tender, 8 to 10 minutes. Carefully transfer the mixture to a blender or food processor and blend until smooth, about 30 seconds. Set aside until ready to use.

MAKE THE DOUGH: In the bowl of a stand mixer fitted with the dough hook, stir together the milk, granulated sugar, and yeast on low speed. Turn off the mixer and let stand until frothy, 5 to 10 minutes. Add the flour, then the salt (this step is super important—always add the flour first so the salt does not harm the yeast you just woke up), and mix on medium-low speed until the flour is mostly incorporated, about 1 minute, stopping to scrape down the sides of the bowl as needed. Add the eggs and mix until the dough forms a ball, about 1 minute. Add the butter in a few additions (I usually do a quarter of it

MAKES 9 BUNS

PLANTAIN FILLING

1 (11-ounce/310 g) soft, ripe black plantain (see Notes, page 170), cut into ½-inch pieces (about 1 cup)

½ cup packed (120 g) light brown sugar

1 teaspoon ground cinnamon

1 teaspoon vanilla extract

½ teaspoon ground ginger

¼ teaspoon kosher salt

¼ teaspoon freshly ground black pepper

¼ teaspoon ground allspice

⅛ teaspoon ground nutmeg

DOUGH

1 cup (240 mL) whole milk, warmed to 96°F

2 teaspoons granulated sugar

1 (¼-ounce/7 g) envelope active dry yeast

3⅓ cups (465 g) all-purpose flour, plus more for dusting

2 teaspoons kosher salt

2 large eggs

6 tablespoons (¾ stick/85 g) unsalted butter, cut into pieces and softened

PAN CARAMEL

½ cup (1 stick/115 g) unsalted butter, plus more for greasing

½ cup packed (120 g) light brown sugar

1 tablespoon light corn syrup

¾ teaspoon kosher salt

¼ teaspoon ground nutmeg

¼ teaspoon ground cinnamon

¼ teaspoon vanilla extract

¾ cup (65 g) chopped pecans

continues ▶

at a time), mixing until the butter is fully incorporated before adding the next addition. Then mix until the dough is smooth and no longer clings to the sides of the bowl, and no butter is visible, about 5 minutes. Cover the bowl with plastic wrap and let stand in a warm, draft-free place until the dough doubles in size, about 1 hour.

MEANWHILE, MAKE THE CARAMEL: Grease a 9-inch square baking pan with butter.

In a medium saucepan, combine the butter, brown sugar, corn syrup, salt, nutmeg, cinnamon, and vanilla. Cook over medium heat, stirring occasionally, until the butter has melted, about 2 minutes (the sugar should not be fully dissolved at this point). Remove from the heat and stir, then pour the caramel into the prepared baking pan, spread it to coat the bottom evenly, and set aside.

Punch down the dough, then turn it out onto a lightly floured work surface and, using a floured rolling pin, roll it out to a 10-inch square. Using an offset spatula or the back of a spoon, spread the filling over the dough all the way to the edges and sprinkle evenly with the pecans. Roll the dough up to form a log, then cut it crosswise into 9 even slices.

Arrange the slices cut-side up in the prepared baking pan (it's OK if they touch). Cover with a clean kitchen towel and let stand in a warm spot until the buns double in size, about 20 minutes.

Preheat the oven to 350°F. Line a rimmed baking sheet with aluminum foil.

Set the pan with the buns on the prepared baking sheet. Bake for 30 to 35 minutes, until the buns are light brown and an instant-read thermometer inserted into the middle of the buns reads 165°F. Alternatively, test the buns by poking one with a toothpick (try to get the dough rather than the filling). If it comes out, well, *doughy*, keep baking. Remove from the oven and let cool in the pan for 5 minutes, then carefully invert the buns onto a platter. Serve warm.

NOTES: *For more on sourcing and working with plantains, see page 23. I really recommend using frozen plantains here because you can be confident that they're perfectly ripe and will break down nicely, creating a smooth filling that won't rip your dough. You can add the frozen plantain straight to the saucepan without defrosting it.*

If you do use fresh plantains, you must first allow them to become overly ripe. The flesh of the plantain should be very sweet and broken down before you make this mixture, as this will ensure that the filling will not taste too starchy.

Zucchini Sticky Buns

Don't be intimidated by the thought of using vegetables in your desserts. I actually used to think that folding zucchini into bread was the only possible use for the ingredient in baking—until the day I made a zucchini rum baba for fun. It was one of the most amazing babas I've ever tried, and ever since, I've been experimenting with zucchini. I soon discovered that adding zucchini to the filling for my tried-and-true plantain sticky buns made the whole thing start to taste like a Greek spoon sweet, an out-of-this-world jam. Satisfying, complex. Perfect.

And this may not be the reason I came up with this variation, but I don't mind being able to sneak in part of my recommended daily dose of veggies by nibbling on a sticky bun.

MAKE THE FILLING: In a small saucepan, combine the plantain, zucchini, brown sugar, ½ cup (120 ml) water, the vanilla, cinnamon, allspice, and salt. Cook over medium heat, stirring occasionally, until the plantain softens, the liquid starts to thicken, and the whole mixture becomes very tender, 8 to 10 minutes. Transfer the mixture to a blender or food processor and blend until smooth, about 30 seconds. Set aside until ready to use.

MAKE THE DOUGH: In the bowl of a stand mixer fitted with the dough hook, stir together the milk, granulated sugar, and yeast on low speed. Turn off the mixer and let stand until frothy, 5 to 10 minutes. Add the flour, then the salt (this step is super important—always add the flour first so the salt does not harm the yeast you just woke up), and mix on medium-low speed until the flour is mostly incorporated, about 1 minute, stopping to scrape down the sides of the bowl as needed. Add the eggs and mix until the dough forms a ball, about 1 minute. And the zucchini and mix until fully incorporated. Add the butter in a few additions (I usually do a quarter of it at a time), mixing until the butter is fully incorporated before adding the next addition. Then mix until the dough is smooth and no longer clings to the sides of the bowl, and no butter is visible, about 5 minutes. Cover the bowl with plastic wrap and let stand in a warm, draft-free place until the dough doubles in size, about 1 hour.

MAKES 9 BUNS

PLANTAIN FILLING

1 (11-ounce/310 g) soft, ripe, black plantain (see Notes, opposite), cut into ½-inch pieces (about 1 cup)

½ cup (85 g) shredded zucchini (about ½ medium)

½ cup packed (120 g) light brown sugar

1 teaspoon vanilla extract

1 teaspoon ground cinnamon

¼ teaspoon ground allspice

¼ teaspoon kosher salt

DOUGH

1 cup (240 mL) whole milk, warmed to 96°F

2 teaspoons granulated sugar

1 (¼-ounce/7 g) envelope active dry yeast

3⅓ cups (465 g) all-purpose flour, plus more for dusting

2 teaspoons kosher salt

2 large eggs

½ cup (125 g) drained shredded zucchini (about 1 medium; see Note, page 172)

6 tablespoons (¾ stick/85 g) unsalted butter, cut into pieces and softened

PAN CARAMEL

½ cup (1 stick/115 g) unsalted butter, plus more for greasing

½ cup packed (120 g) light brown sugar

1 tablespoon light corn syrup

1 teaspoon kosher salt

¼ teaspoon vanilla extract

continues ▶

MEANWHILE, MAKE THE CARAMEL: Grease a 9-inch square baking pan with softened butter.

In a medium saucepan, combine the butter, brown sugar, corn syrup, salt, and vanilla. Cook over medium heat, stirring occasionally, until the butter has melted, about 2 minutes (the sugar should not be fully dissolved at this point). Remove from the heat and stir, then pour the caramel into the prepared baking pan and set aside.

Punch down the dough, then turn it out onto a lightly floured work surface and, using a floured rolling pin, roll it out to a 10-inch square. Using an offset spatula or the back of a spoon, spread the filling over the dough all the way to the edges. Roll the dough up to form a log, then cut it crosswise into 9 even slices.

Arrange the slices cut-side up in the prepared baking pan (it's OK if they touch). Cover with a clean kitchen towel and let stand in a warm spot until the buns double in size, about 20 minutes.

Preheat the oven to 350°F. Line a rimmed baking sheet with aluminum foil.

Set the pan with the buns on the prepared baking sheet. Bake for 30 to 35 minutes, until the buns are light brown and an instant-read thermometer inserted into the middle of the buns reads 165°F. Alternatively, test the buns by poking one with a toothpick (try to get the dough rather than the filling). If it comes out, well, *doughy*, keep baking. If it comes out relatively clean, they're good to go. Remove from the oven and let cool in the pan for 5 minutes, then carefully invert the buns onto a platter. Serve warm.

NOTE: *To drain the shredded zucchini of excess moisture, wrap it in extra-sturdy paper towels or a clean kitchen towel and wring it with your hands over the sink.*

Thai Tea Sticky Buns

MAKES 9 BUNS

PLANTAIN FILLING

1 (11-ounce/310 g) soft, ripe black
    plantain (see Notes, page 170),
    cut into ½-inch pieces (about
    1 cup)
½ cup packed (120 g) light brown
    sugar
¼ cup (60 mL) sweetened
    condensed milk
3 tablespoons loose Thai tea leaves
1 teaspoon vanilla extract
1 teaspoon imitation lemon extract
    (see page 20)
¼ teaspoon ground star anise
¼ teaspoon kosher salt

DOUGH

1 cup (240 mL) whole milk
1 tablespoon sweetened
    condensed milk
2 teaspoons granulated sugar
1 (¼-ounce/7 g) envelope active
    dry yeast
3⅓ cups (465 g) all-purpose flour,
    plus more for dusting
2 teaspoons kosher salt
2 large eggs
6 tablespoons (¾ stick/85 g)
    unsalted butter, cut into pieces
    and softened

PAN CARAMEL

½ cup (1 stick/115 g) unsalted
    butter, plus more for greasing
½ cup packed (120 g) light brown
    sugar
1 tablespoon light corn syrup
1 teaspoon kosher salt
¼ teaspoon vanilla extract

This riff on my plantain sticky buns celebrates the similarities between Thai and Caribbean flavors. At the heart of the recipe is a filling that combines condensed milk, a favorite of many in both regions, with the strength and spice of black tea. The final result is a decadent sticky bun with a super bright and flavorful Thai-iced-tea twist. I decided not to explain how to make your own version of a Thai tea blend at home; instead, just visit your local Asian market and pick up a prepackaged loose-leaf Thai tea blend. My hack is nowhere near as good anyhow.

MAKE THE FILLING: In a small saucepan, combine the plantain, brown sugar, condensed milk, tea, vanilla, lemon extract, star anise, and salt. Cook over medium heat, stirring occasionally, until the plantain softens, the liquid starts to thicken, and the whole mixture becomes very tender, 8 to 10 minutes. Transfer the mixture to a blender or food processor and blend until smooth, about 30 seconds. Set aside until ready to use.

MAKE THE DOUGH: In a small saucepot, combine the whole milk and condensed milk and warm over medium-low heat until it reaches 96°F.

Transfer the warmed milk mixture to the bowl of a stand mixer fitted with the dough hook. Add the granulated sugar and yeast and stir on low speed to combine. Turn off the mixer and let stand until frothy, 5 to 10 minutes. Add the flour, then the salt (this step is super important—always add the flour first so the salt does not harm the yeast you just woke up), and mix on medium-low speed until the flour is mostly incorporated, about 1 minute, stopping to scrape down the sides of the bowl as needed. Add the eggs and mix until the dough forms a ball, about 1 minute. Add the butter in a few additions (I usually do a quarter of it at a time), mixing until the butter is fully incorporated before adding the next addition. Then mix until the dough is smooth and no longer clings to the sides of the bowl, and no butter is visible, about 5 minutes. Cover the bowl with plastic wrap and let stand in a warm, draft-free place until the dough doubles in size, about 1 hour.

MEANWHILE, MAKE THE CARAMEL: Grease a 9-inch square baking pan with butter.

In a medium saucepan, combine the butter, brown sugar, corn syrup, salt, and vanilla. Cook over medium heat, stirring occasionally, until the butter has melted, about 2 minutes (the sugar should not be fully dissolved at this point). Remove from the heat and stir, then pour the caramel into the prepared baking pan.

Punch down the dough, then turn it out onto a lightly floured work surface and, using a floured rolling pin, roll it out to a 10-inch square. Using an offset spatula or the back of a spoon, spread the filling over the dough all the way to the edges. Roll the dough up to form a log, then cut it crosswise into 9 even slices.

Arrange the slices cut-side up in the prepared baking pan (it's OK if they touch). Cover with a clean kitchen towel and let stand until the buns double in size, about 20 minutes.

Preheat the oven to 350°F. Line a rimmed baking sheet with aluminum foil.

Set the pan with the buns on the prepared baking sheet. Bake for 30 to 35 minutes, until the buns are light brown and an instant-read thermometer inserted into the middle of the buns reads 165°F. Alternatively, test the buns by poking one with a toothpick (try to get the dough rather than the filling). If it comes out, well, *doughy*, keep baking. If it comes out relatively clean, they're good to go. Remove from the oven and let cool in the pan for 5 minutes, then carefully invert the buns onto a platter to cool completely.

WHILE THE BUNS COOL, MAKE THE GANACHE: Place the white chocolate in a heatproof bowl. In a small saucepan, bring the cream and tea to a simmer over medium-low heat, then turn off the heat and let steep for 10 minutes. Strain the cream through a fine-mesh sieve into a clean saucepan, then reheat over medium heat until the cream reaches 100°F. Add the corn syrup and salt and stir.

Pour the warmed cream mixture over the chocolate and whisk until the chocolate has melted and the mixture is smooth.

Drizzle the ganache over the Thai tea sticky buns and serve.

THAI TEA GANACHE

1 cup (170 g) white chocolate pieces (discs, fèves, or chopped from a bar)
1 cup (240 mL) heavy cream
2 tablespoons loose-leaf Thai tea blend
2 tablespoons corn syrup
Pinch of kosher salt

Cafecito Sticky Buns

MAKES 9 BUNS

PLANTAIN FILLING

1 (11-ounce/310 g) soft, ripe black plantain (see Notes, page 170), cut into ½-inch pieces (about 1 cup)

½ cup packed (120 g) light brown sugar

3 tablespoons instant espresso granules

1 tablespoon vanilla bean paste

½ teaspoon ground cinnamon

½ teaspoon freshly ground black pepper

¼ teaspoon kosher salt

⅛ teaspoon ground nutmeg

DOUGH

1 cup (240 mL) whole milk, warmed to 96°F

2 teaspoons granulated sugar

1 (¼-ounce/7 g) envelope active dry yeast

3⅓ cups (465 g) all-purpose flour, plus more for dusting

¼ cup (30 g) malted milk powder

2 teaspoons kosher salt

2 large eggs

6 tablespoons (¾ stick/85 g) unsalted butter, cut into pieces and softened, plus more for greasing

MALTED MILK SUGAR

1 cup (200 g) granulated sugar

2 tablespoons malted milk powder

ICING

½ cup (120 mL) evaporated milk

1 pound (455 g) unsifted powdered sugar

½ teaspoon kosher salt

Put down the croissant for a second so you can meet your new favorite breakfast pastry. Inspired by the typical morning routines of many in the Spanish-speaking world, this bun is the ideal companion for your morning cafecito. I can't stress this enough: Dunk the Cafecito Sticky Bun into all the coffee things. Sure, these would be fantastic served à la mode with my banana dulce sherbet (page 257), but in my opinion, there's truly something special about doubling down on the saborcito del cafe. You will be in heaven.

MAKE THE FILLING: In a small saucepan, combine the plantain, brown sugar, ½ cup (120 ml) water, the espresso granules, vanilla, cinnamon, pepper, salt, and nutmeg. Cook over medium heat, stirring occasionally, until the plantain softens, the liquid starts to thicken, and the whole mixture becomes very tender, 8 to 10 minutes. Transfer the mixture to a blender or food processor and blend until smooth, about 30 seconds. Set aside until ready to use.

MAKE THE DOUGH: In the bowl of a stand mixer fitted with the dough hook, stir together the milk, granulated sugar, and yeast on low speed. Turn off the mixer and let stand until frothy, about 5 minutes. Add the flour and malted milk powder, then the salt (this step is super important—always add the flour first so the salt does not harm the yeast you just woke up) and mix on medium-low speed until the flour is mostly incorporated, about 1 minute, stopping to scrape down the sides of the bowl as needed. Add the eggs and mix until the dough forms a ball, about 1 minute. Add the butter in a few additions (I usually do a quarter of it at a time), mixing until the butter is fully incorporated before adding the next addition. Then mix until the dough is smooth and no longer clings to the sides of the bowl, and no butter is visible, about 5 minutes. Cover the bowl with plastic wrap and let stand in a warm, draft-free place until the dough doubles in size, about 1 hour.

Grease a 9-inch square baking pan with softened butter.

MEANWHILE, MAKE THE MALTED MILK SUGAR: In a small bowl, whisk together the granulated sugar and malted milk powder.

Punch down the dough, then turn it out onto a lightly floured work surface and, using a floured rolling pin, roll it out to a 10-inch square.

Using an offset spatula or the back of a spoon, spread the filling over the dough all the way to the edges and sprinkle evenly with the malted milk sugar. Roll the dough up to form a log, then cut it crosswise into 9 even slices.

Arrange the slices cut-side up in the prepared baking pan (it's OK if they touch). Cover with a clean kitchen towel and let stand until the buns double in size, about 20 minutes.

Preheat the oven to 350°F. Line a rimmed baking sheet with aluminum foil.

Set the pan with the buns on the prepared baking sheet. Bake for 30 to 35 minutes, until the buns are light brown and an instant-read thermometer inserted into the middle of the buns reads 165°F. Alternatively, test the buns by poking one with a toothpick (try to get the dough rather than the filling). If it comes out, well, *doughy*, keep baking. If it comes out relatively clean, they're good to go. Remove from the oven and let cool in the pan for 5 minutes, then carefully invert the buns onto a platter.

MAKE THE ICING: In a medium bowl, whisk together the evaporated milk, powdered sugar, and salt. Drizzle the icing over the buns while they are still slightly warm, then serve.

Strawberry Sticky Buns

Strawberries, strawberries, strawberries. Like a lot of the fixations we have as kids, I can't fully explain why I was so obsessed with strawberries when I was growing up. (Honestly, it could have just been because they were pink.) All I can tell you is that even to this day, when the ice cream truck drives by in the summer, strawberry shortcake ice pops are still at the top of my list. Back when I was a kid, whenever I earned a reward for good grades, I would ask for strawberry Nesquik. And whenever my parents splurged for a tub of no-name-brand Neapolitan ice cream, I would make the pink-colored column disappear before bothering with its neighbors.

This recipe is a modern ode to my lasting love for that wonderful fruit. Pro tip: If you really want to double down on the berry notes, make sure to top these with the strawberry ganache. It's listed as optional, but come on, you *know* it's worth the effort.

MAKE THE FILLING: In a small saucepan, combine the plantain, brown sugar, strawberry puree, ½ cup (120 ml) water, the lemon extract, cinnamon, grains of paradise, salt, and citric acid. Cook over medium heat, stirring occasionally, until the plantain softens, the liquid starts to thicken, and the whole mixture becomes very tender, 8 to 10 minutes. Transfer the mixture to a blender or food processor and blend until smooth, about 30 seconds. Set aside until ready to use.

MAKE THE DOUGH: In a small saucepan, stir together the milk and strawberry puree and warm over medium heat until it reaches 96°F, then transfer to the bowl of a stand mixer fitted with the dough hook. Add the granulated sugar and yeast and stir on low speed to combine. Turn off the mixer and let stand until frothy, 5 to 10 minutes. Add the food coloring (if using). Add the flour, then the salt (this step is super important—always add the flour first so the salt does not harm the yeast you just woke up) and mix on medium-low speed until the flour is mostly incorporated, about 1 minute, stopping to scrape down the sides of the bowl as needed. Add the eggs and mix until the dough forms a ball, about 1 minute. Add the butter in a few additions (I usually do a quarter of it at a time), mixing until the butter is fully incorporated before adding the next addition. Then mix until the

continues ▶

MAKES 9 BUNS

PLANTAIN FILLING

1 (11-ounce/310 g) soft, ripe black plantain (see Notes, page 170), cut into ½-inch pieces (about 1 cup)

½ cup packed (120 g) light brown sugar

½ cup (120 g) strawberry puree

1 teaspoon imitation lemon extract (see page 20)

½ teaspoon ground cinnamon

¼ teaspoon ground grains of paradise

¼ teaspoon kosher salt

⅛ to ¼ teaspoon citric acid (depending on how acidic you like your desserts)

DOUGH

¾ cup (180 mL) whole milk

¼ cup (60 g) strawberry puree

2 teaspoons granulated sugar

1 (¼-ounce/7 g) envelope active dry yeast

3 or 4 drops red food coloring (optional)

3⅓ cups (465 g) all-purpose flour, plus more for dusting

2 teaspoons kosher salt

2 large eggs

6 tablespoons (¾ stick/85 g) unsalted butter, cut into pieces and softened

PAN CARAMEL

½ cup (1 stick/115 g) unsalted butter, plus more for greasing

½ cup packed (100 g) light brown sugar

1 tablespoon light corn syrup

1 teaspoon kosher salt

¼ teaspoon ground nutmeg

¼ teaspoon imitation vanilla extract, preferably Dominican

STRAWBERRY SUGAR
1 cup (200 g) granulated sugar
¼ cup (30 g) freeze-dried
  strawberry powder

Ganache from Strawberry Donas
  (page 194; optional, but highly
  recommended)

dough is smooth and no longer clings to the sides of the bowl, and no butter is visible, about 5 minutes. Cover the bowl with plastic wrap and let stand in a warm, draft-free place until the dough doubles in size, about 1 hour.

MAKE THE CARAMEL: Grease a 9-inch square baking pan with butter.

In a medium saucepan, combine the butter, brown sugar, corn syrup, salt, nutmeg, and vanilla. Cook over medium heat, stirring occasionally, until the butter has melted, about 2 minutes (the sugar should not be fully dissolved at this point). Remove from the heat and stir, then pour into the prepared baking pan.

MAKE THE STRAWBERRY SUGAR: In a small bowl, whisk together the granulated sugar and strawberry powder.

Punch down the dough, then turn it out onto a lightly floured work surface and, using a floured rolling pin, roll it out to a 10-inch square. Using an offset spatula or the back of a spoon, spread the filling over the dough all the way to the edges and sprinkle evenly with the strawberry sugar. Roll the dough up to form a log, then cut it crosswise into 9 even slices.

Arrange the slices cut-side up in the prepared baking pan (it's OK if they touch). Cover with a clean kitchen towel and let stand until the buns double in size, about 20 minutes.

Preheat the oven to 350°F. Line a rimmed baking sheet with aluminum foil.

Set the pan with the buns on the prepared baking sheet. Bake for 35 to 40 minutes, until the buns are light brown and an instant-read thermometer inserted into the middle of the buns reads 165°F. Alternatively, test the buns by poking one with a toothpick (try to get the dough rather than the filling). If it comes out, well, *doughy*, keep baking. If it comes out relatively clean, they're good to go. Remove from the oven and let cool in the pan for 5 minutes, then carefully invert the buns onto a platter. Use a spoon to drizzle ganache on top, if desired. Serve warm.

NOTE: *Don't skip the citric acid in this recipe; it adds a much-needed pop of acidity that is going to make these sticky buns super bright yet decadent and amazing.*

Doña Dona

This is my first, my last, my everything when it comes to making brioche donuts; the mother recipe that serves as the foundation for all the variations included in this book—and hopefully, those you will feel inspired to come up with yourself at home. For those of you who are not well versed in the world of donut-baking, this recipe is an excellent way to get your feet wet. If you overproof it, it'll taste great. If you underproof it, guess what? It'll also taste great.

Before you go on your merry way to becoming a dona master, just know that I like a hearty donut. I do not enjoy eating air. So these are BIG! If you're looking at the photo on page 183 and thinking, *Holy s—, this donut is too big* . . . well, I don't know if we can be friends. (Just kidding!) If you want a daintier donut, I'll allow it—just cut the dough into smaller circles and squares to yield more donuts.

In the bowl of a stand mixer fitted with the dough hook, stir together the warm milk, sugar, and yeast on low speed. Turn off the mixer and let stand until frothy, 5 to 10 minutes—it'll look like a little yeast latte!

Add the flour, then the salt (this step is super important—always add the flour first so the salt does not harm the yeast you just woke up), and mix on medium-low speed until the flour is mostly incorporated, about 1 minute, stopping to scrape down the sides of the bowl as needed. Add the eggs and mix until the dough forms a ball, about 1 minute. Add the butter in a few additions (I usually do a quarter of it at a time), mixing until the butter is fully incorporated before adding the next addition. Then mix until the dough is smooth and no longer clings to the sides of the bowl, and no butter is visible, about 5 minutes. Cover the bowl with plastic wrap and let stand in a warm, draft-free place until the dough doubles in size, 1 to 2 hours.

Line two large baking sheets with parchment paper.

Punch down the dough, then transfer it to a lightly floured work surface and, using a lightly floured rolling pin, roll it out to a 9-inch square. Cut into your desired donut shape (I do 9 pretty little squares, roughly 3 by 3 inches each, because squares don't waste any dough, but you could use a 3-inch pastry ring to cut round donuts, if you prefer). Place the cut dough on the prepared baking sheets and punch

continues ▶

MAKES 9 DONAS

2 cups (480 mL) whole milk, warmed to 96°F

4 teaspoons sugar, plus more for coating the donuts (optional)

2 (¼-ounce/7 g) envelopes active dry yeast

6 cups (840 g) all-purpose flour, plus more for dusting

4 teaspoons kosher salt

4 large eggs

½ cup plus 2 tablespoons (1¼ sticks/140 g) unsalted butter, cut into pieces and softened

4 cups (1 L) vegetable oil, for frying

out the center of each piece with a 1-inch cookie cutter or the wide end of a large round piping tip. Cover with plastic wrap and place in the fridge to proof overnight for wonderful flavor and height.

When you're ready to fry the donas, in a large heavy-bottomed pot, caldero, or Dutch oven, heat the oil over medium-high heat until it reaches 350°F on a deep-fry thermometer. Set two wire racks within arm's reach.

Remove the donas from the fridge. Loosen the plastic wrap and just kinda drape it over the donas so they can breathe. Let them sit for 10 to 15 minutes.

When the oil is up to temperature, do the "spring test": Lightly poke the surface of the donas. If the dough dimples without springing back immediately, they're ready. If it completely collapses under the pressure of your finger, whoops! They're probably overproofed.

Working in batches of three, use a spider and/or a slotted spoon to carefully lower the donas into the hot oil. Fry until golden on both sides, 3 to 5 minutes per side. Use the spider to transfer the donas to the wire racks to drain. Repeat to fry the remaining donas.

You can enjoy the donas as is, but for a more traditional sugar-coated dona, pour some sugar into a shallow bowl. Let the donas drain for 3 minutes after frying, then lay them in the sugar one at a time and scoop sugar over the top to coat completely.

Chinola (Passion Fruit) Donas

I just love how the punchy passion fruit icing counterbalances the fluffy, slightly savory dough of these donas. But then again, it's hard for me to dislike any recipe that features passion fruit. My family has a giant passion fruit tree in their backyard in the Dominican countryside, and some of my fondest childhood memories are of sitting perched on the edge of our rainwater well, snacking on the fresh fruits.

Make and fry the donas as instructed on page 181. Let cool.

In a medium bowl, whisk together the powdered sugar, 2 tablespoons of the passion fruit puree, the salt, and the citric acid. Add more passion fruit puree if needed to achieve a smooth, pourable consistency.

Pour the icing over donas, or dip half of each dona into the icing, then place back on the baking sheet to set. If desired, sprinkle black sesame seeds over the icing before it sets or fan out some slices of fresh passion fruit and place on top of each donut before the icing sets. Let stand until the icing sets, then serve.

NOTE: *I sometimes like to make a second decorative icing to pipe on top of the donas, like in the photo at left. To do this, set aside a small bowl of icing and tint it with a few drops of yellow food coloring. Stir to mix, then transfer it to a small piping bag and pipe it onto the donas, or just use a spoon or fork to drizzle it over the donas.*

MAKES 9 DONAS

1 recipe Doña Dona (page 181)
2 cups (250 g) unsifted powdered sugar
2 to 4 tablespoons passion fruit puree
Pinch of kosher salt
Pinch of citric acid
Black sesame seeds, or 1 fresh passion fruit, halved and sliced, for garnish (optional)

Dulce de Leche Donas

Dough for 1 recipe Doña Dona
(page 181)

TOPPING
1 cup (60 g) plantain chips
2 tablespoons unsalted butter,
   softened
2 tablespoons granulated sugar
1½ teaspoons kosher salt
½ teaspoon ground cinnamon

ICING
2 cups (250 g) unsifted powdered
   sugar
3 tablespoons dulce de leche,
   homemade (page 281) or store-
   bought
2 tablespoons whole milk
½ teaspoon kosher salt
¼ teaspoon freshly ground black
   pepper

This is a fun take on dulce de leche that I top with delicious candied plantain chips for a sweet-and-salty vibe. These donuts are an instant classic that were always one of the first to sell out during my Doña Dona pop-up days, and I'm super excited to share this recipe with you here.

Make and shape the dona dough as instructed on page 181, but do not fry them yet.

MAKE THE TOPPING: Preheat the oven to 300°F. Line a large baking sheet with parchment paper.

Place the plantain chips in a large metal bowl. In a small saucepan, melt the butter over medium heat, then pour it over the plantain chips and mix with a rubber spatula to coat. Add the granulated sugar, salt, and cinnamon and mix until the chips are coated.

Transfer the plantain chips to the prepared baking sheet and bake for 10 to 15 minutes, until you see slightly crystallized sugar on top of the plantain chips. Remove from the oven and let cool to room temperature. The chips will firm up as they cool.

Meanwhile, fry the donas as instructed on page 182.

WHEN THE DONAS ARE COOL, MAKE THE ICING: Place the powdered sugar in a medium bowl and make a well in the center. In a microwave-safe bowl, combine the dulce de leche and milk and microwave on full power for 30 seconds. Stir to combine, then stir in the salt and pepper. Pour the mixture into the well in the powdered sugar and mix until combined.

Hold a dona in your hand and dip the top into the bowl of the icing to coat, then top the icing with pieces of plantain chips. Repeat with the remaining donas. Let the icing set, then serve.

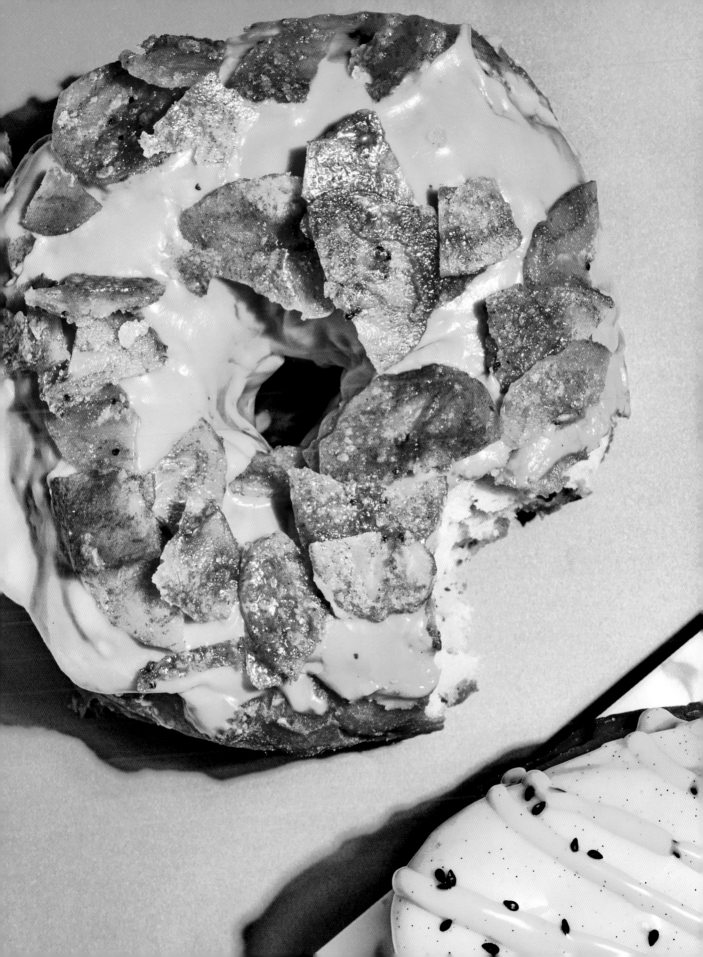

Quesito Donas

This is an homage to quesitos, a Puerto Rican puff pastry delicacy with a sweet cheesy filling. For a subtler effect, I fill mine with tangy cream cheese and top with luscious evaporated milk icing.

Make and shape the donas as instructed on page 181, but do not cut holes in the center. Fry as instructed and let cool completely.

MEANWHILE, MAKE THE TOPPING: Preheat the oven to 400°F. Line a large baking sheet with parchment paper.

If your puff pastry is frozen, remove it from the freezer and let it sit at room temperature for 5 to 10 minutes, until it's pliable. Roll out the puff pastry to ⅛ inch thick. Place the pastry on the prepared baking sheet. Dock the pastry by pricking it all over with a fork, then, using a pastry brush, brush the surface with the cream and sprinkle the granulated sugar over the top.

Bake for 25 to 35 minutes, until deep golden brown. Remove from the oven and let cool completely, then break the pastry into pieces. Set aside.

MEANWHILE, MAKE THE FILLING: In the bowl of a stand mixer fitted with the paddle attachment (or using one of the alternate methods on page 25), beat the cream cheese on medium speed until, well, creamy! This should take 3 to 4 minutes. Add the granulated sugar and mix until fluffy and smooth, about 4 minutes. Transfer the filling to a piping bag fitted with a large round tip.

To fill the donas, use a paring knife to cut a small X into the side of each dona. Place your index finger into a dona and press to create a cavity for your filling. Hold the dona so the X is facing up and pipe ample filling into the cavity; when you start to feel a little pressure or resistance, stop piping. Do not overfill the dona, or it might burst. Set the filled dona aside on a tray and repeat to fill the remaining donas.

MAKE THE ICING: Pour the powdered sugar into a medium bowl and make a little well in the center. Add 2 tablespoons of the evaporated milk and salt to the well, then whisk to incorporate. Add more evaporated milk if needed to achieve a smooth, pourable consistency.

Dip the top of a dona into the bowl of icing to coat, then decorate with pieces of the puff pastry topping. Place the dona on a tray and repeat with the remaining donas. Let the icing set, then serve.

1 recipe Doña Dona (page 181)

CANDIED PUFF PASTRY TOPPING
4 ounces (115 g) puff pastry, homemade (page 277) or store-bought
¼ cup (60 mL) heavy cream
¼ cup (50 g) granulated sugar

FILLING
8 ounces (225 g) cream cheese
¼ cup (50 g) granulated sugar

ICING
2 cups (250 g) unsifted powdered sugar
2 to 3 tablespoons evaporated milk
Pinch of kosher salt

Tasty Orange Donas

1 recipe Doña Dona (page 181)
7½ ounces (210 g) Marshmallow
    Fluff (see Note)

ORANGE ICING
2 cups (250 g) unsifted powdered
    sugar
1 tablespoon fresh orange juice,
    plus more if needed
½ teaspoon imitation lemon
    extract (see page 20)
¼ teaspoon orange extract
1 or 2 drops orange food coloring

DECORATIVE ICING
¼ cup (30 g) unsifted powdered
    sugar
1 to 2 teaspoons whole milk

NOTE: *Some parts of the country, like the Northeast and the South, love Fluff, so it's easier to find it sold in 7½-ounce (210 g) containers. Depending on where you live (and shrinkflation), you might have to buy two smaller containers to get your healthy dose of Fluff.*

When I was a kid, I used to eat jarred Marshmallow Fluff by the spoonful, the way some kids eat peanut butter. Or I'd spread it on toasted white bread, my bodega-sourced version of fancy toast. Even now I just love the convenience of premade marshmallow cream. Here I make Fluff even fancier by pairing it with lemon and orange extracts. The end result is like the nostalgic flavor of Hostess Orange Cupcakes—if you don't know it, I feel *very* sorry for you.

Make and shape the donas as instructed on page 181, but do not cut holes in the center, since these donas will be filled. Fry as instructed and let cool completely.

To fill the donas, use a paring knife to cut a small X into the side of each dona. Place your index finger into the dona and press to create a cavity for your filling.

Fill a piping bag fitted with a large round tip with the Fluff. Hold a dona so the X is facing up, then pipe ample Fluff into the cavity; when you start to feel a little pressure or resistance, stop piping. Do not overfill the dona, or it might burst. Set the filled dona aside on a tray and repeat to fill the remaining donas.

MAKE THE ORANGE ICING: Pour the powdered sugar into a medium bowl and make a little well in the center. Add the orange juice, lemon extract, orange extract, and food coloring to the well, then whisk to incorporate. Add more orange juice if needed to achieve a smooth, pourable consistency.

MAKE THE DECORATIVE ICING: In a small bowl, whisk together the powdered sugar and milk until the mixture has the consistency of runny toothpaste (clean your whisk first so you don't accidentally dye this orange!). Transfer the icing to a piping bag fitted with a small round tip.

To decorate your donas, hold one in your hand and dip the top into the bowl of orange icing to coat. Repeat with the remaining donas and set aside until the icing is set, 5 to 10 minutes.

Pipe the decorative icing on top of the orange icing in nice little loopity-loop squiggles. Let set for 2 to 5 minutes before serving.

Arnold Palmer Donas

I have a stutter. You may not notice it because I mask it really well, but I can assure you, it's there. Just ask me to say "Arnold Palmer." I get tongue-tied and nervous. Anyway, where were we? Here: As both drink and dona, the Arnold Palmer is a wonder of balance. Subtle tannins give way to notes of bright citrus and sweetness. But tasting notes aside, it's just a damn good donut.

Make and shape the donas as instructed on page 181, but do not cut holes in the center. Fry as instructed and let cool completely.

MEANWHILE, MAKE THE FILLING: In a small saucepan, combine ½ cup (120 mL) of the milk and the cream. Bring to a simmer over medium heat, then turn off the heat, add the black tea, and steep for 5 to 7 minutes, depending on how strong you want the tea flavor to be.

In a medium bowl, whisk together the remaining 2 tablespoons milk, the cornstarch, and the egg yolks until smooth. While whisking continuously, slowly add a ladleful of the hot milk mixture to the eggs and whisk vigorously until combined. Pour the egg mixture into the saucepan with the milk mixture, add the sugar, and cook over medium heat, stirring often, until the temperature registers 185°F. Strain through a fine-mesh sieve into a clean bowl, then add the bourbon and the butter and mix by hand until completely smooth. Cover the filling with a piece of plastic wrap pressed directly against the surface and refrigerate until completely cool, at least 2 hours or up to overnight. Transfer the chilled filling to piping bag fitted with a large round tip.

To fill the donas, use a paring knife to cut a small X into the side of each dona. Place your index finger into the dona and press to create a cavity for your filling. Hold a dona so the X is facing up and pipe ample filling into the cavity; when you start to feel a little pressure or resistance, stop piping. Do not overfill the dona, or it might burst. Set the filled dona aside on a tray and repeat to fill the remaining donas.

MAKE THE ICING: Pour the powdered sugar into a medium bowl and make a little well in the center. Add the lemon juice, food coloring, and citric acid to the well, then whisk to incorporate. Add more lemon juice if needed to achieve a smooth, pourable consistency.

Dip the top of a dona into the icing to coat. Place it on a tray and repeat with the remaining donas. Let the icing set for 5 to 10 minutes before serving.

MAKES 9 DONAS

1 recipe Doña Dona (page 181), made with 1 tablespoon lemon zest added with the flour

FILLING
½ cup plus 2 tablespoons (150 mL) whole milk
3 tablespoons heavy cream
2 tablespoons loose black tea leaves
2 tablespoons cornstarch
2 large egg yolks
¼ cup (50 g) granulated sugar
1 tablespoon bourbon
3 tablespoons unsalted butter, softened

ICING
2 cups (250 g) unsifted powdered sugar
2 tablespoons fresh lemon juice, plus more if needed
5 drops yellow food coloring
Pinch of citric acid

Strawberry Donas

1 recipe Doña Dona (page 181)

FILLING
16 ounces (450 g) dulce de leche,
    homemade (page 281) or store-
    bought
1 cup (160 g) diced strawberries

GANACHE
8 ounces (225 g) Valrhona
    Inspiration Fraise chocolate
    fèves
¾ cup (180 mL) heavy cream
2 tablespoons corn syrup
Pinch of kosher salt
Pinch of citric acid

12 whole strawberries, for garnish

When a dulce de leche dona is somehow not enough, kick it up a notch: Fill it with fresh strawberry pieces and coat it in an other-worldly chocolate-strawberry ganache for an absolute showstopper.

Make and shape the donas as instructed on page 181, but do not cut holes in the center, since these donas will be filled. Fry as instructed and let cool completely.

MEANWHILE, MAKE THE FILLING: Place the dulce de leche in a medium bowl and stir it with a rubber spatula. The friction should warm it up and make it more malleable. Add the strawberries and fold them into the dulce de leche. Transfer the filling to a piping bag fitted with a large round tip.

To fill the donas, use a paring knife to cut a small X into the side of each dona. Place your index finger into the dona and press to create a cavity for your filling. Hold a dona so the X is facing up and pipe ample filling into the cavity; when you start to feel a little pressure or resistance, stop piping. Do not overfill the dona, or it might burst. Set the filled dona aside on a tray and repeat to fill the remaining donas.

MAKE THE GANACHE: Place the strawberry chocolate in a medium bowl. In a small stainless-steel or other nonreactive pot, combine the cream and corn syrup and warm it over medium heat until it's slightly warmer than your body temperature. Pour the hot cream over the chocolate and let stand for a minute or two, then whisk until the chocolate has melted and the ganache is smooth. Add the salt and citric acid and stir to incorporate.

To decorate your donas, hold one in your hand and dip the top into the bowl of ganache to coat. Place the dona on a tray and repeat with the remaining donas. Top each with a whole strawberry before serving.

Dulce de Leche Babka

The Riverdale Diner on Kingsbridge Avenue was a very special place. It ticked off all the diner boxes: ridiculously long menu, late hours, tight booths. But it was different, in that it was also a mirror into the community it served. Where else could you get flapjacks, black-and-white cookies, babka, mangu, and queso frito in the same place, as part of the same meal? The Riverdale was New York at its best.

I've eaten a lot of babka in my day, including a couple that were maybe sitting out for a bit too long. But to me, every babka—even old babkas—is a doughy, chocolaty masterpiece. And if I were to develop my version of a Bronx babka right now? Well, I'd want to take a page out of Riverdale Diner's book and make one that stands out by combining the unique cultures represented in my neighborhood.

What does this look like? A dulce de leche babka. I find that dulce de leche is sweeter and more balanced than cinnamon sugar, and not as heavy as chocolate. Plus, the dough absorbs the moisture from the dulce de leche and comes out super fluffy as a result, with every flake, nook, and cranny absolutely laced with deliciousness.

MAKE THE DOUGH: In the bowl of a stand mixer fitted with the dough hook, stir together the warm milk, sugar, and yeast on low speed. Turn off the mixer and let stand until frothy, about 10 minutes.

Add the vanilla, then the flour, salt, nutmeg, and cinnamon. Mix on medium-low speed until the flour is mostly incorporated, about 1 minute, stopping to scrape down the sides of the bowl as needed. Add the eggs and mix until the dough forms a ball, about 1 minute. Add the butter in a few additions (I usually do a quarter of it at a time) and mix until incorporated, then mix until the dough is smooth and no longer clings to the sides of the bowl, and no butter is visible, about 5 minutes. Cover the bowl with plastic wrap and let stand in a warm, draft-free place until the dough doubles in size, 1 to 2 hours.

Punch down the dough, then cover the bowl and refrigerate for 1 to 2 hours, until the dough is firm and cold to the touch. (This will make the dough easier to handle later so you can make perfect twists.)

MAKES 1 BABKA

BABKA DOUGH
½ cup (120 mL) whole milk, warmed to 96°F
¼ cup (50 g) sugar
1 (¼-ounce/7 g) envelope active dry yeast
2 teaspoons vanilla bean paste
3¼ cups (455 g) all-purpose flour, plus more for dusting
½ teaspoon kosher salt
½ teaspoon ground nutmeg
¼ teaspoon ground cinnamon
4 large eggs
½ cup (1 stick/115 g) unsalted butter, cut into pieces and softened
Vegetable oil cooking spray

FILLING
½ cup (130 g) toasted white chocolate chunks or fèves (see Note, page 36), plus more if needed
¼ cup (60 mL) heavy cream
½ cup (150 g) dulce de leche, homemade (page 281) or store-bought
3 tablespoons corn syrup
2 teaspoons ground cinnamon
1½ teaspoons kosher salt

SPRINKLING SUGAR AND SYRUP
¾ cup (150 g) sugar
1 teaspoon ground cinnamon

continues ▶

MEANWHILE, MAKE THE FILLING: Place the white chocolate in a heatproof medium bowl. In a medium saucepan, combine the cream, dulce de leche, corn syrup, cinnamon, and salt and bring to a simmer over medium heat. Cook, stirring frequently, until the dulce de leche fully incorporates into the cream, about 3 minutes. Pour the warmed cream over the chocolate and stir with a spatula until the chocolate has melted and the mixture is a smooth paste that resembles a loose peanut butter. Your goal is something soft and spreadable that won't rip the dough; if it's too loose, add a bit more chocolate and stir to melt and combine. Let cool completely.

Preheat the oven to 350°F. Grease a 1-pound loaf pan with cooking spray.

Transfer the chilled dough to a lightly floured work surface and roll it out to a 12 by 6-inch rectangle. Use an offset spatula to spread the filling over the dough in a ⅛-inch-thick layer that extends all the way to the edge. Sprinkle with ½ cup (100 g) of the sugar and the cinnamon. Starting from one long side, roll up the dough into a log. Using a serrated knife, cut the dough in half lengthwise to create two ropes. Rotate the ropes so the exposed filling faces up, then coil them together tightly without stretching the dough, keeping the filling facing up.

Place the coiled rope of dough in the prepared loaf pan and cover with plastic wrap or a kitchen towel. Let stand until doubled in size, about 20 minutes.

Bake the babka for 45 minutes to 1 hour, until the dough's internal temperature reaches 185°F.

Just before the babka finishes baking, in a small saucepan, combine the remaining ¼ cup (50 g) sugar and ¼ cup (60 mL) water and bring to a boil, stirring to dissolve the sugar. Remove from the heat and cover the syrup to keep warm until the babka comes out of the oven.

Remove the babka from the oven and immediately brush it with the syrup. Let cool to room temperature before serving. Alternatively, wrap the cooled babka tightly in plastic wrap and freeze for up to 1 month.

Ponche Babka

In America, it's eggnog. In Mexico, it's rompope. In Puerto Rico, it's coquito. In Haiti, it's kremas. And in the Dominican Republic it's ponche. Some have rum, others brandy; some feature spices, others amp up the citrus. But the vibe is the same: a creamy, comforting, milky beverage. I happen to believe that ponche and its cousins can and should be served year-round, whenever you crave it. This recipe is one of the strongest cases I can make for that argument.

Make the babka dough and refrigerate as instructed on page 197.

MAKE THE FILLING: Place the chocolate in a heatproof bowl and microwave in 30-second intervals, stirring after each, until completely melted and smooth. Add the butter and stir with a rubber spatula until completely melted. Add the nutmeg, rum, salt, vanilla, and cinnamon and mix. The filling should be soft and spreadable. Let cool completely.

Preheat the oven to 350°F. Grease a 1-pound loaf pan with cooking spray.

Transfer the chilled dough to a lightly floured work surface and roll it out to a 12 by 6-inch rectangle. Use an offset spatula to spread the cooled filling over the dough in a ⅛-inch-thick layer all the way to the edges. Starting from one long side, roll up the dough into a log. Using a serrated knife, cut the dough in half lengthwise to create two ropes. Rotate the ropes so the exposed filling faces up, then coil them together tightly without stretching the dough, keeping the filling facing up.

Place the coiled dough in the prepared pan and cover with plastic wrap or a kitchen towel. Let stand until doubled in size, about 20 minutes.

Bake for 45 minutes to 1 hour, until the babka's internal temperature reaches 185°F.

JUST BEFORE THE BABKA FINISHES BAKING, MAKE THE GLAZE: In a small saucepan, combine the sugar, rum, and ¼ cup (60 mL) water and bring to a boil, stirring to dissolve the sugar. Remove from the heat and cover to keep warm until the babka comes out of the oven.

Remove the babka from the oven and immediately brush it with the glaze. Let cool to room temperature before serving. Alternatively, wrap the cooled babka tightly in plastic wrap and freeze for up to 1 month.

MAKES 1 BABKA

1 recipe Babka Dough (see page 197)

FILLING
1 cup (165 g) white chocolate chunks or fèves
4 tablespoons (½ stick/55 g) unsalted butter
1 teaspoon ground nutmeg
1 teaspoon dark rum
½ teaspoon kosher salt
½ teaspoon vanilla bean paste
¼ teaspoon ground cinnamon
Vegetable oil cooking spray

GLAZE
¼ cup (50 g) sugar
½ teaspoon rum

Blossom Funnel Cake

FUNNEL CAKES
2 cups (480 mL) vegetable oil, for
    deep-frying
2 tablespoons light brown sugar
2 large eggs
½ teaspoon orange blossom water
½ teaspoon coconut extract
1 teaspoon dark rum
½ cup (120 mL) full-fat coconut
    milk
1¼ cups (175 g) all-purpose flour
1½ teaspoons baking powder
1 teaspoon ground nutmeg
½ teaspoon kosher salt
¼ teaspoon ground cinnamon
1 tablespoon Baker's Angel Flake
    coconut flakes (see page 20),
    toasted
1 tablespoon lime zest

**COCONUT ICING
(OPTIONAL)**
2 cups (250 g) unsifted powdered
    sugar
1 tablespoon full-fat coconut milk
1 tablespoon evaporated milk, plus
    more if needed
1 teaspoon coconut extract
¼ teaspoon ground nutmeg
¼ teaspoon kosher salt
2 drops orange food coloring
⅛ teaspoon citric acid

Powdered sugar, for sprinkling
    (optional)

If you're in the market for a treat, it's hard to beat a good state fair. When I was growing up, my parents took me to quite a few of them. In the city, instead of big county or state fairs, we have street fairs that usually take place on Sundays in the spring, summer, and early fall. They close down this or that avenue from morning to sunset. Booths and stands will sell grilled corn, gyros, fresh juices, and fried confections.

One of my absolute street fair favorites is FUNNEL CAKE. Funnel cake is God's gift to Earth, although it could just as easily have been engineered in a lab as a vehicle for getting powdered sugar on people. To be honest, though, dodging the mess is half the fun. Funnel cake captivated me so much as a kid. The smell of fried dough, any fried dough, really, will instantly take me back to the joys of digging into a fresh funnel cake at one of those local fairs, the most famous of which might be the Feast of San Gennaro, a historic eleven-day festival spanning Little Italy's eleven blocks, that was founded a century ago by immigrants.

While it's hard to improve on funnel cake, I humbly present my "more adult" version, with lime and orange delivering Tutti Frutti flavors and rum serving as the Caribbean anchor. Need more convincing? It's a one-bowl situation. I hate washing dishes. And you do too. I've heard that there *are* people who will say otherwise, but I have yet to meet them.

MAKE THE FUNNEL CAKES: In a large heavy-bottomed pot, caldero, or Dutch oven, heat the oil over medium-high heat until it registers 375°F on a deep-fry thermometer. Set a wire rack over a plate or baking sheet.

In a large bowl, whisk together the brown sugar and the eggs until slightly pale and fluffy, 3 to 4 minutes. Add the orange blossom water, coconut extract, and rum and whisk to combine. Add the coconut milk and 2 tablespoons water and whisk until homogeneous.

In a separate large bowl, whisk to combine the flour, baking powder, nutmeg, salt, cinnamon, coconut flakes, and lime zest. Add this to the wet ingredients, then whisk until no clumps of flour are visible. The batter should be thin—thinner than pancake batter. Transfer the

continues ▶

batter to a spouted liquid measuring cup or a piping bag fitted with a medium round tip.

Steadily, with control, pour or pipe the batter into the hot oil, starting in the center of the oil and swirling around to coat the surface with batter in an irregular shape almost like a bird's nest or a spiderweb. You'll use about one-third of the batter for each funnel cake (although you can always use less to make smaller funnel cakes!). Cook, watching carefully, until the funnel cake turns a deep tan color on the bottom, about 3 minutes, then flip with tongs, a fork, or a spider halfway and cook until deep tan on the second side, about 3 minutes more. Using the tongs or fork or a large slotted spoon, transfer the funnel cake to the wire rack to drain.

MAKE THE COCONUT ICING (IF USING): Pour the powdered sugar into a medium bowl and make a little well in the center. Add the coconut milk, evaporated milk, coconut extract, nutmeg, salt, food coloring, and citric acid to the well, then whisk to incorporate. Add more evaporated milk if needed to achieve a smooth, pourable consistency.

When the funnel cake has cooled slightly, use a fork or spoon to drizzle the icing over the top, or just sprinkle with powdered sugar and serve.

Hibiscus Donut Bites

Making incredible donuts doesn't have to be difficult. In fact, it can be very easy. Here's an example: To prepare these donut bites, which have a lovely sweet-and-sour flavor and beautiful bright red hue, you don't need to roll them out on a counter, cool them, or spend all that time cleaning a stand mixer. Just fry them. For an added touch, feel free to decorate them with sprinkles or even edible flowers, if you're feeling inspired.

MAKE THE DONUTS: In a large heavy-bottomed pot, caldero, or Dutch oven, heat the oil over medium-high heat until it reaches 350°F on a deep-fry thermometer. Set a wire rack over a baking sheet.

Meanwhile, in a small pan, melt the butter over medium heat, stirring occasionally, then cook until it is fragrant and small golden brown bits of milk solids form on the bottom of the pan, about 2 minutes. Transfer the browned butter to a small bowl and let cool slightly.

In the same pan you used for the butter, heat the milk over medium heat until bubbles form around the edge of the pan and the milk reaches 180°F, about 5 minutes. Add the hibiscus flowers and remove from the heat. Let steep while you make the batter, 5 to 10 minutes.

In the bowl of a stand mixer fitted with the paddle attachment (or using one of the alternate methods on page 25), combine the flour, granulated sugar, cinnamon, baking powder, and salt and mix on low speed until just combined.

Transfer the hibiscus milk to a blender. Blend on high speed until smooth.

Add the hibiscus milk, yogurt, cooled browned butter, and eggs to the dry ingredients and mix on low until just incorporated. The dough will be slightly damp.

Working in batches of 5 or 6, drop leveled 1-ounce scoops of the dough directly into the hot oil. (Alternatively, scoop 2-tablespoon portions of dough and roll each gently between very lightly oiled palms to form them into rounds, then add them to the hot oil.) Fry the donuts, adjusting the heat as needed to maintain the oil temperature, until

continues ▶

MAKES 24 DONUT BITES

DONUTS
3 cups (720 mL) vegetable oil, for deep-frying
2 tablespoons unsalted butter
½ cup (120 mL) whole milk
¼ cup (10 g) dried hibiscus flowers
2 cups (280 g) all-purpose flour
¾ cup (150 g) granulated sugar
2 teaspoons ground cinnamon
1½ teaspoons baking powder
1 teaspoon kosher salt
¾ cup (210 g) plain full-fat Greek yogurt
2 large eggs

HIBISCUS ICING
Juice of 1 lemon
¼ cup (20 g) hibiscus powder
2 cups (250 g) unsifted powdered sugar
1 tablespoon vanilla bean paste
Pinch of kosher salt
Dried edible flowers or sprinkles, for garnish (optional)

they are golden brown (or begin to crack open on the surface) and cooked through, 3 to 5 minutes. Use a spider or slotted spoon to transfer the donuts to the wire rack and let cool completely. Repeat with the remaining dough, letting the oil return to 350°F between batches.

MAKE THE ICING: In a small bowl, stir together the lemon juice and hibiscus powder (the lemon juice will activate the bold pink color).

Pour the powdered sugar into a medium bowl and make a little well in the center. Add the vanilla, salt, and half the hibiscus-lemon mixture to the well, then whisk to combine. Add more of the hibiscus-lemon mixture as needed to achieve a smooth, pourable consistency (if you run out before the icing is smooth, switch to water).

Use a fork or spoon to drizzle the icing over the donut bites, then decorate with dried edible flowers or sprinkles. Let the icing set, then serve.

Yuca Donuts

DONUTS

3 cups (720 mL) vegetable oil, for
   frying
2 tablespoons unsalted butter
2 cups (280 g) all-purpose flour
¾ cup (150 g) sugar
2 teaspoons ground cinnamon
1½ teaspoons baking powder
1 teaspoon kosher salt
¾ cup (210 g) plain full-fat Greek
   yogurt
¼ cup (50 g) mashed boiled yuca
   (see Note)
2 large eggs

SYRUP

2 cups (400 g) sugar
3 cinnamon sticks
1 tablespoon lemon zest
Juice of 1 lemon
1 tablespoon vanilla bean paste
1 tablespoon golden or dark rum

Yuca (also known as cassava) is a root vegetable with incredible nutritional properties that is absolutely beloved throughout Latin America. Most people know yuca for its savory applications as a starchy side that rounds out any meal perfectly—boiled yuca with plenty of mojo often accompanies a protein. It isn't an ingredient commonly used in sweets, but when I realized that the tapioca pearls in boba tea are actually made from cassava, my mind began to race as I wondered what other methods and applications were possible.

These donut bites are a great example. The easiest way to describe them is as buñuelos that are lighter, fluffier, and much easier to prepare than the traditional variety, with a stretchy, chewy texture that makes them just so much fun to eat.

MAKE THE DONUTS: In a large heavy-bottomed pot, caldero, or Dutch oven, heat the oil over medium-high heat until it reaches 350°F on a deep-fry thermometer. Set a wire rack over a baking sheet.

Meanwhile, in a small pan, melt the butter over medium heat, stirring occasionally, then cook until it is fragrant and small golden brown bits of milk solids form on the bottom of the pan, about 2 minutes. Transfer the browned butter to a small bowl and let cool slightly.

In the bowl of a stand mixer fitted with the paddle attachment (or using one of the alternate methods on page 25), combine the flour, sugar, cinnamon, baking powder, and salt and mix on low speed until just combined.

Add the yogurt, cooled browned butter, yuca, and eggs to the dry ingredients and mix on low until just incorporated. The dough will be slightly damp.

Working in batches of 5 to 6, drop leveled 1-ounce scoops of the dough directly into the hot oil. (Alternatively, scoop 2-tablespoon portions of dough and roll each gently between very lightly oiled palms to form them into rounds, then add them to the hot oil.) Fry the donuts, adjusting the heat as needed to maintain the oil temperature, until they are golden brown (or begin to crack open on the surface) and cooked through, 3 to 5 minutes. Use a spider or slotted spoon to transfer the donuts to the wire rack and let cool completely. Repeat with the remaining dough, letting the oil return to 350°F between batches.

MAKE THE SYRUP: In a medium saucepan, combine the sugar, cinnamon sticks, lemon zest, lemon juice, vanilla, and 1½ cups (360 mL) water and and bring to a boil over high heat. Boil, stirring occasionally, until viscous and slightly thicker than simple syrup, 3 to 5 minutes. Remove from the heat, add the rum, and stir.

Pour the syrup over the donuts (while they're still on the rack, or prepare for a mess!) and serve.

NOTE: *You can use frozen or fresh yuca. If using fresh, peel it and cut into chunks. Boil the yuca (fresh or frozen) in a small pot of lightly salted water until fork-tender, 30 to 45 minutes, before using.*

Pitaya Churros

CHURROS

2 cups (480 mL) vegetable oil, for
    frying
1 teaspoon Dominican imitation
    vanilla extract
1 teaspoon lemon zest
1 teaspoon dragon fruit powder
1 teaspoon sugar
½ teaspoon kosher salt
1 cup (140 g) all-purpose flour

MILK CHOCOLATE SAUCE

5 ounces (140 g) milk chocolate,
    chopped (1 cup)
1 cup (240 mL) evaporated milk
1 tablespoon corn syrup
1 tablespoon Maizena cornstarch
1 teaspoon kosher salt
1 teaspoon dark rum
½ cup (100 g) chopped rainbow
    sprinkles

Pretty much everyone loves churros. But how many people can say they have had churros infused with the flavors of dragon fruit?! All dressed up with a rum-infused Maizena chocolate sauce and topped with rainbow sprinkles, these churros will definitely feel bonita. (Note to the reader: Yes, I did "meme" that, haha!)

MAKE THE CHURROS: In a large heavy-bottomed pot, caldero, or Dutch oven, heat the oil over medium-high heat until it reaches 350°F on a deep-fry thermometer. Set a wire rack over a baking sheet.

Meanwhile, in a stainless-steel medium pot, combine the vanilla, lemon zest, dragon fruit powder, sugar, salt, and 1¼ cups (300 mL) water and bring to a simmer over medium heat.

Remove from the heat, add the flour, and vigorously whisk (or stir with a firm rubber spatula that isn't floppy at the tip) until the flour is no longer visible. Cook the dough over medium heat, stirring, until a film appears on the bottom of the pan, 3 to 5 minutes. The dough will become super soft and turn a darker shade of pink.

Transfer the dough to the bowl of a stand mixer fitted with the paddle attachment and let cool for 4 minutes. Mix on low speed until the dough is completely cool and super thick, 8 to 10 minutes. It will have the consistency of soft Play-Doh. Transfer the dough to a piping bag fitted with a 1-inch star or round tip and refrigerate for 30 minutes to 1 hour.

Working in batches so as not to crowd the pan, pipe the dough directly into the hot oil in 1 by 2-inch strips and fry until golden, about 4 minutes. Use a spider or tongs to transfer the churros to the wire rack.

MAKE THE SAUCE: Place the chocolate in a heatproof bowl. In a small or medium stainless-steel pot, combine the evaporated milk, corn syrup, cornstarch, and salt and bring to a boil. Pour the hot milk mixture over the chocolate. Add the rum and stir until the chocolate has melted and the mixture is well combined and smooth.

Dip the warm churros into the chocolate sauce, then scatter the sprinkles on top and enjoy.

NOTE: *If you're nervous about burning yourself on hot oil, do it this way: Working one at a time, pipe the dough onto a sheet of parchment paper, then slide the churro off the parchment into the hot oil and fry.*

Dominican Brioche (Pan Sobao)

One of my favorite facets of life in the Dominican Republic is the panaderías and the bread they are known for, which is soft and smooth, like someone has been gently petting it. We don't typically bake our own bread. We prefer to support our local bakeries, making a stop at the panadería or colmado a part of our daily routine. It's the perfect way to start your morning: cafecito and a treat. That being said, I think there's something very special about having the power to make things for yourself. This recipe is my ideal rendition of the bakery classic. Enjoy these pancitos with a side of sliced mild cheddar (queso de papa in the Dominican Republic), or fill these kipferl-style rolls with cheddar for the ultimate pan sobao experience. But remember, just because you'll learn how to make them yourself doesn't mean you should stop supporting the places making these yeasty treats.

MAKES 12 ROLLS

- ½ cup (120 mL) evaporated milk, warmed to 96°F
- ½ cup (120 mL) warm water (96°F)
- 1 tablespoon sugar
- 2 (¼-ounce/7 g) envelopes active dry yeast
- 3 cups (420 g) all-purpose flour, plus more for dusting
- 2 teaspoons kosher salt
- 4 large egg yolks
- 6 tablespoons (¾ stick/85 g) unsalted butter, cut into pieces and softened
- 1 large egg

In the bowl of a stand mixer fitted with the dough hook, stir together the warm milk, warm water, sugar, and yeast. Let stand until frothy, about 10 minutes.

Add the flour, then the salt (this step is super important—always add the flour first so the salt does not harm the yeast you just woke up), and mix on medium-low speed until the flour is mostly incorporated, about 1 minute, stopping to scrape down the sides of the bowl as needed.

Add the egg yolks and mix until the dough forms a ball, about 1 minute. Add the butter in a couple of additions, mixing after each, then mix until the dough is smooth and no longer clings to the sides of the bowl, about 2 minutes. Cover the bowl with plastic wrap and let stand in a warm, draft-free place until the dough doubles in size, 1 to 2 hours.

Line a baking sheet with parchment paper.

Punch down the dough, then transfer it to a lightly floured work surface and, using a lightly floured rolling pin, roll it out to a 13 by 9-inch rectangle. Cut the dough into 12 pretty triangles, then roll up the triangles, starting from the wide base, so they look like little croissants

continues ▶

or pigs in a blanket (minus the pigs). Place the rolled dough on the prepared baking sheet, point-side down (this helps seal the shape). Cover with a kitchen towel and let stand until the dough triangles have doubled in size, 10 to 15 minutes.

Preheat the oven to 350°F.

In a small bowl, whisk the egg with 1 tablespoon water. Lightly brush the dough with the egg wash and bake for 15 to 20 minutes, until golden. Remove from the oven, let cool slightly, and then enjoy warm.

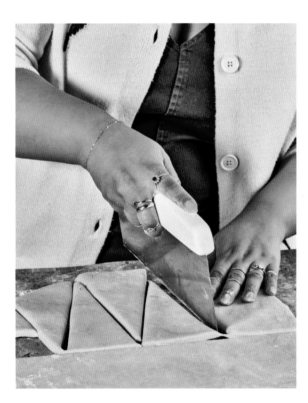

Pan de Agua

1 cup (240 mL) warm water (96°F)
1½ tablespoons light brown sugar
½ teaspoon granulated sugar
1 (¼-ounce/7 g) envelope active dry
    yeast
2½ cups (375 g) bread flour
2 tablespoons all-purpose flour,
    plus more for dusting
1 teaspoon cornstarch
1½ teaspoons kosher salt
1 tablespoon vegetable oil

All it takes is water and a bit of vegetable oil to achieve the consistency that makes this crumbly, flaky bread so versatile and irresistible. It's toasty on the outside and impossibly soft within. Use it as the base for your take on the popular Dominican chimi sandwiches, or slather it with butter to dip in your morning coffee.

In the bowl of a stand mixer fitted with the dough hook, stir together the warm water, brown sugar, granulated sugar, and yeast on low speed. Turn off the mixer and let stand until frothy, about 10 minutes.

Add the bread flour, all-purpose flour, and cornstarch, then the salt (this step is super important—always add the flour first so the salt does not harm the yeast you just woke up), and mix on medium-low speed until the flour is mostly incorporated, about 1 minute, stopping to scrape down the sides of the bowl as needed.

Mix until the dough forms a ball, about 1 minute longer. Add the oil and mix until the dough is smooth and no longer clings to the sides of the bowl, about 2 minutes. Cover the bowl with plastic wrap and let stand in a warm, draft-free place until the dough doubles in size, 1 to 2 hours.

Punch down the dough, then transfer it to a lightly floured work surface and portion it into 1-ounce (2-tablespoon) balls. Working with one at a time, roll each ball tightly between your palm and the work surface until the surface of the dough is smooth, then set the ball on a plate and cover with a kitchen towel. Repeat with the remaining dough. Let the dough balls rest for 5 minutes to relax the gluten.

Preheat the oven to 375°F. Line a baking sheet with parchment paper.

Using a small, lightly floured rolling pin, roll the dough balls on a lightly floured surface. The technique is cool but a bit different than what you might be used to. Basically, we're trying to roll the balls into little ovoid shapes with a seam down the middle. They'll look like awkward lips. To do this, with your hands, shape the spherical ball into roughly a football (American football!) shape. Turn it so the long side is facing you, then, working from the center (where the laces would be on the football), roll down with the rolling pin so one lengthwise half of the football is smooshed. So now you have a

football with one half inflated and one half deflated. Use your hands to roll the side that you just deflated in a little curl until it meets the inflated side of the dough at the center. When you've finished rolling, it should look like a pair of lips. Smooch!

Place the dough pieces seam-side down on the prepared baking sheet. Cover with a kitchen towel and let proof for 15 minutes.

Bake the pan de agua for 15 minutes, then reduce the oven temperature to 350°F and bake for 10 minutes more, or until the bottoms are completely golden brown. Remove from the oven and let stand for 5 minutes before eating.

The Flan
Familia

"Never Been to Italy" Panna Cotta

4 cups (1 L) heavy cream
1 tablespoon unflavored gelatin powder (from two ¼-ounce/7 g packets)
⅓ cup (80 mL) honey
1 teaspoon vanilla bean paste
½ teaspoon kosher salt
¼ teaspoon ground nutmeg

"Have you even been to Italy?" asked a lady once while I was at work in my first "official" pastry chef gig. I could tell she knew my answer and had already formed preconceived notions of me when I walked out of the kitchen with my high Afro puff tucked into my bandanna. I said, "No, but I've been to Little Italy in the Bronx," and giggled at my own joke (as I normally do). She stared in awe of my response and noted that this was the best panna cotta she's ever had. And so, I proudly present to you all this humbly playful panna cotta.

Pour ⅓ cup (80 mL) of the cream into a large bowl, sprinkle the gelatin over the top, and stir to combine. Set aside for 5 minutes to bloom the gelatin.

Pour the remaining cream into a large saucepan and add the honey, vanilla, salt, and nutmeg. Heat over medium heat until bubbles form around the edge of the pan and the mixture reaches 180°F. Immediately pour the hot cream mixture over the bloomed gelatin and whisk until the gelatin has melted. Let cool until just barely warm to the touch.

Put six 6-ounce ramekins on a small baking sheet. Pour the cream mixture into the ramekins. Cover the baking sheet with plastic wrap. Poke a few holes in the plastic wrap to let any residual heat escape, then refrigerate overnight.

When ready to serve, warm a butter knife with hot water and run it around the inside of the ramekins. Unmold the panna cottas onto individual plates and serve, or cover the tops of the ramekins with plastic wrap and refrigerate for up to 1 week before serving.

Flan de Calabaza

I love gourds. I love the way they grow in the soil. I love seeing them on display in the fall. I love roasting them with a touch of honey. I love pepitas even more. This flan captures all that yummy calabaza goodness I've just described, highlighting the actual flavor of the gourd instead of falling back on the pumpkin spice trick. This recipe is a great reminder of just how amazing pumpkins can be.

MAKE THE FLAN: Preheat the oven to 325°F.

In a blender, combine the eggs, condensed milk, whole milk, pumpkin puree, vanilla, brown sugar, salt, ginger, cinnamon, nutmeg, allspice, and pepper and blend until a light froth forms on top of the mixture, about 3 minutes. Strain the custard through a fine-mesh sieve into a large bowl. Cover the bowl with plastic wrap and place in the fridge to chill for 15 minutes.

Meanwhile, put the granulated sugar in a small saucepan and add a splash of water; it should look like wet sand. Cook over medium heat, without stirring, until the caramel is dark golden brown and reaches 365°F on a candy thermometer, about 5 minutes. If sugar crystals start to form and creep up the sides of the pan while the caramel is cooking, brush them down with a pastry brush dipped in water.

Immediately and carefully pour the caramel into a 9-inch round cake pan. Using kitchen towels or oven mitts, slightly tilt the pan in a circular motion to evenly distribute the caramel over the bottom. Let cool completely.

Pour the custard into the pan over the caramel. Cover the pan with aluminum foil. Set the cake pan in a roasting pan.

Run water from the tap until the water is very hot. Add enough hot water to the roasting pan to come halfway up the sides of the cake pan, being careful not to get any water in the cake pan. The cake pan should not be floating.

Carefully transfer the roasting pan to the oven and bake for 1 hour. Remove the foil to check the center of the flan; it should jiggle when

FLAN

7 large eggs

1 (14-ounce/400 g) can sweetened condensed milk

1¾ cups (420 mL) whole milk

¼ cup (60 g) pumpkin puree

2 tablespoons Dominican imitation vanilla extract

¼ cup lightly packed (50 g) light brown sugar

1 tablespoon kosher salt

1 tablespoon grated fresh ginger

1 teaspoon ground cinnamon

¼ teaspoon ground nutmeg

¼ teaspoon ground allspice

¼ teaspoon freshly ground black pepper

1 cup (200 g) granulated sugar

PEPITAS

½ cup (65 g) shelled pepitas

2 tablespoons honey

1 tablespoon avocado oil

½ teaspoon ground ginger

¼ teaspoon ground cinnamon

¼ teaspoon ground nutmeg

¼ teaspoon cayenne pepper

¼ teaspoon freshly ground black pepper

continues ▶

tapped but not be liquidy. If the flan is not yet ready, return it to the oven, uncovered, and bake for 15 minutes before testing again. Remove from the oven, remove the cake pan from the roasting pan, and let cool to room temperature. Cover and refrigerate overnight.

MEANWHILE, TOAST THE PEPITAS: In a large dry nonstick skillet, toast the pepitas over medium heat until toasty and golden, about 3 minutes. Add the honey and oil and stir with a rubber spatula until the honey melts and coats the pepitas. Remove from the heat. Add the ginger, cinnamon, nutmeg, cayenne, and black pepper and vigorously toss until evenly coated. Spread the seeds over a baking sheet and let them sit overnight or until dry.

To unmold, run a thin blunt knife under very hot water to heat it up. Run it around the edge of the pan between the flan and the pan. Place a plate with a lip over the pan and very carefully flip the pan and plate together so the flan slips out onto the plate. Lightly tap the pan before removing it. Serve, topping each portion of flan with spiced pepitas for crunch, or lightly cover the flan with plastic wrap or a clean kitchen towel and return it to the fridge until ready to serve.

Flan Casero

7 large eggs

2 cups (480 mL) whole milk

1 (14-ounce/400 g) can sweetened
condensed milk

¼ cup lightly packed (50 g) light
brown sugar

2 tablespoons Dominican imitation
vanilla extract

1 tablespoon kosher salt

1 cup (200 g) granulated sugar

This is the flan you get at Dominican restaurants, just more complex and a touch lighter. Keeping the sweetness in check means
you can savor a few slices instead of a few bites, and I love that
for us.

Preheat the oven to 325°F.

In a blender, combine the eggs, whole milk, condensed milk, brown
sugar, vanilla, and salt and blend until a light froth forms on top of
the mixture, about 3 minutes. Strain the custard through a fine-mesh
sieve into a large bowl. Cover the bowl with plastic wrap and place in
the fridge to chill for 15 minutes.

Place the granulated sugar in a small saucepan and add a splash of
water; it should look like wet sand. Set over medium heat and cook,
without stirring, until the caramel is dark golden brown and reaches
365°F on a candy thermometer, 3 to 5 minutes. If sugar crystals start
to form and creep up the sides of the pan while the caramel is cooking, brush them down with a pastry brush dipped in water.

Immediately and carefully pour the caramel into a 9-inch round cake
pan. Using kitchen towels or oven mitts, slightly tilt the pan in a circular motion to evenly distribute the caramel. Let cool completely. Pour
the chilled custard into the pan over the caramel. Cover the pan with
aluminum foil, then set it in a roasting pan.

Add enough very hot tap water to the roasting pan to come halfway
up the sides of the cake pan, being careful not to get any water in the
cake pan. The cake pan should not be floating.

Carefully transfer the roasting pan to the oven and bake for 1 hour.
Remove the foil to check the center of the flan; it should jiggle when
tapped but not be liquidy. If the flan is not yet ready, return it to
the oven, uncovered, and bake for 15 minutes before testing again.
Remove from the oven, remove the cake pan from the roasting pan,
and let cool to room temperature. Cover and refrigerate overnight.

Run a thin blunt knife under very hot water to heat it up. Run it
around the edge of the pan between the flan and the pan. Place a
plate over the pan and very carefully flip the pan and plate together
so the flan slips out onto the plate. Lightly tap the pan before removing it. Serve immediately, or loosely cover the flan with plastic wrap
or a clean kitchen towel and refrigerate until ready to serve.

Black & White Cookie Charlotte

My childhood apartment in the Bronx was just blocks away from the Stella d'Oro factory, which emanated intoxicating aromas of baked goods around the clock and probably had a little something to do with my chosen career path. I'd walk by the facility early in the morning or late at night, and if the lights were on, my mind would wander and I'd imagine all the glorious things happening inside. Some of my fondest memories are of picking up boxes of freshly baked ladyfingers right at the source, allowing us the rare opportunity to eat them warm and at their airiest. In a lot of ways, Stella d'Oro was my local bakery.

To this day, I could down a whole stack of ladyfingers in minutes. Here I've taken the idea of a traditional British charlotte and twisted it on its head. I filled the center with a pastry cream that evokes the flavors of a black-and-white cookie, and stacked the base and surrounded the exterior with ladyfingers. I'm all for substituting ingredients in a pinch, but come on, don't make this if you aren't going to use Stella d'Oro.

MAKE THE VANILLA PASTRY CREAM: Place 2 tablespoons of the milk in a small bowl and sprinkle the gelatin over the surface. Stir, then set aside for 5 minutes to bloom the gelatin.

In a medium saucepan, combine ½ cup (120 mL) of the milk, the cream, sugar, and vanilla and heat over medium heat until bubbles form around the edge of the pan and the mixture reaches 180°F.

In a small bowl, combine the remaining 2 tablespoons milk with the cornstarch and stir until smooth.

In a medium bowl, lightly whisk together the egg yolks and cornstarch slurry. While whisking continuously, slowly add a ladleful of the hot milk mixture to the eggs and whisk vigorously to combine. Pour the tempered egg mixture into the saucepan with the hot milk mixture and cook, stirring, until it reaches 185°F. Strain through a fine-mesh sieve into clean bowl. Add the butter and stir until completely smooth.

continues ▶

VANILLA PASTRY CREAM
¾ cup (180 mL) whole milk
2 tablespoons unflavored gelatin powder (from two ¼-ounce/7 g packets)
½ cup (120 mL) heavy cream
¼ cup plus 2 tablespoons (75 g) sugar
1 teaspoon vanilla bean paste
2 tablespoons cornstarch
3 large egg yolks
4 tablespoons (½ stick/55 g) unsalted butter, softened

FILLING
¼ cup (25 g) black (noir) cocoa powder
1½ cups (360 mL) heavy cream
¼ cup (22 g) chocolate curls

VANILLA SYRUP
1 cup (200 g) sugar
1 teaspoon vanilla bean paste
1 teaspoon rum

16 Italian ladyfinger cookies, preferably Stella d'Oro

Add the bloomed gelatin to the pastry cream and stir until the gelatin has dissolved. Let cool to room temperature before using. (You can make the pastry cream up to 1 week in advance and store it, covered with plastic wrap, in the refrigerator.)

MAKE THE FILLING: Divide the vanilla pastry cream between two medium bowls (you should have 1 cup/150 g of pastry cream in each). Add the cocoa powder to one bowl and stir until evenly incorporated.

In the bowl of a stand mixer fitted with the whisk attachment or in a large bowl using a hand mixer or a stick blender, whip the heavy cream to stiff peaks, 3 to 5 minutes. Divide the whipped cream evenly between the vanilla and chocolate pastry creams and fold it in. Fold three-quarters of the chocolate curls into the chocolate pastry cream (reserve the rest for garnish). Transfer the pastry creams to separate piping bags, each fitted with a large round tip. Refrigerate until it's time to pipe.

MAKE THE SYRUP: In a small saucepan, combining the sugar, vanilla, and ½ cup (120 mL) water and bring to a boil over high heat. Cook, stirring, until the sugar has dissolved, 3 to 5 minutes. Remove from the heat, stir in the rum, and let cool slightly.

ASSEMBLE THE CHARLOTTES: Line the bottoms of four 4-inch mini springform pans or one 10-inch springform pan with parchment paper cut to fit.

Dunk the ladyfingers in the warm vanilla syrup, then place them rounded-side down over the bottom of the prepared pans. Repeat to line the circumference of the pans, standing the ladyfingers vertically around the edge (see Note).

Place both of the pastry cream piping bags into a single, larger piping bag. Pipe the filling over the ladyfingers in a swirl pattern, filling each pan to just under the top of the edge of the vertical ladyfingers. Top the filling evenly with the remaining chocolate curls.

Loosely cover with plastic wrap or a clean kitchen towel and refrigerate for at least 6 hours or preferably overnight before serving.

NOTE: *If you'll be making mini charlottes, trim the ladyfingers so they fit in the pans with the tips poking out (you'll likely cut them in half). For a 10-inch springform pan, trim off about one-quarter of the ladyfingers so just the rounded tips poke out over the top of the pan.*

Avocado Crème Brûlée

Avocado is a fruit! Should I say that again? Avocado. Is. A. Fruit. Now that I have your attention, here's one more hot take: Everyone should have at least one avocado dessert in their arsenal.

Crème brûlée and avocado sound like an odd pairing, but trust me. Consider making this for a dinner party when you care about impressing your guests—they'll be as satisfied as they are surprised.

Preheat the oven to 300°F.

In a small saucepan, heat the cream and milk over medium heat until steaming, about 5 minutes.

Fill a large bowl with ice and water and set it nearby. In a separate large bowl, whisk together the egg yolks and superfine sugar until combined, about 3 minutes. While whisking continuously, slowly pour a ladleful of the hot cream into the egg mixture and whisk vigorously to combine. Pour the egg mixture into the saucepan with the cream mixture. Bring to a simmer and cook until the temperature reaches 184°F. Place the pan over the ice bath to cool completely.

Transfer the mixture to a blender and add the lemon juice, avocado, and vanilla. (Fun science note: Adding the avocado when the mixture is cool prevents browning. And adding the lemon prevents the mixture from turning into clotted cream. In other words, don't skip this step unless you want to make avocado cheese.) Blend until smooth, then strain the mixture through a fine-mesh sieve into a large liquid measuring cup or other vessel with a spout.

Pour the mixture into four small ramekins and set the ramekins in a roasting pan. Run water from the tap until the water is very hot. Add enough hot water to the roasting pan to come halfway up the sides of the ramekins, being careful not to get any water in the ramekins. The ramekins should not be floating. Carefully transfer the roasting pan to the oven and bake for 30 to 45 minutes, until the custard has set into a soft but wobbly-in-the-center texture. Remove from the oven and remove the ramekins from the roasting pan. Refrigerate until completely chilled before serving, at least 4 hours or up to overnight.

Just before serving, sprinkle the brown sugar over the surface of each custard and use a kitchen torch to melt and crystallize the sugar into a hard shell. (Alternatively, you can slide them directly under the broiler for 1 to 2 minutes to brûlée the sugar—just keep an eye on them.)

SERVES 4

1¼ cups (300 mL) heavy cream
¼ cup (60 mL) whole milk
3 large egg yolks
¼ cup (50 g) superfine sugar
1 teaspoon fresh lemon juice
½ Hass avocado, mashed
1 tablespoon vanilla bean paste
½ cup firmly packed (100 g) light
    brown sugar, for topping

Rum-amisù

RUM SYRUP
½ cup (100 g) sugar
½ cup (120 mL) dark rum

MASCARPONE MIXTURE
6 large eggs, separated
1 cup (200 g) sugar
2 cups (900 g) mascarpone
¼ teaspoon kosher salt

30 Italian ladyfinger cookies,
   preferably Stella d'Oro, or as
   needed
2 tablespoons caramel dust, for
   topping (see Note)
Whipped cream, for serving

NOTE: *Caramel dust is a fun little DIY project. In a nonstick skillet, heat 1 cup (200 g) granulated sugar over medium-high heat, stirring only if you see dark spots, until it melts into a golden brown caramel, 5 to 6 minutes. Pour it onto a parchment-lined baking sheet in a thin layer, then let it harden. Break the hardened caramel into pieces and transfer to a food processor. Blitz until you have dust! Store in an airtight container at cool room temperature for up to 2 days.*

"But tiramisù is already rum-forward!" you say. Not enough, in my opinion. I need you to taste the dark-rum-soaked ladyfingers in my version. Goodness gracious, I feel like making this the minute I start thinking about that electric jolt of rum at the end of each bite.

MAKE THE RUM SYRUP: In a small saucepan, combine the sugar, half the rum, and ¼ cup (60 mL) water. Cook over medium heat, stirring, until the sugar has dissolved, then add the remaining rum. Remove from the heat and set aside.

MAKE THE MASCARPONE MIXTURE: Set up a baño maría (double boiler) by placing a heatproof bowl over a pot of boiling water (the bottom of the bowl should not touch the water). Place the egg whites in the heatproof bowl. Cook, whisking continuously, until the egg whites reach 160°F. Remove the bowl from the pot and set aside.

Place the egg yolks in a separate heatproof bowl, set it over the pot, and cook, whisking continuously, until they reach 160°F. Remove the bowl from the pot.

In a large bowl, combine the tempered egg yolks and the sugar and beat with a hand mixer until pale yellow, about 5 minutes. (Alternatively, you can do this in a stand mixer fitted with the whisk attachment.) Use a spatula to fold in the mascarpone and set aside.

Degrease your beaters (see page 26). Add the salt to the tempered egg whites and use the hand mixer to whip them to stiff peaks, about 10 minutes. Add the whipped egg whites to the egg-mascarpone mixture and fold with a spatula to combine.

Spread a thin layer of the mascarpone mixture over the bottom of a 9 by 13-inch or 8-inch square baking dish. (This is a flexible recipe—use what you have.) Lightly soak the ladyfingers in the rum syrup, then arrange them flat-side down on top of the mascarpone layer, trimming them as needed to fit. Repeat these layers with the remaining mascarpone and cookies, ensuring that the final layer is mascarpone. Top with the caramel dust.

Refrigerate, covered, for at least 4 hours or preferably overnight, then serve, topped with whipped cream.

PB&J Pots de Crème

Pot de crème is a fancy French term for "pudding," which is an ideal vehicle for the very American flavors of a PB&J. In this case, it's guava jelly, because #caribbean.

In a blender, combine the half-and-half and peanuts and blend on high until the mixture is homogeneous, about 3 minutes, then strain through a fine-mesh sieve into a medium saucepan.

Spread ¼ cup (50 g) of the sugar in a dry nonstick skillet. Add 2 tablespoons water and heat over medium heat without stirring. As it begins to get warm, you will see large bubbles form and the mixture will begin to change color from light amber to golden amber. Stir only if you start to see dark spots—the caramel is done when it turns a golden brown color. Timing varies but it should be ready in 5 to 6 minutes.

Add the vanilla to the half-and-half mixture and bring to a simmer over medium heat, then pour it into the skillet with your caramel and whisk vigorously until the caramel melts into the dairy. Remove from the heat.

In a large bowl, whisk together the egg yolks and remaining ¼ cup (50 g) sugar until the mixture turns pale yellow and has thickened a bit, about 3 minutes. While whisking continuously, slowly pour a ladleful of the hot caramel mixture into the bowl with the egg mixture and whisk vigorously to combine. Pour the tempered egg mixture into the saucepan with the caramel mixture and whisk to combine. Heat over medium heat until the mixture reaches 165°F on an instant-read thermometer.

Place the milk chococalte in a large heat-resistant bowl, then pour the hot caramel mixture over the top. Whisk until the chocolate has melted, then add the salt and whisk to combine. Strain the mixture through a fine-mesh sieve into a large liquid measuring cup or other vessel with a spout. Pour the mixture into four large (10-ounce) ramekins or eight smaller ramekins. Set the ramekins in a roasting pan.

2 cups (480 mL) half-and-half
¼ cup (40 g) unsalted roasted
    peanuts
½ cup (100 g) sugar
2 tablespoons vanilla bean paste
6 large egg yolks
4 ounces (115 g) milk chocolate
¼ teaspoon kosher salt

GUAVA JELLY

¼ cup (60 mL) fresh lemon juice
1 teaspoon unflavored gelatin
    powder (from one ¼-ounce/7 g
    packet)
1 cup (310 g) guava paste

continues ▶

Run water from the tap until the water is very hot. Add enough hot water to the roasting pan to come halfway up the sides of the ramekins, being careful not to get any water in the ramekins. The ramekins should not be floating.

Carefully transfer the roasting pan to the oven and bake for 30 to 55 minutes, until the mixture is set and the center is firm but still wobbles a little bit. If it still looks liquid, keep baking. Remove from the oven and remove the ramekins from the roasting pan. Let cool for 10 minutes, or until the pots de crème are no longer warm to the touch, then cover each loosely with plastic wrap and refrigerate until completely chilled before serving, at least 2 hours or up to overnight. (They can be stored in the refrigerator for up to 1 week.)

MEANWHILE, MAKE THE GUAVA JELLY: Place the lemon juice in a small bowl and sprinkle the gelatin over the surface. Stir to combine and set aside for 5 minutes to bloom the gelatin.

In a medium saucepan, combine the guava paste and ½ cup (120 mL) water and bring to a boil over high heat, stirring to dissolve the guava paste. Reduce the heat to medium-low and add the bloomed gelatin mixture. Stir until the mixture is fully incorporated and sets into a soft jelly. Remove from the heat and refrigerate until cooled before serving.

Spoon some cooled guava jelly over each pot de crème and enjoy.

Avena Caliente

Avena is actually "oatmeal" in Spanish. We love to drink oatmeal, so the ratio of oats to water is different for us than in American-style oatmeal dishes. Ours is smoother and a bit sweeter, and has more spices. Although avena caliente is not technically a dessert, I'm taking liberties and deeming it close enough. It's important for me to carve out space for this unassuming beverage in the book because it's the one thing my grandmother would make for me every morning. You see, I had a lot of anxiety growing up, and the warm oats and milk laced with cinnamon have some magical calming properties that always seem to comfort me. It fills you up, yet it's not too heavy. Although it's in the same family as arroz con leche, it lives in a universe all its own. I hope that you love it as much as I do.

In a medium saucepan, combine the oats, brown sugar, cinnamon sticks, orange zest, cloves, milk, and 1 cup (240 mL) water. Bring to a boil over medium heat, then reduce the heat to maintain a simmer and cook for 5 minutes, or until fragrant.

The avena can be drizzled with honey and served hot—right away! Or you can transfer it to an airtight container and refrigerate for up to 1 day, then serve it chilled, over ice, if you like.

SERVES 1

¼ cup (40 g) rolled oats
¼ cup lightly packed (50 g) light brown sugar
3 cinnamon sticks
Orange zest, to taste
2 whole cloves
3 tablespoons oat milk or almond milk (or whole milk, if you're not lactose-intolerant like me)
Honey, for drizzling

Majarete

MAJARETE

2 ears white corn, shucked

1½ cups (360 mL) evaporated milk

1 Ceylon cinnamon stick

¼ teaspoon ground nutmeg

¼ teaspoon kosher salt

¼ cup lightly packed (50 g) light brown sugar

2 tablespoons cornstarch

CORN SPOON SWEETS

1 ear corn, shucked

¼ cup (50 g) granulated sugar

¼ cup (60 mL) honey

Zest of 1 lemon, cut into strips

¼ cup (60 mL) fresh lemon juice

Can I be honest here for a second? It wasn't easy to trim down the "setlist" for my debut collection of recipes. But before I even put pen to paper, I knew that if I didn't throw some majarete into the mix, I would be spending the rest of my life getting angry letters from the Dominican embassy (and my mom). JK . . . although they'd have very good reason to remind me of my oversight: Majarete, a corn porridge with a lovely color, is king in the Dominican Republic. I kept this version fairly close to the traditional recipe, but leaned in a bit more into warming spice notes (my love language) and used fresh corn. I want to show you the fullest expression of what majarete can be so you can start making this simple, tasty treat at home, too.

MAKE THE MAJARETE: Cut the kernels from 1 ear of corn and transfer to a blender. Blend until smooth, then set the pureed corn aside. Cut the kernels off the other ear of corn and set the whole corn kernels aside as well.

In a medium saucepan, combine the evaporated milk and cinnamon stick and bring to a boil over medium heat. Remove from the heat and let steep until fragrant, 5 to 7 minutes. Add the pureed corn, whole corn kernels, nutmeg, salt, brown sugar, and cornstarch and bring to a gentle boil over medium heat, stirring frequently with a rubber spatula to prevent the bottom of the marjarete from sticking to the pan. Gently boil, stirring, until the marjarete has a thick, puddinglike consistency, 10 to 15 minutes.

Transfer the marjarete to a large liquid measuring cup or other vessel with a spout. Pour it into four small ramekins (or one larger serving dish, if you prefer). Loosely cover the ramekins with plastic wrap and refrigerate until completely chilled, at least 4 hours or up to a week.

MEANWHILE, MAKE THE SPOON SWEETS: Preheat the oven to 400°F. Roast the ear of corn directly on the oven rack for about 25 minutes, until golden brown. Remove from the oven and set aside until cool enough to handle, then cut the kernels off the cob.

In a small pot, combine the roasted corn kernels, granulated sugar, honey, lemon zest, and lemon juice. Cook over medium-high heat until the corn is soft and the liquid has reduced by half, 8 to 10 minutes. Remove from the heat and refrigerate for 4 to 6 hours, until chilled.

Serve the spoon sweets on top of the majarete.

Jalea de Batata Mousse

GANACHE
8 ounces (225 g) white chocolate
(chips, fèves, or chopped from
a bar)
½ cup (120 mL) heavy cream
1 cup (240 mL) Jalea (recipe
follows)

ITALIAN MERINGUE
4 large egg whites
1 cup (200 g) sugar

1 cup (240 mL) heavy cream, plus
more for serving, if desired

Many would agree that a sweet potato isn't much to look at from the outside. But just as it is with human beings, it's what's on the inside that counts. Sweet potatoes' rough, craggy exteriors give way to beautifully fluffy interiors with irresistible flavor. I've always been fond of everything about sweet potatoes, especially the white-fleshed variety. You can't escape the intoxicating aromas of people roasting them on the roadside or at home if you spend any amount of time in the Dominican Republic. This jalea de batata recipe takes those intense flavors and transforms the humble roasted sweet potato into a creamy pudding.

MAKE THE GANACHE: Place the white chocolate in a heatproof medium bowl. In a small saucepan, warm the cream over medium heat until steaming, then pour it over the white chocolate and whisk until the chocolate has melted and the mixture is smooth. Add the jalea and whisk until the ganache is smooth. Set aside.

MAKE THE MERINGUE: Degrease the equipment you are going to use to whip your egg whites (see page 26).

In the bowl of a stand mixer fitted with the whisk attachment, whip the egg whites on medium-high speed until frothy, 5 to 8 minutes.

Meanwhile, in a medium saucepan, combine the sugar and ½ cup (120 mL) water. Cook over medium heat without stirring until the syrup reaches 240°F on a candy thermometer, about 10 minutes. (Keep a small bowl with ½ cup/120 mL water and a pastry brush on the side to brush away any crystallization that might appear on the inside of the pan.)

When the syrup reaches 240°F, with the mixer on medium-low speed, slowly stream it into the egg whites, pouring it down the inside edge of the bowl (avoid the whisk—you don't want hot syrup flying around!). When all the syrup has been added, raise the mixer speed to medium-high and whip until the meringue is cool to the touch, 8 to 10 minutes.

Add the meringue to the ganache and fold to combine.

Wipe out the bowl of the stand mixer. Pour the cream into the bowl and, using the whisk attachment, whip on medium-high speed until stiff peaks form, 5 to 8 minutes. Fold the whipped cream into the meringue-ganache mixture.

Pour the mousse into your preferred serving vessel (individual cups or ramekins or a large serving bowl all work) and refrigerate for at least 4 hours or preferably overnight before serving. Serve with additional whipped cream, if desired.

Jalea (Sweet Potato Pudding)

Bring a medium pot of lightly salted water to a boil. Add the sweet potato and boil until fork-tender, 20 to 30 minutes.

Drain the sweet potato and transfer to a blender. Add the coconut milk, clotted cream, evaporated milk, sugar, cloves, cinnamon, and a pinch of salt and blend until smooth.

Transfer the mixture to a large saucepan and cook over medium heat, stirring frequently as it starts to thicken so you don't scorch the bottom, until it has a puddinglike consistency, 20 to 30 minutes. Set aside to cool to room temperature, then transfer to an airtight container and store in the refrigerator for up to 1 week.

MAKES ABOUT 3 CUPS (700 G)

Kosher salt

4 ounces (115 g) white sweet potato, peeled and chopped into chunks

½ cup (120 mL) full-fat coconut milk

½ cup (120 mL) clotted cream or crème fraîche

½ cup (120 mL) evaporated milk

¼ cup (50 g) sugar

½ teaspoon ground cloves

¼ teaspoon ground cinnamon

Dulce de Leche Cortada

For those who associate dulce de leche with caramel and caramel alone, this may catch you off guard. You may be suspicious. What is this dish? Why's it look like the surface of Mars? I promise you: these caramelized curdles of crumbly, creamy, ever-so-lemony joy are going to knock your socks off. Just like my grandmother, after trying this you'll end up keeping jars of the stuff in the fridge. You will thank me.

In a medium saucepan, combine the milk, sugar, raisins, nutmeg, and cinnamon sticks. Heat over low heat until the milk curds start to separate, then stir and cook until the mixture is steaming but not quite at a boil. Stir in the lime zest, lime juice, orange zest, and lemon zest. Give it one stir and then, still over low heat, bring to a simmer, without stirring, and cook until a syrup forms at the top of the mixture, about 10 minutes. Increase the heat to medium-low and simmer, still without stirring, until the milk solids caramelize and the liquid reduces by half, about 15 minutes more. As it cooks, the citrus will separate the dairy into curds, which will begin to turn tannish or light golden brown.

Transfer the cortada to a serving vessel or an airtight container, cover, and refrigerate for at least 6 hours or up to 1 week before serving. Serve chilled.

MAKES ABOUT 2 CUPS

3 cups (720 mL) whole milk
1 cup (200 g) sugar
¼ cup (50 g) golden raisins
¼ teaspoon ground nutmeg
3 cinnamon sticks
1 tablespoon lime zest
¼ cup (60 mL) fresh lime juice
1 teaspoon orange zest
1 teaspoon lemon zest

Chilled Habichuela Soufflé

MAKES FOUR OR FIVE
6-OUNCE SOUFFLÉS

1½ cups (250 g) Habichuela con
   Dulce (recipe follows)
1 tablespoon unflavored gelatin
   powder (from one ¼-ounce/7 g
   packet)

SWISS MERINGUE
4 large egg whites
1 cup (200 g) granulated sugar

GARNISH
½ cup (55 g) crushed crumbs from
   Dominican milk crackers, such
   as Guarina Galletas Dulces Ideal
   con Leche
½ cup (50 grams) desiccated
   coconut, toasted
¼ cup (25 grams) powdered sugar,
   for dusting

A fondness for sweet red beans is something my people share with many Asian cultures. Habichuela con dulce, made by boiling the beans and blending them with milk, sweet potato, raisins, and spices, is a staple on our Easter table. The anglaise-like dessert is typically served with some Guarina galletas dulces (Dominican sweet milk cookies) for dipping. I've included a traditional version of this dish as a subrecipe here—if you've never tried the original, you should definitely make it.

Place the habichuela con dulce in a small pot. Sprinkle the gelatin over the top, then set aside for 5 minutes to bloom. After the gelatin has bloomed, place the pot over medium heat and cook, stirring, just until the gelatin has dissolved. Remove from the heat and set aside to cool.

MEANWHILE, MAKE THE SWISS MERINGUE: Degrease the equipment you are going to use to whip your egg whites (see page 26).

Set up a baño maría (double boiler) by placing a heatproof bowl over a pot of boiling water (the bottom of the bowl should not touch the water). Place the egg whites and sugar in the heatproof bowl. Cook, stirring continuously with a rubber spatula, until you can no longer feel sugar granules when you rub the mixture in between your index finger and thumb, about 5 minutes.

Transfer the cooked egg whites to the bowl of a stand mixer fitted with the whisk attachment and whip on medium-low speed until frothy, 4 to 5 minutes. Increase the speed to medium-high and whip until medium peaks form and the meringue is glossy and doubled in volume, about 8 minutes.

Use a rubber spatula to gently fold the habichuela con dulce into the meringue—it's okay if you see some meringue streaks.

Line the edges (but not the bottoms) of four or five 6-ounce ramekins with aluminum foil, making sure the foil extends 4 to 6 inches above the top of the ramekin (this provides additional support for the soufflé as it sets in the fridge). Use a spatula to divide the habichuela-meringue mixture among the ramekins, smoothing the top of each. Transfer to the refrigerator and chill for at least 3 hours or up to overnight. To serve, remove the foil and then top with milk crackers, toasted coconut, and powdered sugar.

Habichuela con Dulce

1 medium white sweet potato
1 cup (180 g) cooked or canned
    red kidney beans (drained and
    rinsed, if canned)
1 cup (240 mL) heavy cream
¾ cup (180 mL) full-fat coconut
    milk
½ cup (120 mL) evaporated milk
¼ cup (50 g) granulated sugar
1 teaspoon ground cinnamon
¼ teaspoon ground cloves
¼ teaspoon Dominican imitation
    vanilla extract
¼ teaspoon kosher salt

Preheat the oven to 450°F.

Using a fork, generously poke the sweet potato all over. Wrap the sweet potato tightly in aluminum foil and bake directly on the oven rack for 30 to 40 minutes, until soft, tender, and with visible steam coming out. (The texture of the sweet potato after mashing should be silky and soft, so when in doubt, err on the side of more cook time, since you want to release sweetness and make sure the starch is fully cooked out.) Remove from the oven and set aside until cool enough to handle, then halve the sweet potato. Score and scoop the flesh into a medium bowl. Use a fork to lightly mash the flesh. Place ¼ cup (50 g) of the mashed sweet potato in a small bowl and reserve it for later.

In a medium pot, combine the remaining sweet potato, beans, cream, coconut milk, evaporated milk, granulated sugar, cinnamon, cloves, vanilla, and salt. Bring to a boil over medium heat, and cook, stirring occasionally, until the beans are fork-tender and not grainy, and the mixture is fragrant, 15 to 20 minutes. Transfer the mixture to a blender along with the reserved ¼ cup (50 grams) mashed sweet potato. Blend until smooth, then strain through a fine-mesh sieve into a clean bowl. You can either eat this warm or chilled. Store, covered, in the refrigerator for up to 3 days.

Torta Dominicana, aka Arepa Dominicana

In the Dominican Republic, this is a classic, classic, classic delight—a robust and custardy cornbread with rum-soaked raisins that people in my province call a torta but is elsewhere referred to as an arepa. Every family has their own recipe, and I owe much of the inspiration for my version to my mother-in-law. I humbly submit that it might be the best one ever made. (You hear that, Dominican Embassy? Llamame!)

Preheat the oven to 350°F. Grease a 12-inch springform pan (see Note). Wrap the exterior of the pan (bottom and sides) with a single sheet of aluminum foil (this will protect it in the water bath later).

In a small saucepan, heat the rum over medium heat until warm (or warm it in the microwave). Put the raisins in a small bowl and pour the warm rum over them. Let stand, uncovered, until the raisins absorb the rum and are cool to the touch.

In a large nonstick pot, combine the evaporated milk and coconut milk and heat over medium heat until bubbles form around the edge of the pan and the mixture reaches 180°F. Add the cinnamon sticks, then turn off the heat, cover the pot, and let it sit on the burner for 10 minutes to infuse the milk with the cinnamon. Fish out and discard the cinnamon.

Add the cornmeal, brown sugar, granulated sugar, salt, and vanilla to the milk mixture and cook over medium heat, stirring periodically, until the mixture thickens to a puddinglike consistency, about 10 minutes. Add the butter and stir until melted. Drain the remaining rum from the raisins, then stir the rum-soaked raisins into the cornmeal mixture and remove from the heat. Transfer the mixture to the prepared springform pan. Set the springform pan in a roasting pan.

Run water from the tap until the water is very hot. Add enough hot water to the roasting pan to come halfway up the sides of the springform pan, being careful not to get any water in the springform pan. The springform pan should not be floating.

MAKES ONE 12-INCH TORTA

Vegetable oil cooking spray, for greasing
⅓ cup (80 mL) golden rum
¼ cup (50 g) raisins or golden raisins
2 cups (480 mL) evaporated milk
1 cup (240 mL) full-fat coconut milk
6 cinnamon sticks
2 cups (160 g) fine cornmeal
¾ cup lightly packed (180 g) light brown sugar
½ cup (100 g) granulated sugar
¼ teaspoon kosher salt
2 teaspoons vanilla bean paste
2 tablespoons unsalted butter
Cinnamon Cornflakes (recipe follows), for topping (optional)

continues ▶

Carefully transfer the roasting pan to the oven and bake for 40 minutes, or until a cake tester inserted into the center comes out clean. Remove from the oven, immediately top with cinnamon cornflakes, if desired, and let cool for 5 minutes before serving.

NOTE: *You can make this in a 10-inch springform pan, if you prefer—just add 5 to 7 minutes to the cook time.*

Cinnamon Cornflakes

Preheat the oven to 350°F. Line a baking sheet with parchment paper.

In a medium bowl, combine the sugar and cinnamon. Add the cornflakes. Pour in the melted butter and gently mix to combine. Spread the cornflakes over the prepared baking sheet and bake for 10 minutes, or until the coated cornflakes look golden brown and the sugar has created a glaze on each flake. Remove from the oven and let cool before using.

MAKES ½ CUP (150 G)

¼ cup (50 g) sugar
½ teaspoon ground cinnamon
½ cup (15 g) cornflakes cereal
4 tablespoons (½ stick/55 g)
    unsalted butter, melted

Ponlo en el Freezer!

(Put It in the Freezer!)

Washington Heights Icicle Pops

When the weather is sweltering and it's so hot it feels like your shoes are sticking to the asphalt, there's nothing in the world more refreshing than an ice pop. Even though I grew up enjoying the bright, neon-colored versions, my current favorites are made with fresh, ripe fruits that really bring the flavors to life. I've offered three suggestions here, but I encourage you to play around with your favorite fruit or flavor combinations. Treat this as a template and experiment with abandon.

MAKES ABOUT 8 OF EACH

Piña Pops

In a medium bowl, combine the pineapple juice, coconut water, and simple syrup and stir with a kitchen whisk or spoon. Taste the mixture with a clean spoon and add the citric acid if you'd like a more sour flavor.

Funnel the mixture into ice pop bags (see Notes). If you don't have a funnel, you can use a spouted liquid measuring cup. Do not overfill the bags or they might pop in the freezer. Add the pineapple chunks and edible flowers (if using) to the bags, seal according to the manufacturer's instructions, and freeze for 24 hours.

1 cup (240 mL) fresh or canned pineapple juice
2 cups (480 mL) coconut water
½ cup (120 mL) Simple Syrup (page 280)
Pinch of citric acid (optional)
1 cup (240 g) finely diced pineapple
Edible flowers (optional)

continues ▶

Cherry Pops

2 cups (480 mL) unsweetened
   cherry juice
½ cup (120 mL) Simple Syrup
   (page 280)
½ cup (120 mL) fresh lemon juice
Pinch of citric acid

In a medium bowl, combine the cherry juice, simple syrup, ½ cup (120 mL) water, the lemon juice, and the citric acid and stir with a whisk or spoon to combine.

Funnel or pour the mixture into ice pop bags (see Notes), seal according to the manufacturer's instructions, and freeze for 24 hours before serving.

Cotton Candy Pops

2 teaspoons finger lime powder
   (see Notes)
¼ teaspoon ground cloves
½ cup (120 mL) honey
2 cups (480 mL) blood orange juice
½ cup (120 mL) fresh or canned
   pineapple juice
¼ cup (60 mL) fresh lime juice

In a small saucepan, combine the finger lime powder, cloves, and ¼ cup (60 mL) water and bring to a simmer over medium heat. Remove from the heat, add the honey, and stir until it has dissolved. Let cool to room temperature.

Add the blood orange, pineapple, and lime juices and stir to combine. Strain the mixture through a fine-mesh sieve into a clean bowl or spouted liquid measuring cup. Funnel or pour the mixture into ice pop bags (see Notes), seal according to the manufacturer's instructions, and freeze for 24 hours before serving.

NOTES: *Look for finger lime powder online. As an alternative, use dried lime zest.*

If you're not able to order ice pop bags—which I highly recommend you do, they're so fun!—use small resealable sandwich bags. Fill each with 3 to 3½ ounces of liquid and seal tightly.

Since it's harder to taste things that are super cold, remember to taste everything as you go, but recognize that the fruit flavor will mellow out and be less intense when the pops are frozen.

Strawberry Semifrio with Stuffed Wafers

I'd have probably gone to church more often if they gave you strawberry wafers instead of communion wafers. Both melt in your mouth, but that's about as far as the similarities go. Strawberry wafers are impossible to improve upon, in my opinion. Like Stella d'Oro ladyfingers, they are just a flawless food for me. In this recipe, I fold wafer pieces into a semifrio, providing little nuggets of added texture and flavor throughout.

Line a 9-inch square baking pan with parchment paper or aluminum foil, leaving a few inches of parchment or foil overhanging two sides (alternatively, you can use an 8-inch square pan or a 1-pound loaf pan).

Set up a baño maría (double boiler) by placing a large heatproof bowl over a pot of boiling water (the bottom of the bowl should not touch the water). Place the sugar, cornstarch, and egg yolks in the bowl and cook over medium-high heat, whisking continuously to make sure the yolks do not curdle, until very thick, 4 to 5 minutes. The mixture should coat the back of a metal spoon, and if you drag a finger down the back of the spoon, the gap should remain.

Add the browned butter, citric acid, and salt and vigorously whisk until the butter is incorporated. Add the jam and mix again until all is incorporated. Remove the bowl from the pot. Cover with plastic wrap and let sit on the countertop until the custard is completely cool to the touch.

Meanwhile, pour ¼ cup (60 mL) of the cream into a small bowl. Sprinkle the gelatin over the surface, stir to combine, and set aside for 5 minutes to bloom the gelatin.

Microwave the gelatin mixture in 15-second bursts, stirring after each, until the gelatin has completely dissolved. (Alternatively, heat the mixture in a small saucepan over medium-low heat, stirring occasionally, to dissolve the gelatin.)

When the custard is completely cool, pour the remaining ¾ cup (180 mL) cream into the bowl of a stand mixer fitted with the whisk

1 cup (200 g) sugar
1½ teaspoons cornstarch
5 large egg yolks
½ cup (115 g) Browned Butter (page 277)
1 teaspoon citric acid
1 teaspoon kosher salt
1¼ cups (340 g) strawberry jam
2 cups (480 mL) heavy cream
1 (¼-ounce/7 g) packet unflavored gelatin powder
2 cups chopped strawberry-filled crispy wafers (from one 5-ounce/140 g package)

continues ▶

attachment. With the mixer on low speed, slowly drizzle in the cream-gelatin mixture. Increase the speed to medium-high and whip until you achieve medium peaks, 3 to 5 minutes.

Add one-quarter of the whipped cream to the custard and mix vigorously until all the cream is incorporated. Add the remaining whipped cream and very gently fold it together—there should still be visible white streaks. Add the wafer pieces and fold until they are incorporated.

Pour the mixture into the prepared pan and cover with a layer of parchment. Freeze overnight.

Use the overhanging parchment to lift the semifrio out of the pan and place it on a cutting board. Cut it into 9 pieces with a warmed dry knife (if you used a loaf pan, cut it into slices). Immediately return the semifrio to the freezer until ready to serve.

Two-Ingredient Creamy Ice Pops

Here's my advice to you: Freeze these, forget them, and eat them as a snack whenever the mood strikes. This might be the easiest recipe in the book. Two ingredients. Blend. Strain. Pour. Freeze. That's it. Who says you need a fancy ice cream maker to make delicious frozen treats at home?

In a blender, combine the evaporated milk and the chocolate spread or the dulce de leche. Blend on high speed until fully incorporated. Strain the mixture through a fine-mesh sieve into a bowl to remove any unincorporated bits of spread.

Pour the mixture into sturdy ice pop molds, add sticks, and freeze for at least 5 hours or preferably overnight before serving.

MAKES 5 ICE POPS

1 (12-ounce/360 mL) can evaporated milk

½ cup (120 mL) chocolate spread, such as Nutella, or ½ cup (115 g) dulce de leche, homemade (page 281) or store-bought

Helado de Batata

MAKES ABOUT 7 POPS

1 pound (455 g) white sweet
    potatoes (3 or 4 medium)
½ cup (120 mL) evaporated milk,
    plus more if needed
½ (7-ounce/210 mL) can
    unsweetened coconut cream
½ cup (120 mL) sweetened
    condensed milk
¼ to ½ cup lightly packed (50 to
    100 g) light brown sugar, to taste
1 tablespoon vanilla bean paste
1 teaspoon ground cinnamon
¼ teaspoon ground cloves

I totally understand if you're wondering: "Can she just cool it with the sweet potatoes?" By now, though, you should be able to understand why I cannot. If this iconic, top-tier Dominican ice cream flavor laced with my favorite warming spices—not about to cool it on those, either—doesn't convince you, then we need to have a word.

Preheat the oven to 450°F.

Using a fork, generously poke the sweet potatoes all over. Wrap the sweet potatoes tightly in aluminum foil and bake directly on the oven rack for 30 to 40 minutes, until soft, tender, and with visible steam coming out. (The texture of the sweet potato after mashing should be silky and soft, so when in doubt, err on the side of more cook time, since you want to release sweetness and make sure the starch is fully cooked out before making the helado.) Remove from the oven and set aside until cool enough to handle.

Halve the sweet potatoes and scoop the flesh into a large bowl. Use a fork to lightly mash the flesh. Transfer 2 cups (300 g) of the mashed sweet potato to a blender. (Reserve the rest for another use.)

Add the evaporated milk, coconut cream, condensed milk, ¼ cup (50 g) of the brown sugar, the vanilla, cinnamon, and cloves to the blender. Blend on high speed until pureed. Taste and adjust the sweetness with more brown sugar, if desired. If the mixture is too thick, add more evaporated milk, a spoonful at a time, to achieve a pourable consistency.

Strain the mixture through a fine-mesh sieve into a clean bowl or large spouted liquid measuring cup, then pour it into rounded ice pop molds. Freeze overnight before enjoying.

Banana Dulce Sherbet

A sherbet is a sorbet with the slightest bit of milk, but definitely nowhere near enough to qualify as ice cream. In this rendition, I use a blended frozen banana as the emulsifier, which gives a smooth and silky mouthfeel right up there with that of the finest ice creams.

In a blender, combine the frozen bananas, evaporated milk, dulce de leche, salt, and ascorbic acid and blend until smooth. Transfer to a freezer-safe container and freeze while you make the whipped cream.

In a large bowl, combine the cream and vanilla and, using a hand mixer or a whisk, whip until it forms soft peaks, 4 to 5 minutes.

Transfer the banana mixture to a separate large bowl and add one-quarter of the whipped cream. Fold with a spatula until the cream is incorporated, then fold in the rest of the whipped cream. Transfer the mixture to a freezer-safe airtight container, cover the top with a layer of parchment paper and the lid, and freeze overnight.

Scoop into chilled mugs or stemmed ice cream dishes and serve.

NOTE: *If you have an ice cream maker, skip freezing the bananas and whipping the cream. Instead, combine all the ingredients in a blender and blend on high until incorporated. Transfer the mixture to the ice cream maker and churn according to the manufacturer's instructions for sherbet, then scoop into a freezer-safe container and freeze overnight.*

SERVES 8 (MAKES 4 CUPS)

3 ripe large bananas, peeled, sliced, and frozen overnight
½ cup (120 mL) evaporated milk
1 cup (230 g) dulce de leche, homemade (page 281) or store-bought
Pinch of kosher salt
Pinch of ascorbic acid or citric acid (to prevent the ice cream from turning gray)
½ cup (120 mL) heavy cream
1 teaspoon Dominican imitation vanilla extract

Frio Frio & Syrups

3 cups ice cubes, for serving

COCONUT SYRUP

1 cup (240 mL) Simple Syrup
(page 280)
1 cup (70 g) unsweetened coconut
flakes, toasted (see Note)
1 tablespoon vanilla extract

LEMON SYRUP

1 cup (240 mL) Simple Syrup
(page 280)
½ cup (120 mL) fresh lemon juice
Citric acid, to taste (optional)

COLA

2 cups (480 mL) cola soda
Zest of 1 lemon, removed with a
vegetable peeler
1 teaspoon vanilla extract
1 cinnamon stick

NOTE: *A nice, no-oven way to toast coconut flakes is to put them in a dry skillet and cook over medium-heat, stirring, until they start to change color, 3 to 5 minutes. Watch them carefully and don't walk away—they go from barely toasted to burnt very quickly!*

Frio frio (Spanish for "cold cold") is a quintessential summer treat made from shaved ice covered in your choice of syrups. The first thing I need to point out is the texture here is somewhere between shaved and crushed ice, but it is not snow. This is a super important point because texture is one of the most important qualities to consider when you're craving an arctic treat.

The second point I'd like to make is that this recipe is a really good way to learn how to make "real" ingredients deliver the same feeling as commodified ones. It's a subject I had the surreal honor of discussing with sustainability students at Yale: Put finger lime, blood orange, and a touch of vanilla in the same room, for example, and you've got yourself an unadulterated Tutti Frutti flavor. Here are a few simpler examples.

Put the ice in a high-powered blender and pulse slowly until the ice is evenly crushed. Transfer the crushed ice to a freezer-safe container and freeze while you make the syrups or for at least 1 hour.

MAKE THE COCONUT SYRUP: In a medium pot, bring the simple syrup to a simmer over medium heat. Add the coconut flakes and vanilla, cover, and remove from the heat, then let stand for 30 minutes, or until fragrant. Strain the syrup into a jar and discard the coconut flakes, then cover and set aside until ready to use. (The syrup can be stored in the fridge for up to 1 week.)

MAKE THE LEMON SYRUP: In a medium bowl, stir together the simple syrup and lemon juice to combine. If you like it more acidic, feel free to stir in a touch of citric acid. Transfer to an airtight container and store in the fridge for up to 1 week.

MAKE THE COLA SYRUP: In a medium pot, combine the cola, lemon peel, vanilla, and cinnamon stick and bring to a simmer over medium heat. Simmer for 30 minutes, or until reduced by half. Let cool to room temperature, then transfer to an airtight container and store in the fridge for up to 1 week.

When ready to serve, remove the crushed ice from the freezer. With a large metal cooking spoon, scrape the crushed ice and spoon it into cups. Drizzle with the syrups as desired. (A friend of mine recommends the cola and lemon syrups together in one cup, to which I say, hell yeah!) Serve immediately with a spoon and a straw.

Morir Soñando Sherbet

Morir soñando (which means "to die dreaming") is one of those drinks that doesn't make sense on paper, but you just have to try it. Your first sip of the chilled mixture of orange juice, milk, and sugar instantly transports you to a beachside bar, shaded from the powerful Caribbean sun. Doubling down on the chilled-out vibes, here I freeze the orange mixture, put it in a blender, and blitz it to make a sherbet version! (If you have an ice cream maker, see the note on page 257 for an alternative method.) You'll use a bit more milk for this sherbet compared to the banana version on page 257 to compensate for the citrus's relative lack of richness.

In a medium bowl, combine the orange juice, condensed milk, coconut milk, vanilla, cinnamon, nutmeg, and salt and whisk until smooth. Place in the freezer while you make the whipped cream.

In a large bowl using a hand mixer or a whisk, whip the cream until it forms soft peaks, 4 to 5 minutes.

Remove the orange juice mixture from the freezer. Add one-quarter of the whipped cream and fold with a spatula until the cream is incorporated. Fold in the rest of the whipped cream until incorporated. Transfer the mixture to a freezer-safe airtight container, cover the top with a layer of parchment paper and the lid, and freeze overnight.

Scoop into chilled mugs or stemmed ice cream dishes and serve.

SERVES 9 (MAKES ABOUT 4½ CUPS)

2 cups (480 mL) orange juice (preferably freshly squeezed, but store-bought is OK, too)
1 (14-ounce/400 g) can sweetened condensed milk
½ cup (120 mL) full-fat coconut milk
1 tablespoon Dominican imitation vanilla extract
1 teaspoon ground cinnamon
¼ teaspoon ground nutmeg
Pinch of kosher salt
½ cup (120 mL) heavy cream

Lime-Elderflower Granita

SERVES 10
(MAKES ABOUT 5 CUPS)

1 cup (240 mL) nonalcoholic
    elderflower cordial
1 cup (240 mL) fresh lime juice
1 teaspoon vanilla bean paste
Pinch of kosher salt
Pinch of citric acid
3 cups ice cubes
¼ cup (60 mL) Simple Syrup
    (page 280), or as needed

For this granita, which highlights more "grown-up" flavors I certainly wasn't aware of as a child, you don't need a blender. Just use a fork. In order to make the granita texture, scrape the pulverized ice as much or as little as you like. At the end of the day, we're talking about ice and juice. The only things that matter are that it is cold and flavorful.

In a large bowl, combine the elderflower cordial, lime juice, vanilla, salt, and citric acid and mix until combined.

Put the ice in a high-powered blender and pulse slowly while drizzling in the elderflower mixture through the hole in the lid until the ice is evenly crushed. Taste the granita and add as much simple syrup as you'd like to achieve the sweetness you desire.

Transfer the granita to a square, shallow, roughly quart-size airtight container (freezer-safe is best, but a square baking pan works here, too) and spread it evenly. Immediately cover and freeze overnight.

With a large metal cooking spoon or two forks, scrape the frozen granita until fluffy granules form. Alternatively, working in batches, transfer the granita to the blender in chunks and blend for a smoother texture.

To serve, use a spoon to scrape and scoop the granita into frozen cups or coupe glasses.

Hibiscus-Pineapple Sorbet

Had to include at least one sorbet for posterity. But if you know anything about me by now, it's that I'm all for keeping it simple. Freeze the ingredients together, put 'em in a Ziploc, break it all up with the back of a spoon (or however you like), and then throw it in a blender. To me, the hibiscus flower—which transforms into a soft and chewy, almost candy-like texture—is like a gummy bear au naturel.

Place 2 cups (420 g) of the pineapple in a freezer bag and freeze.

In a medium saucepan, combine the hibiscus flowers (reserve a few for garnish), 1¼ cups (300 mL) water, and the sugar and cook over medium heat until the hibiscus flowers release a beautiful purple color, about 4 minutes. Add the remaining 2 cups (420 g) pineapple and cook until the pineapple is infused with hibiscus, 3 to 4 minutes.

Use a slotted spoon to transfer the pineapple chunks from the hibiscus mixture to a freezer bag (it can be the same bag as the frozen pineapple) and freeze for at least 24 hours. Transfer the hibiscus and syrup to an airtight container and refrigerate to use for garnish.

Transfer all the frozen pineapple to a blender and blend until completely smooth. If needed, you can add a bit of tap water 1 teaspoon at a time to reach sorbet consistency. Transfer to a freezer-safe container and freeze for 2 to 4 hours, at which point the mixture should be the perfect sorbet consistency.

Scoop into bowls and serve topped with a drizzle of olive oil, some hibiscus syrup, and a hibiscus flower.

SERVES 6
(MAKES ABOUT 3½ CUPS)

4 cups (840 g) diced fresh
    pineapple (from 1 large)
½ cup (20 g) dried edible hibiscus
    flowers
¼ cup (50 g) sugar
Extra-virgin olive oil, for serving
    (optional)

Brooklyn Black & White Semifrio

1 cup (200 g) sugar

1½ teaspoons cornstarch

5 large egg yolks

½ cup (115 g) Browned Butter (page 277)

1 teaspoon citric acid

1 teaspoon kosher salt

¼ cup (25 g) black (noir) cocoa powder

1 tablespoon vanilla bean paste

2 cups (480 mL) heavy cream

1 (¼-ounce/7 g) packet unflavored gelatin powder

1 cup (125 g) crumbled chocolate cake pieces (from page 149, for example), frozen (optional)

½ cup (120 mL) DIY Chocolate Shell (page 281; optional)

Decadent, fun to make, and stunning to eat. The cool thing about recipes that deal with frozen dairy is that you can keep the affair really simple and still get an incredible complex, captivating richness in the final product.

Line a 9-inch square baking pan with parchment paper or aluminum foil, leaving a few inches of parchment or foil overhanging two sides (alternatively, you can use an 8-inch square pan or a 1-pound loaf pan).

Set up a baño maría (double boiler) by placing a large heatproof bowl over a pot of boiling water (the bottom of the bowl should not touch the water). Place the sugar, cornstarch, and egg yolks in the bowl and cook over medium-high heat, whisking continuously to make sure the yolks do not curdle, until very thick, 4 to 5 minutes. The mixture should coat the back of a metal spoon, and if you drag a finger down the back of the spoon, the gap should remain.

Add the browned butter, citric acid, and salt and vigorously whisk until the butter is incorporated into the custard. Add the cocoa powder and vanilla and stir. Remove the bowl from the pot. Cover with plastic wrap and let sit on the countertop until the custard is completely cool to the touch.

Meanwhile, put ¼ cup (60 mL) of the cream in a small bowl. Sprinkle the gelatin over the surface, stir, and set aside for 5 minutes to bloom the gelatin.

Microwave the gelatin mixture in 15-second bursts, stirring after each, until the gelatin has completely dissolved. (Alternatively, heat the mixture in a small saucepan over medium-low heat, stirring occasionally, to dissolve the gelatin.)

When the custard is completely cool, pour the remaining ¾ cup (180 mL) cream into the bowl of a stand mixer fitted with the whisk attachment. With the mixer on low speed, slowly drizzle in the cream-gelatin mixture. Increase the speed to medium-high and whip until you achieve medium peaks, 3 to 5 minutes.

Add one-quarter of the whipped cream to the custard and mix vigorously until all the cream is incorporated. Add the remaining whipped cream and very gently fold it together—there should still be white

streaks visible. Add the cake pieces and chocolate shell (if using), and fold until the cake is incorporated.

Pour the mixture into the prepared pan and cover with a layer of paper. Freeze overnight.

Use the overhanging parchment to lift the semifrio out of the pan and place it on a cutting board. Cut it into 9 pieces with a warmed dry knife (if you used a loaf pan, cut it into slices). Immediately return the semifrio to the freezer until ready to serve.

Creamy Vanilla Gelato

My gelatos all originate from a traditional crème anglaise base, so consider this your mother gelato recipe moving forward. What's really fun is that once you master this recipe, you can start to experiment with different flavors and ingredients and really make it your own. For your sake, I also purposefully made all my gelato recipes no-churn. The gelatin stabilizes, the condensed milk and whipped cream provide the fluffiness, and the egg in the crème anglaise hammers home the gelato-y feeling. Remember, you don't need fancy machines to make beautiful gelato at home (unless you consider a blender a fancy machine . . . in which case, yes, you'll need one).

SERVE 8
(MAKES ABOUT 4 CUPS)

1 recipe Crème Anglaise (page 280), cooled
¼ cup (60 mL) sweetened condensed milk
2 cups (480 mL) heavy cream

In a large bowl, stir together the cooled crème anglaise and condensed milk to combine.

In the bowl of a stand mixer fitted with the whisk attachment (or using one of the alternate methods on page 25), whip the heavy cream on medium speed until medium peaks form, 3 to 5 minutes. Use a spatula to fold the whipped cream into the crème anglaise mixture.

Transfer to a freezer-safe container and freeze overnight before serving.

Malted Salted Chocolate Gelato

SERVES 8
(MAKES ABOUT 4 CUPS)

1 recipe Chocolate Crème Anglaise
  (see page 280), cooled
¼ cup (60 mL) sweetened
  condensed milk
¼ cup (30 g) malted milk powder
¼ teaspoon kosher salt
2 cups (480 mL) heavy cream

I am a big fan of chocolate gelato, but I figured I'd show you how to easily add depth and nuance to a classic—or, as I like to put it, make it taste like Whoppers.

In a large bowl, stir together the cooled crème anglaise, condensed milk, malted milk powder, and salt to combine.

In the bowl of a stand mixer fitted with the whisk attachment (or using one of the alternate methods on page 25), whip the heavy cream on medium speed until medium peaks form, 3 to 5 minutes. Use a spatula to fold the whipped cream into the crème anglaise mixture.

Transfer to a freezer-safe container and freeze overnight before serving.

Sweet Plantain Gelato

A tropical twist on a chilled classic. The flavors here may remind you of butter pecan ice cream, which is why you could add nuts to this, if you like.

In a large bowl, stir together the cooled crème anglaise and condensed milk to combine.

In the bowl of a stand mixer fitted with the whisk attachment (or using one of the alternate methods on page 25), whip the heavy cream on medium speed until medium peaks form, 3 to 5 minutes. Use a spatula to fold the whipped cream into the crème anglaise mixture.

Transfer half the cream mixture to a freezer-safe container, then layer the plantain filling on top. Add the remaining cream mixture and use a knife or wooden dowel to swirl the cream and plantains (but don't overswirl—you want some contrast). Freeze overnight before serving.

SERVES 8
(MAKES ABOUT 4 CUPS)

1 recipe Crème Anglaise (page 280), cooled
¼ cup (60 mL) sweetened condensed milk
2 cups (480 mL) heavy cream
1 cup (200 g) Plantain Filling (see page 169)

Passion Fruit Gelato

SERVE 8
(MAKES ABOUT 4 CUPS)

1 recipe Crème Anglaise (page 280), cooled
¼ cup (50 g) passion fruit powder (see Note)
¼ cup (60 mL) sweetened condensed milk
2 cups (480 mL) heavy cream

Passion fruit's acidity and vibrancy give the gelato base a pop of tropical freshness.

In a large bowl, combine the cooled crème anglaise, passion fruit powder, and condensed milk. Whisk until all the passion fruit powder is well incorporated.

In the bowl of a stand mixer fitted with the whisk attachment (or using one of the alternate methods on page 25), whip the heavy cream on medium speed until medium peaks form, 3 to 5 minutes. Use a spatula to fold the whipped cream into the crème anglaise mixture.

Transfer to a freezer-safe container and freeze overnight before serving.

NOTE: *If you can't find or order passion fruit powder, you can substitute passion fruit puree—but since the puree is more liquidy, the mouthfeel will be different. I'm biased, since this is my recipe, but I think the powder is worth seeking out!*

Basics

Browned Butter

MAKES A LITTLE LESS THAN 2 CUPS

2 cups (4 sticks/450 g) unsalted butter

In a medium saucepan, melt the butter over medium heat. When it begins to foam, cook, whisking frequently and watching carefully so it doesn't burn, until the butter is brown and smells nice and toasty and the milk solids have browned and settled to the bottom of the pan, about 10 minutes. Immediately remove from the heat and transfer the browned butter to a nonreactive bowl so it doesn't keep browning from the residual heat of the pan. Let cool to room temperature before using. Store in a nonreactive airtight container in the refrigerator for up to 1 week or in the freezer for up to 3 months.

Puff Pastry

MAKES ABOUT 1½ POUNDS (700 G)

1 cup (2 sticks/225 g) unsalted butter, softened
2¼ cups (315 g) all-purpose flour
1½ teaspoons kosher salt

Cut two 9 by 13-inch pieces of parchment paper. Place the butter on one piece of parchment and top with the second. Roll or press the butter into a rectangle just a bit smaller than the parchment, roughly 6 by 12 inches. It doesn't have to be perfectly smooth, but it should be an even thickness. You can use a bench scraper to even out the edges of the butter, if you like (I do this while the butter is sandwiched in the parchment to make it less messy).

Place the parchment-sandwiched butter on a large rimmed baking sheet and refrigerate until cold, about 1 hour.

Meanwhile, in a medium bowl, stir together the flour, salt, and ¾ cup (180 mL) water until it forms a smooth ball, 5 to 10 minutes. (Alternatively, combine the ingredients in the bowl of a stand mixer fitted with the dough hook and mix, starting at low and gradually bringing the speed up to medium, until the dough comes together, about 5 minutes.) You may need to add a few drops of water to bring the dough together or a dusting of flour if the dough is too sticky.

Cover the bowl and let the dough rest for 15 minutes. (This will make it easier to roll out.)

On a lightly floured work surface, roll out the dough to an 18 by 12-inch rectangle, working from the center outward. Remove both sheets of parchment from the butter and place the block of butter in the center of the dough rectangle. Fold the sides of the dough over the butter. The goal is to encase the butter completely without too much dough overlap. Use a rolling pin to smack the seams of the dough to close them tight.

Gently roll the dough lengthwise until it is 12 inches long. Fold the dough in thirds like you're folding a letter—fold the bottom 4 inches up, and the top 4 inches down—wrap in plastic wrap, and place in the refrigerator until chilled, 15 to 30 minutes.

Unwrap the dough and spin it around so a short edge is facing you. (Every time you roll the dough, you're trying to spread the butter in a different direction from the previous turn.) Use your rolling pin to smack the dough up and down a few times, then roll it out so it's 12 inches long again. Fold it into thirds, then wrap in plastic and refrigerate until chilled. Repeat the process of rolling, folding, and refrigerating 4 more times (for 6 folds total), rolling the dough out smooth-side (i.e., the side that was in contact with the work surface) up. Wrap again in plastic and refrigerate for at least 30 minutes before using.

If you want to store your puff pastry for later, wrap it tightly in parchment and then fold it so it will fit in a freezer-safe airtight container. Freeze for up to 1 year. Defrost the frozen puff pastry in the refrigerator overnight before using. If you're in a rush, you can defrost it on your counter (this should take 30 to 60 minutes, depending on the room temperature). If it gets too tacky, soft, and malleable, you'll want to pop it in the fridge for 15 minutes to firm up again. Sticky, tacky puff pastry is the enemy of crunchy, flaky layers!

Lazy Girl Piecrust

MAKES DOUGH FOR ONE 10-INCH SINGLE-CRUST PIE

3¼ cups (455 g) all-purpose flour

1½ cups (3 sticks/340 g) cold unsalted butter, cut into cubes

¼ cup (50 g) sugar

2 teaspoons kosher salt

8 teaspoons (40 mL) white rum

¼ to ½ cup (60 to 120 mL) ice-cold water, or as needed

In the bowl of a stand mixer fitted with the paddle attachment (or using one of the alternate methods on page 25), combine the flour, butter, sugar, and salt and mix on medium speed until the butter forms pea-size balls, 3 to 4 minutes. Chill the bowl in the fridge for 15 minutes.

Return the bowl to the mixer. With the mixer running on low speed, add all the rum, then slowly stream in ¼ cup (60 mL) water and mix until the

dough forms a smooth ball, about 5 minutes. If the dough needs more hydration, add more water a few tablespoons at a time.

Remove the dough from the bowl, form it into a disc, and wrap in plastic wrap. Refrigerate for up to 1 week or freeze for up to 3 months.

Dominican Cake Batter

MAKES ENOUGH FOR THREE 8-INCH ROUND CAKES

1 cup (200 g) granulated sugar

¼ cup lightly packed (50 g) light brown sugar

4 tablespoons (½ stick/55 g) unsalted butter, softened

¼ cup (60 mL) vegetable oil

¼ cup (50 g) vegetable shortening

6 large eggs

2 cups (280 g) all-purpose flour

½ cup (65 g) cornstarch

2 teaspoons baking powder

½ teaspoon kosher salt

1 cup (240 mL) evaporated milk

1 tablespoon Dominican imitation vanilla extract

1 teaspoon apple cider vinegar

In the bowl of a stand mixer fitted with the paddle attachment (or using one of the alternate methods on page 25), combine the granulated sugar, brown sugar, butter, oil, and shortening and beat on medium speed until fluffy and pale, about 8 minutes.

Reduce the mixer speed to medium and add the eggs one at a time, mixing until incorporated and scraping down the sides and bottom of the bowl with a rubber spatula after each addition. Beat until glossy and well combined, 5 to 8 minutes.

In a medium bowl, whisk together the flour, cornstarch, baking powder, and salt to combine. Add half the dry ingredients to the mixer bowl with the wet ingredients and pulse the mixer on and off, almost like you're trying to jump-start a car, so the flour gets gradually incorporated without flying all over your kitchen. When the dry ingredients are mostly combined, mix on low to incorporate them fully, about 3 minutes.

Pour in the evaporated milk and mix until just incorporated. Repeat with the vanilla and then the vinegar. Scrape down the bowl. Add the remaining flour mixture and mix on low speed for 3 minutes, then increase the speed to medium and mix until smooth, 2 to 3 minutes more.

Bake as instructed in whatever recipe you're using!

The Only Rum Cake Recipe You'll Ever Need

MAKES ONE 10-INCH CAKE

Vegetable oil cooking spray
1 cup (225 g) Browned Butter (page 277)
2½ cups (450 g) granulated sugar
¼ cup lightly packed (50 g) light brown sugar
4 large eggs
1 teaspoon vanilla bean paste
1 tablespoon dark rum
2½ cups (600 mL) heavy cream
2½ cups (350 g) all-purpose flour
8 teaspoons (20 g) cornstarch
½ teaspoon baking soda
¼ teaspoon kosher salt

Preheat the oven to 350°F. Line a 10-inch round cake pan with parchment paper and spray it with cooking spray.

In the bowl of a stand mixer fitted with the paddle attachment, beat the browned butter, granulated sugar, and brown sugar on medium-low speed until aerated and paler in color, 4 to 5 minutes. Reduce the mixer speed to low and add the eggs one at a time, scraping down the sides and bottom of the bowl with a rubber spatula after each

addition, and mix until glossy and combined. Add the vanilla and rum and mix to incorporate. Add 1¼ cups (300 mL) of the cream and mix until incorporated.

In a medium bowl, whisk together the flour, cornstarch, baking soda, and salt. Turn off the mixer and add half the dry ingredients to the bowl with the wet ingredients. Pulse the mixer on and off, almost like you're trying to jump-start a car, so the flour gets gradually incorporated without flying all over your kitchen. Add the remaining 1¼ cups (300 mL) cream, mix until incorporated, then add the remaining flour mixture and mix until the flour is incorporated. Scrape down the bowl and mix on low speed for 1 minute more to make sure any remaining flour is incorporated.

Pour the batter into the prepared pan and bake for 25 to 30 minutes, until a cake tester inserted into the center comes out clean. Do not overbake this cake (pretty please)! Remove from the oven and let cool completely, then proceed as directed in the recipe.

Suspiro, aka Dominican Meringue

MAKES ABOUT 3½ QUARTS

⅔ cup (150 g) egg whites (from about 5 large eggs)
¼ teaspoon citric acid
1½ cups plus 2 tablespoons (325 g) sugar
1 teaspoon kosher salt

Degrease the equipment you are going to use to whip your egg whites (see page 26). In the bowl of a stand mixer fitted with the whisk attachment, combine the egg whites and citric acid. Using the whisk attachment, gently stir them together by hand and then attach the bowl to the mixer and turn the mixer on to the lowest speed to let the egg whites begin to mix, very gently.

Meanwhile, in a medium saucepan, combine the sugar and ½ cup (120 mL) water and stir gently. (Keep a small bowl with ½ cup/120 mL water and a pastry brush on the side to brush away any crystallization that might appear on the inside of the pan.) Bring to a boil over medium-high heat, then boil until the syrup reaches 240°F on a candy thermometer.

When the syrup reaches 240°F, increase the mixer speed to medium-high and slowly stream in the syrup, pouring it down the inside edge of the bowl (avoid the whisk—you don't want hot syrup flying around!). When all the syrup has been added, turn the mixer up to the highest speed and mix until completely cool. The suspiro should be super glossy. Use immediately.

Simple Syrup

MAKES ABOUT 1⅓ CUPS (320 ML)

1 cup (200 g) sugar

In a small saucepan, combine the sugar and 1 cup (240 mL) water. Heat over medium-high heat, stirring frequently, until the sugar has dissolved. Let cool to room temperature, then transfer to an airtight container and store in the refrigerator for up to 1 month.

Crème Anglaise

MAKES ENOUGH FOR 1 BATCH OF GELATO

1½ cups (360 mL) whole milk
½ cup (100 g) sugar
2 tablespoons vanilla bean paste
1 strip of lemon peel
Pinch of kosher salt
6 large egg yolks

In a large pot, combine the milk, sugar, vanilla, lemon peel, and salt and bring to a gentle simmer over medium heat.

Place the egg yolks in a medium bowl. While whisking continuously, slowly pour in a ladleful of the warm milk mixture and whisk vigorously so the eggs don't scramble. Keep whisking in more of the milk mixture, one ladle at a time, until the egg mixture has turned pale and yellow, almost beige. Pour the tempered egg mixture into the pot with the milk mixture and cook, whisking, until the mixture reaches 185°F. Remove from the heat.

Remove and discard the lemon peel, then carefully transfer the mixture to a blender and blend until completely smooth. Strain through a fine-mesh sieve into a bowl. Fill a larger bowl with ice and set the bowl with the crème anglaise over the ice until it cools completely. Store in an airtight container in the refrigerator for up to 2 days.

NOTE: *To make Chocolate Crème Anglaise, omit the lemon peel and add ½ cup (90 g) chopped dark chocolate (64% cacao) to the blender with the tempered egg mixture.*

Tamarind Jam

MAKES 2 TO 3 CUPS (650 TO 975 G)

1 (14-ounce/400 g) block seedless tamarind paste

In a small saucepan, combine the tamarind paste with an equal quantity (400 mL, or about 1⅔ cups) of water. Bring to a boil over medium-high heat, whisking until the tamarind block melts into a nice, tender jam consistency, about 10 minutes. If the block won't soften, you can add a little more water, cook longer, and press it apart with a metal or wooden spoon. It's a thick block and requires a little TLC.

Working in batches, strain the tamarind jam through a fine-mesh sieve into a clean bowl, pressing on the solids to extract the jam; discard the solids.

Let cool, then transfer to an airtight container and store in the refrigerator for up to 1 week or in the freezer for up to 1 year.

Dulce de Leche

MAKES ABOUT 1¼ CUPS

1 (14-ounce/400 g) can sweetened condensed milk

Preheat the oven to 350°F.

Pour the condensed milk into a loaf pan, then set the loaf pan in a larger baking dish.

Run water from the tap until the water is very hot. Add enough hot water to the baking dish to come halfway up the sides of the loaf pan, being careful not to get any water in the loaf pan. The loaf pan should not be floating.

Carefully transfer the baking dish to the oven and bake for 3 hours, VERY carefully stirring every 30 minutes or so. (The dulce de leche is hot and caramel burns are not fun.) Remove from the oven and let cool to room temperature, then transfer the dulce de leche to an airtight container and store in the refrigerator for up to 2 weeks.

DIY Chocolate Shell

MAKES ABOUT 1¼ CUPS

10 ounces (285 g) dark chocolate (65 to 70% cacao), melted (see page 29)

1 to 2 tablespoons coconut oil or food-grade cocoa butter, melted

In a large bowl, combine the melted chocolate and melted coconut oil and mix until smooth. Use immediately, while still melted.

Sunflower Seed Paste

MAKES ABOUT 2 CUPS (400 GRAMS)

1 cup (200 g) shelled sunflower seeds, toasted

1 cup (125 g) unsifted powdered sugar

1 medium egg white

In a food processor, blitz the sunflower seeds until pureed, about 2 minutes, then add the powdered sugar and egg white. Process until you have a completely smooth paste, about 3 minutes more. Store in an airtight container in the freezer for up to 3 months.

Acknowledgments

I never in a million years would have thought I'd get to write a book, but I'm so honored I got to go on this journey, and thankful for the people who made it happen.

I chose to work with Union Square & Co. because I believed in the prowess of editor Caitlin Leffel and editorial director Amanda Englander. You are both geniuses, and I couldn't have gotten to the finish line without your vision. Thank you to Allison Chi and Jennifer Halper, the talented designer and photography director who, along with art director Renée Bollier and creative director Lisa Forde, turned my words into something beautiful. And to Ivy McFadden, our brilliant copyeditor—thank you for making sure those words made sense!

This book is as beautiful as it is because of our photo team: photographer Lauren Vied Allen (and her baby, who I consider part of the team because they were on set with us in Lauren's belly a few weeks before they officially entered the world!); Jacqui McDonald, Beth Kircher, and the team at All Opal; food stylist Hadley Sui and her team of Erica Santiago (and baby), Katherine Sprung, and Albane Sharrard; prop stylist Summer Moore; and prop assistant Sappo Hocker.

I of course have to thank my Bakers Against Racism family: Rob Rubba, who supported me throughout the BAR journey, and the whole community of bakers who are still baking the world a better place.

To my book team: Michelle Fadden, thank you for your hard work and the A game you bring to every project we've worked on together! Thank you to Gabe Ulla for helping me with the proposal; without your contribution, we wouldn't be here today. To Marvelous Mary Dodd: Thank you for being much more than just my recipe tester. You were a shoulder to lean on, a voice of reason, a breath of fresh air, and just overall the most marvelous person I've met in a while. Emily Timberlake, you are a godsend. We worked our tuchuses off on the scariest, most challenging project I've faced in a while. But we dove in headfirst and made magic—that's the only way I can describe it. When I read through this book, I can hear our jokes, and our laughter. My literary agent, Rica Allannic, is the best agent a girl could ask for—you push me to be better, and truly have represented me like none other. Thank you for showing me that there are still good people in this world.

When I was a young savory cook in NYC, I watched Christina Tosi with admiration: She was every young pastry cook's hero. When I moved to DC from NYC, I emailed the New York Milk Bar team and they immediately offered me a position in their new DC location. Chef Tosi had no idea how heartsick I was feeling, but she still took the time to help and guided me, and to always check in and make sure I was okay, without me even having to ask. She's the ultimate "hardbody," as we used to say at Milk Bar, and she taught me that there are kind and joyful leaders in our industry. She reminded me that I don't have to burn any bridges to reach the top. I'm forever thankful for you, Christina.

Thank you, Chef Jacques, Chef Hasty, Chef Ken, and my greatest friend, the lovely, friendly Italian giant Chef Paul. You taught me how to navigate this industry, and taught me to be bold and take chances on flavors. You rewarded my work ethic with kindness, love, and support. Thank you for honoring me by giving me the title of pastry sous chef at the age of twenty-one. (And also for letting me make Chef Jacques Pépin's favorite treats: chocolate-covered Oreos.)

DeAndra Bailey, your passion, heart, and light supported me and guided me throughout every single marquee we've worked at. I'm grateful that work couldn't keep us apart and that you became my friend in the real world, too. I will always be here to support you.

To my mom, Lala; my mother's husband, Eli; my mother-in-law, Rebecca; and my father-in-law, Hector Sr.: Throughout this whole journey, you've championed me—and picked me back up when I didn't think I could possibly finish this book. I cried a lot of tears—tears of joy, anxiety, frustration, and, ultimately, relief. You mean everything to me, and I'm grateful God placed you in my life. *Yo le doy gracias a Dios todo los días por ser su hija. Te quiero muchísimo. Gracias por ser mis padres en esta vida. No sé si podría vivir sin ustedes, y estoy súper agradecida por ustedes.* Papa Hector, thank you for being my bestie. Every time I see the gallery wall of my accomplishments, I can't believe this is my life—not because of the accomplishments, but because you love me as if I were your own daughter. *Rebecca y Lala, Dios es tan bueno porque él me dio dos mamás. El amor y cariño que me dan me inspira a ser una buena mujer, una buena esposa y algún día una buena mamá. Mi deseo es ser la mitad del modelo a seguir que son para mí, para mis hijos y para las personas que conoceré en el futuro.*

To Aba, Ashley, and Stef, thank you for being here with me throughout this journey. I cannot wait to continue building with you ladies. To Karla, Jeremy, Yanique, Wesley, Jamilia, Melissa, and Brian, we have gone through so much in life together—weddings, babies, and new jobs. Thank you for never giving up on our friendship. You are all family until the day that I am no longer here on Earth.

To my husband, Hector: You are my rock. Everything I've been able to do, I've done because you hold me and love me when I falter and am weak. Growing up, I didn't think that the world could understand my quirky brain, or understand me as a human. Until I met you. We were basically kids when we met, and somehow the universe kept bringing us together. Finally realized that you were my person in this life. The bond that we share leads me to believe that we've loved each other in every iteration of the lives we've lived. Your joy is my joy, and my joy is yours. Every day, my faith in humanity is restored when I look into your eyes and you tell me you love me. You and your family took me and my mom in and gave me everything I didn't know I needed. Thank you, Hector, for loving me the way you do, and thank you for loving my mom the way you do. I know that if anything were to ever happen to me, she is in safe hands. Plus, you're her favorite anyway, haha.

And to you, the reader—yes, you! Thank you for buying this book. I hope it inspires you to be a better baker, but also know that you are not alone in this life. I'm here with you, baking and loving you with every single gram of butter, flour, and sugar. Your quirkiness is not a negative thing, the way you see the world is beautiful, and I hope that I can inspire you to be exactly who you are. Without your support, I wouldn't be here today. I just make cake. You make all this happen. And for that, I'm grateful for you.

Index

Note: Page references in *italic* indicate photographs.